Advance Praise

"At last we have a solidly research-based text on the Enterprise Governance of IT that successfully fuses business and IT perspectives. With its emphasis on the creation of business value, and on the use of relevant metrics, this book offers a distinctive view of these key processes. The authors, whose reputation and experience in the field is second to none, have created a guide to the strategic management of IT that will be an essential source for managers."
Professor James W. Bryant
Centre for Individual & Organisational Development
Sheffield Hallam University
United Kingdom

"IT governance is a hot topic today and this book provides a wealth of practical and useful information. Regardless of whether you are concerned about compliance issues, or worried about the alignment of your IT investment with the corporate goals, this book will provide guidance to assist your efforts. As well as academic models and practice oriented frameworks such as CobiT, Val-IT and balanced scorecard, the volume includes recent case studies illustrating how the concepts and frameworks are applied in real life companies. I strongly recommend this book to Corporate and IT Managers as well as MBA and IT Graduate students."
Aileen Cater-Steel, PhD
Senior Lecturer (Information Systems)
School of Information Systems
University of Southern Queensland
Australia

"The control of IT within enterprise systems has an ambiguous pattern of mismanagement and associated horror stories for new players. This book confronts the most serious problem facing enterprise managers today with instruction, case studies and solutions. It is a must read and a must use for those seeking to extract top value from the IT investment in a control challenged work place."
Brian O. Cusack, PhD
Director CRISM Security

School of Mathematics & Computer Sciences
University of Auckland
New Zealand

"This text is a commendable exposition of Enterprise Governance of IT by one of the pioneers of the field, Wim Van Grembergen, together with one of its rising stars, Steven De Haes. The important theoretical insights presented by the authors are skillfully balanced with practical application in the form of several highly informative case studies. Anyone interested in the governance of IT, the alignment between the business and IT, and the business value of IT would benefit greatly from this exceptional volume."
Pontus Johnson, PhD
Industrial Information and Control Systems
KTH – Royal Institute of Technology
Sweden

"This book quite appropriately moves the attention from the technology-confined to the enterprise-driven governance of IT. It offers a very complete overview of current thinking about effective IT governance."
Prof. dr ir R. Maes
Dean of the Information Management Program
PrimaVera Program Director
Universiteit van Amsterdam Business School
Sweden

"The shift from IT governance to Enterprise Governance of IT is not just playing with words – it represents a significant cultural change – a change that is essential if enterprises are to realize value from their increasingly significant and complex investments in IT-enabled change. This book provides a valuable resource to anyone who believes that we can and must do better."
John Thorp
President of The Thorp Network Inc.
Author, "The Information Paradox"

Wim Van Grembergen · Steven De Haes

Enterprise Governance of Information Technology

Achieving Strategic Alignment and Value

Springer

Wim Van Grembergen
University of Antwerp
University of Antwerp Management School
Sint Pauwels, Belgium
wim.vangrembergen@ua.ac.be

Steven De Haes
University of Antwerp
University of Antwerp Management School
Malle, Belgium
steven.dehaes@ua.ac.be

ISBN 978 0 387-84881-5 e-ISBN 978-0-387-84882-2
DOI 10.1007/978-0-387-84882-2

Library of Congress Control Number: 2008936215

Printed on acid-free paper

springer.com

Preface

"Enterprise Governance of IT" is a relatively new concept in literature and is gaining more and more interest in the academic and practitioner's world. "Enterprise Governance of IT" is about defining and embedding processes and structures in the organizations that enable both business and IT people to execute their responsibilities in creating value from IT-enabled business investments. As an example of its growing importance, the standardization organization ISO issued in 2008 a new worldwide ISO standard in this domain.

Within the UAMS – ITAG Research Institute (University of Antwerp Management School – IT Alignment and Governance Research Institute), we have been executing applied research in this domain for many years now. With this book, we want to provide a complete and comprehensive overview of what Enterprise Governance of IT entails and how it can be applied in practice. Our conclusions in this book are based on our knowledge obtained in applied research projects, our many years of involvement in the development of COBIT and Val IT, our own hands-on experience in many industries in governance and alignment projects, and international state-of-the art literature. In this way, this manuscript encompasses both academic models and concepts, but also includes practice-oriented frameworks such as COBIT and Val IT and discusses and analyzes many practical case studies in different industries.

The target audience for this book is threefold:

- Master students, for whom this textbook can be used in courses typical on IT strategy, Enterprise Governance of IT, IT management, IT processes, IT and business architecture, IT assurance/audit, information systems management, etc.
- Executive students in business schools, for MBA type of courses where IT strategy or IT management modules are addressed.
- Practitioners in the field, both business and IT managers, who are seeking research-based fundamentals and practical implementation issues related to it in the domain of Enterprise Governance of IT.

This book is organized around eight main chapters. Chapter 1 defines the core concepts around Enterprise Governance of IT as a means to enable business/IT alignment and business value from IT. This chapter also includes detailed research results on how business goals can be translated into/aligned with IT goals and vice versa. Chapter 2 builds on the first chapter and provides an overview of best practices that organizations can leverage to implement Enterprise Governance of IT. A lot of case studies are described in this chapter, as each individual governance implementation will be different depending on the organization's size, sector, geography, etc. Finally, detailed discussions are laid out regarding the effectiveness, ease of implementation and importance of each of the presented practices for Enterprise Governance of IT. In Chapter 3, the impact of Enterprise Governance of IT implementations on business/IT alignment will be discussed. The first question is how an organization can measure and evaluate its current status of business/IT alignment. This discussion is supplemented with a benchmarking case, where business/IT alignment was measured for the Belgian financial services sector. Next, the impact of Enterprise Governance of IT practices on business/IT alignment is analyzed and illustrated with cases. Chapter 4 introduces the IT balanced scorecard as a framework for Enterprise Governance of IT. This chapter discusses the core concepts of the IT BSC and explains how the IT BSC can be used as an instrument for Enterprise Governance of IT. Chapter 4 also includes a detailed case study of a working IT balanced scorecard implementation. Chapter 5 positions COBIT in the field of Enterprise Governance of IT. This chapter discusses in detail all the core elements of the COBIT framework and explains how organizations should leverage them for the purpose of Enterprise Governance of IT. In relation, Chapter 6 continues by discussing how COBIT can also be leveraged as a framework to execute IT assurance/audit assignments. This chapter also offers a lot of hands-on templates that can be used in practice. Where COBIT addresses the IT processes, Val IT covers the IT-related business processes. This Val IT framework is addressed in Chapter 7, against explaining all core concepts and implementation issues. Chapter 8 finally provides some guidelines to get started with Enterprise Governance of IT and outlines a balanced scorecard for Enterprise Governance of IT, to manage and measure the outcome of the governance project.

To support the reader in understanding and absorbing the material provided, each chapter provides (short and long) "assignment boxes" where readers can apply the concepts explained in comprehensive exercises. Also, at the end of each chapter, a summary and study questions are available enabling the reader to cross-check the insights obtained in a chapter. For people who want more information, each chapter provides hooks to more detailed background material by way of literature references and website links. This textbook is heavily based on research executed within the UAMS – ITAG Research Institute. For readers with research interest, "research boxes" are inserted in the text each time giving some background on research methodologies and strategies used in executing the different research assignments.

We hope that with this book, we can contribute to further developing the emerging knowledge domain of Enterprise Governance of IT. This book is one of the outcomes of our activities within the UAMS – ITAG Research Institute. We do invite the readers to visit our website www.uams.be/ITAG, for more information on our research activities and publications. Also, we welcome reactions to this book or sharing experiences in the domain of Enterprise Governance of IT via steven.dehaes@ua.ac.be and wim.vangrembergen@ua.ac.be.

Wim Van Grembergen
Sint Pauwels, Belgium

Steven De Haes
Malle, Belgium

Acknowledgments

We would like to thank all involved in participating in our research and teaching activities and in writing this book. Without the support of these people, the development of this book could not have been satisfactorily completed.

We gratefully acknowledge the business and IT managers who shared their insights and practices on Enterprise Governance of IT and participated in one or more of our research projects. We appreciate the support provided for this project by the Business Faculty of the University of Antwerp (UA) and the University of Antwerp Management School (UAMS) and by our colleagues in these institutions. A special word of appreciation goes to our colleague researcher in the UAMS – ITAG Research Institute, Hilde Van Brempt, who contributed in a very constructive way in the execution of many of our research projects. We would also like to thank our master and executive students and the members of the UAMS IT Management Advisory Board who provided us with many ideas on the subject of Enterprise Governance of IT and its related mechanisms.

We would also like to express our gratitude toward the board of directors, the management committee and all the staff and volunteers of the IT Governance Institute (ITGI). Our involvement in the COBIT and Val IT development activities has been of great value in further progressing our ideas.

We would also like to thank our publisher Springer who showed great interest in our research and book project, and from whom we received magnificent support in managing this project.

Last but not least, we would like to thank our families. Wim would like to extend his gratitude to Hilde, Astrid and Helen who always supported and helped him with every project including this book. Steven wishes to thank Brenda for her loving support and patience and wants to dedicate this book to his children Ruben, Charlotte and Michiel.

Contents

About the Authors

Wim Van Grembergen, PhD, is professor at the Economics and Management Faculty of the University of Antwerp (UA) and executive professor at the University of Antwerp Management School (UAMS). He teaches information systems at bachelor, master and executive levels and researches in IT governance, IT strategy, IT assurance, IT performance management and the IT balanced scorecard. Within his IT Alignment and Governance (ITAG) Research Institute (www.uams.be/itag) he conducts research for ISACA/ITGI on IT governance and supports the continuous development of COBIT. He is also a member of the IT Governance Committee, ISACA/ITGI's strategic committee. Van Grembergen is a frequent speaker at academic and professional meetings and conferences and has served in a consulting capacity in a number of firms. He has several publications in leading academic journals and published books on IT governance and the IT balanced scorecard.

Steven De Haes, PhD, is responsible for the Information Systems Management executive programs and research at the University of Antwerp Management School (UAMS) and is guest lecturer at the University of Antwerp (UA). He has teaching assignments in executive programs in the domain of IT governance & assurance, alignment and IT performance measurement. He is actively engaged in applied research within the IT Alignment and Governance (ITAG) Research Institute (www.uams.be/itag). He performs research and project management assignments for the IT Governance Institute (ITGI) in the domain of IT governance and assurance and, in this capacity, has contributed to many publications of ITGI (COBIT 4, VALIT and IT Assurance Guide). He has several publications on IT governance and business/IT alignment in leading journals and acts as advisor to firms in these domains.

Chapter 1
Concepts of Enterprise Governance of IT

Abstract Enterprise Governance of IT is a relatively new concept in literature and is gaining more and more interest in the academic and practitioner's world. Enterprise Governance of IT addresses the definition and implementation of processes, structures and relational mechanism that enable both business and IT people to execute their responsibilities in support of business/IT alignment and the creation of value from IT-enabled business investments. As an example of its growing importance, the International Organization for Standardization (ISO) issued a new worldwide ISO standard in this domain in 2008. This chapter defines the core concepts around Enterprise Governance of IT as a means to enable business/IT alignment and business value from IT.

1.1 Enterprise Governance of IT

This section addresses the need for governance of IT, defines IT governance and explains the shift from IT governance toward Enterprise Governance of IT.

1.1.1 Why Governance of IT?

Information technology (IT) has become pervasive in current dynamic and often turbulent business environments. While in the past, business executives could delegate, ignore or avoid IT decisions, this is now impossible in most sectors and industries. This major IT dependency implies a huge vulnerability that is inherently present in IT environments. System and network downtime has become far too costly for any organization these days, as doing business globally around the clock has become the standard. Take for example the impact of downtime in the banking sector or in a medical environment. The risk factor is accompanied by a wide spectrum of external threats, such as errors and omissions, abuse, cyber crime and fraud.

W. Van Grembergen, S. De Haes, *Enterprise Governance of Information Technology*, DOI 10.1007/978-0-387-84882-2_1,

IT of course has the potential not only to support existing business strategies, but also to shape new strategies. In this mindset, IT becomes not only a success factor for survival and prosperity, but also an opportunity to differentiate and to achieve competitive advantage. In this viewpoint, the IT department moves from a commodity service provider to a strategic partner.

Information technology also often entails large capital investments in organizations while companies are faced with multiple shareholders that are demanding the creation of business value through these investments. The question of the "productivity paradox," why information technologies have not provided a measurable value to the business world, has puzzled many practitioners and researchers.

All the issues aforementioned point out that the critical dependency on information technology calls for a specific focus on governance of IT. This is needed to ensure that the investments in IT will generate the required business value and that risks associated with IT are mitigated.

However, not everybody seems to agree with the increasing strategic importance of information technology. In his article "IT doesn't matter," Nicolas Carr (2003) makes the comparison between commodities such as water and gas and information technology. He states, "As information technology's power and ubiquity have grown, its strategic importance has diminished. [. . .] By now, the core functions of IT – data storage, data processing, and data transport – have become available to all. Their very power and presence have begun to transform them from potentially strategic resources into commodity factors of production. They are becoming costs of doing business that must be paid by all but provide distinction to none."

After Carr's article, a debate started between opponents and proponents of his ideas. In the context of this book, it is acknowledged that some parts in the IT domain were standardized and became a commodity, but still many systems and technologies are very complex, and IT investments and the way IT is used need to be governed properly. Or, as the General Motors CIO Ralph Szygenda points out as a reaction to Carr's article: "Nicholas Carr may ultimately be correct when he says IT doesn't matter. . .. [But] business-process improvement, competitive advantage, optimization, and business success do matter and they aren't commodities. To facilitate these business changes, IT can be considered a differentiator or a necessary evil. But today, it's a must in a real-time corporation. [. . .] I also agree on spending the minimum on IT to reach desired business results. Precision investment on core infrastructure and process-differentiation IT systems is called for in today's intensely cost-conscious business versus the shotgun approach sometimes used in the past" (Evans, 2003).

1.1.2 From IT Governance to Enterprise Governance of IT

Information technology and its use in business environments has experienced a fundamental transformation in the past decades. Since the introduction of IT in organizations, academics and practitioners conducted research and developed

> "IT governance is the responsibility of executives and the board of directors, and consists of the leadership, organizational structures and processes that ensure that the enterprise's IT sustains and extends the organization's strategy and objectives" (ITGI, 2003).
>
> "IT governance is the organizational capacity exercised by the board, executive management and IT management to control the formulation and implementation of IT strategy and in this way ensure the fusion of business and IT" (Van Grembergen, 2002).

Fig. 1.1 Definitions of IT governance

theories and best practices in this emerging knowledge domain. This resulted in a variety of IT governance definitions of which some are formulated in Fig. 1.1.

After the emergence of the IT governance concept in the late 1990s, the concept received a lot of attention. However, due to the focus on "IT" in the naming of the concept, the IT governance discussion mainly stayed as a discussion within the IT area, while of course one of the main responsibilities is situated at the business side. It is clear that business value from IT investments cannot be realized by IT, but will always be created at the business side. For example, there will be no business value created when IT delivers a new CRM application on time, on budget and within functionalities, and afterward when the business is not integrating the new IT system into its business operations. Business value will only be created when new and adequate business processes are designed and executed, enabling the sales people of the organization to increase turnover and profit.

This discussion raised the issue that the involvement of business is crucial and initiated a shift in the definition, focusing on the business involvement, toward "Enterprise Governance of IT." For this book, we define Enterprise Governance of IT as (Fig. 1.2):

> Enterprise Governance of IT is an integral part of corporate governance and addresses the definition and implementation of processes, structures and relational mechanisms in the organization that enable both business and IT people to execute their responsibilities in support of business/IT alignment and the creation of business value from IT-enabled business investments.

Fig. 1.2 Definition of Enterprise Governance of IT

As an example of its growing importance, the International Organization for Standardization (ISO) released in 2008 a new worldwide ISO standard defined as "Corporate Governance of IT" (ISO/IEC 38500:2008). In this standard, ISO puts forward six principles for governance of IT, as illustrated in Fig. 1.3. The principles express preferred behavior to guide IT-related decision-making and address both business' and IT's roles and responsibilities (Fig. 1.3).
Enterprise Governance of IT clearly goes beyond the IT-related responsibilities and expands toward (IT-related) business processes needed for business value creation. In this book, separate chapters are dedicated to the governance frameworks COBIT and Val IT. Relating to these frameworks, COBIT focuses

Principle 1: Responsibility

Individuals and groups within the organization understand and accept their responsibilities in respect of both supply of, and demand for IT. Those with responsibility for actions also have the authority to perform those actions.

Principle 2: Strategy

The organization's business strategy takes into account the current and future capabilities of IT; the strategic plans for IT satisfy the current and ongoing needs of the organization's business strategy.

Principle 3: Acquisition

IT acquisitions are made for valid reasons, on the basis of appropriate and ongoing analysis, with clear and transparent decision making. There is appropriate balance between benefits, opportunities, costs, and risks, in both the short term and the long term.

Principle 4: Performance

IT is fit for purpose in supporting the organization, providing the services, levels of service and service quality required to meet current and future business requirements.

Principle 5: Conformance

IT complies with all mandatory legislations and regulations. Policies and practices are clearly defined, implemented and enforced.

Principle 6: Human Behavior

IT policies, practices and decisions demonstrate respect for Human Behavior, including the current and evolving needs of all the 'people in the process'.

Fig. 1.3 ISO principles for corporate governance of IT
Adapted from: ISO/IEC 38500:2008 – Corporate Governance of Information Technology.

on the IT processes and Val IT addresses the IT-related business processes. Both provide a strong basis to build a broader framework for Enterprise Governance of IT (Fig. 1.4).

The above-mentioned definition states that Enterprise Governance of IT is an integral part of enterprise or corporate governance. Corporate governance is the system by which organizations are directed and controlled. The business dependency on information technology has resulted in the fact that corporate governance issues can no longer be solved without considering information technology. Corporate governance should therefore drive and set Enterprise Governance of IT. Information technology in its turn can influence strategic opportunities as outlined by the enterprise and can provide critical input to strategic plans. In this way, Enterprise Governance of IT enables the enterprise to take full advantage of its information and can be seen as a driver for

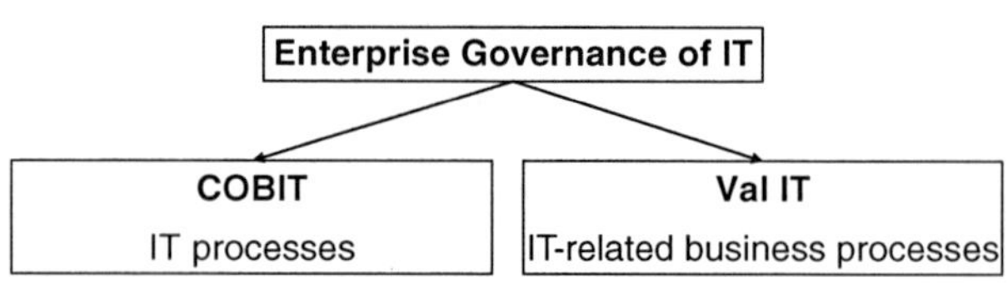

Fig. 1.4 Enterprise Governance of IT related to COBIT and Val IT

corporate governance. Enterprise Governance of IT and corporate governance cannot therefore be considered as pure distinct disciplines and Enterprise Governance of IT needs to be integrated into the overall governance structure.

Using similar argumentations as for Enterprise Governance of IT, a rationale could be built up to promote governance requirements for other key assets in the organization. Typical examples could be "human resources governance" and "financial governance." In this context, Weill and Ross identify six key assets through which an organization can accomplish its strategies and generate business value: human assets, financial assets, physical assets, IP assets, information and IT assets, relationship assets (see Fig. 1.5). Using their words, "Senior executive teams create mechanisms to govern the management and use of each of these assets both independently and together. [...] Governance of the key assets occurs via a large number of organizational mechanisms, for example structures, processes, procedures and audits."

It is important to note that there is a clear distinction between IT governance or Enterprise Governance of IT and IT management. IT management is focused on the effective and efficient internal supply of IT services and products and the management of present IT operations. IT governance/Enterprise Governance of IT in turn is much broader and concentrates on performing and transforming IT to meet present and future demands of the business (internal focus) and business customers (external focus). This "higher-level" focus of IT governance/Enterprise Governance of IT is confirmed in the IT governance definition of ITGI (2003), which states that "IT governance is the responsibility of executives and the board of directors." Pragmatically, one could say that IT management is the prime responsibility of the IT Director while the "Chief Information Officer" (CIO) in co-operation with the business is focused on IT governance/Enterprise Governance of IT.

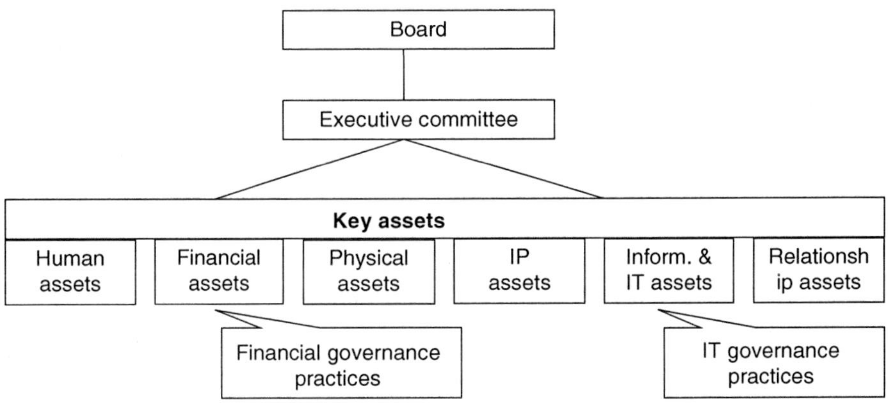

Fig. 1.5 Key asset governance
Adapted from: Weill, P., and Ross, J., 2004, IT Governance: How Top Performers Manage IT Decision Rights for Superior Results. Boston: Harvard Business School Press. Portions reprinted, with permission, from MIT Sloan School Center for Information Systems Research (CISR).

1.2 Enterprise Governance of IT and Business/IT Alignment

The Enterprise Governance of IT definition explicitly underlines that the ultimate outcome of Enterprise Governance of IT is the alignment of information technology with the business. Business/IT alignment in turn is an important driving force to achieve business value through investments in IT, as illustrated in Fig. 1.6. This section will discuss the business/IT alignment concept in more detail and its impact on achieving business value. Note that the relationship between Enterprise Governance of IT and business/IT alignment will be further studied in Chapter 3.

1.2.1 Business/IT Alignment

What does "alignment between the business and IT" exactly mean? Business/IT alignment is the fit and integration among business strategy, IT strategy, business structures and IT structures. It comprises two major questions: How is IT aligned with the business? How is the business aligned with IT? The market research company IDC formulated the following definition: "the process and goal of achieving competitive advantage through developing and sustaining a symbiotic relationship between business and IT." The idea behind strategic alignment is very comprehensive, but the question is how organizations can achieve this ultimate goal.

Henderson and Venkatraman were the first to clearly describe the interrelationship between business strategies and IT strategies in their well-known Strategic Alignment Model or SAM (see Fig. 1.7). Many authors used this model for further research. The concept of the SAM is based on two building blocks: "strategic fit" and "functional integration." *Strategic fit* recognizes that the IT strategy should be articulated in terms of an external domain (how the firm is positioned in the IT marketplace) and an internal domain (how the IT infrastructure should be configured and managed). Strategic fit is of course equally relevant in the business domain. Two types of *functional integration* exist: strategic integration and operational integration. Strategic integration is the link between business strategy and IT strategy reflecting the external components which are important for many companies as IT emerged as a source of strategic advantage. Operational integration covers the internal domain and deals with the link between organizational infrastructure and processes and IT infrastructure and processes.

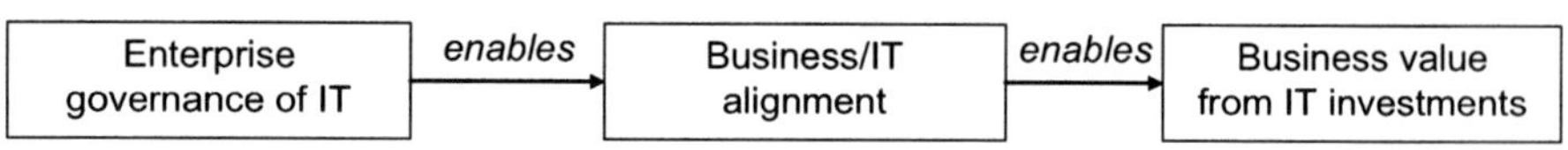

Fig. 1.6 Enterprise Governance of IT, business/IT alignment and business value

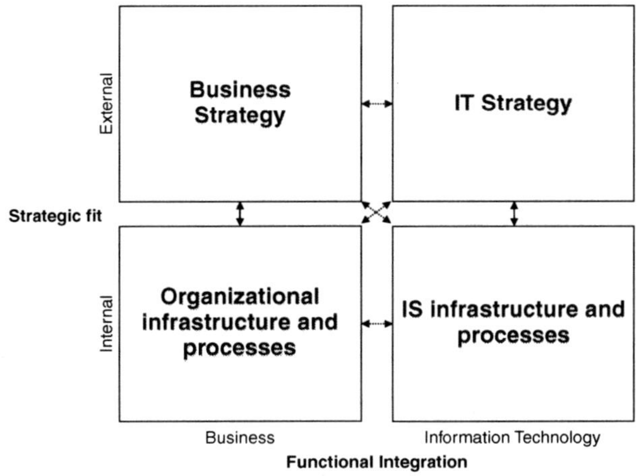

Fig. 1.7 Strategic alignment model
Adapted from: Henderson, J.C., and Venkatraman, N., 1993, Strategic Alignment: Leveraging Information Technology for Transforming Organizations, IBM Systems Journal, vol. 32, no. 1. Portions reprinted, with permission, from IBM Systems Journal.

Henderson and Venkatraman argue that the external and the internal domains are equally important, but that managers traditionally think of IT strategy in terms of the internal domain, since historically IT was viewed as a support function that was less essential to the business. In their research results, Henderson and Venkatraman warn of the problems that may surface when a bivariate approach is undertaken with respect to balancing across the four domains – IT strategy, business strategy, IS infrastructure and organizational infrastructure. For instance, when only external issues – IT strategy and business strategy – are considered, a serious underestimation of the importance of internal issues such as the required redesigning of key business processes might occur. Therefore, SAM calls for the recognition of multivariate relationships, which will always take into consideration at least three out of the four defined domains.

As mentioned before, many authors have used the SAM for further research and have provided comments and additional insights. Maes for example developed an interesting extension to the strategic alignment model (see Fig. 1.8). The basic idea is that the 2×2 dimensions of the strategic alignment model is an oversimplification of reality and needs to be extended to a 3×3 model.

In the first place, the internal domain of the extended strategic alignment model of Maes is subdivided into two separate areas: a structural and an operational level. This results from the observation that the former plays an essential role in the tuning of long-term strategic vision (which is set in the external domain) and the latter serves the short-term operational transformation. The IT domain, in turn, is being reshaped into an information/communication level

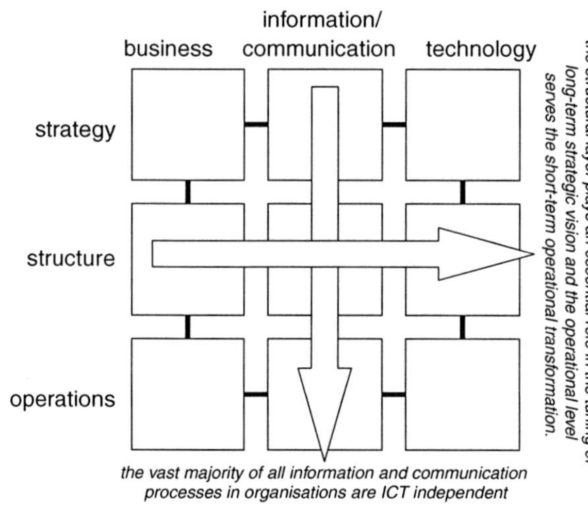

Fig. 1.8 The alignment framework of Maes – an extension of SAM
Adapted from: Maes, R., 1999, Reconsidering Information Management Through a Generic Framework, PrimaVera Working Paper 99–15. Portions reprinted, with permission, from Prima Vera Working Papers.

and a technology level. The split of the IT domain results from the observation that most information and communication processes are IT independent and therefore need to be regarded separately. In this context, reference needs to be made to another new concept that is emerging in the field, under the name Information Governance, stating that it is all in the first place about the information and not the technology. The previous argumentation results in a 3×3 matrix as opposed to the 2×2 matrix first presented by Henderson and Venkatraman.

Both models presented above clearly demonstrate that alignment is a multi-faced and complex construct, often referred to as the alignment challenge. Broadbent and Weill (1998) continue in this domain by depicting a number of difficulties (barriers) that organizations have experienced while aligning business with IT. The *expression barriers* arise from the organization's strategic context and from senior management behavior, including lack of direction in business strategy. This results in insufficient understanding of and commitment to the organization's strategic focus by operational management. *Specification barriers* arise from the circumstances of the organization's IT strategy such as lack of IT involvement in strategy development and business and IT management conducting two independent monologues. This ends up in a situation where business and IT strategies are setin isolation and are not adequately related. The nature of the organization's current IT portfolio creates *implementation barriers* which arise when there are technical, political or financial constraints on the current infrastructure. A good example of this last barrier is the difficult integration of legacy systems.

- IT is a professional organization that effectively and efficiently manages its resources in alignment with the needs of the organization.
- IT is the exclusive provider of IT services. Outsourcing is always organized in joint partnership between business and IT.
- IT is pro-actively engaged in further developing and innovating the organization.
- IT primarily develops and maintains competencies that are aligned to and required for supporting the expertise available in the organization.
- The priorities within IT are aligned to the strategic goals of the organizations through integrated planning cycles.
- All IT applications comply with rules and policies as mutually agreed upon by business and IT.
- IT is pro-actively engaged in reviewing and designing efficient business processes.
- IT and the business collaborate based on fixed agreements. Based on a scope definition, impact analysis and capacity reviews, both business and IT commit for timely delivery within quality requirements.
- There is transparency on the required service quality that IT has to deliver to the business, and this service quality is continuously monitored.
- Starting from the initial development of a new business project, the potential impact on IT needs to be analyzed.

Fig. 1.9 Business/IT alignment principles

In practice, organizations often try to express a number of "business/IT principles," which clearly state how business and IT will collaborate in the organization. These principles are to be defined jointly by business and IT and constitute a kind of contract between business and IT. Examples of principles used in real-life organizations are provided in Fig. 1.9. Each of these principles of course requires more detailed definitions and descriptions of what exactly the implications are toward both business and IT.

Assignment Box 1.1: Understanding business/IT alignment principles

Discuss in group the meaning of the alignment principles as depicted in Fig. 1.9. Describe in a paper what exactly the implications are for both business and IT. Present and discuss the results to the class.

1.2.2 Aligning Business Goals and IT Goals

To provide practitioners with hands-on guidance in the business/IT alignment domain, a research project by the UAMS – ITAG Research Institute and the IT Governance Institute worked on developing pragmatic insights into how concrete business goals can drive IT goals and vice versa, as visualized in Fig. 1.10. If "maintaining the enterprise reputation and leadership" is an important

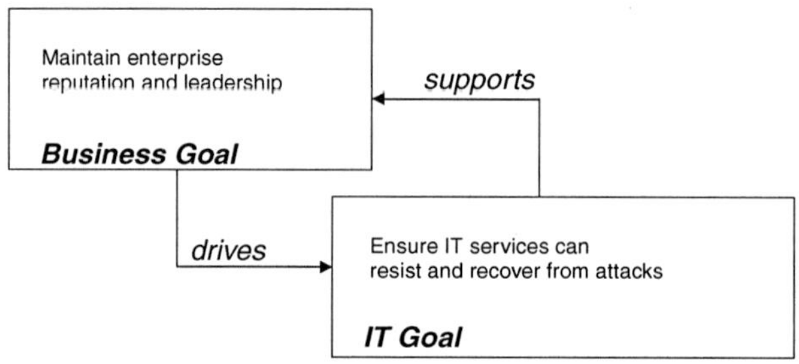

Fig. 1.10 Business goals driving IT goals

business goal, a supporting IT goal could be "ensuring IT services can resist and recover from attacks." Some outcomes of this research are discussed below, and the research methodology (delphi methodology) is described in Research Box 1.1.

In practice, every enterprise will have its own distinct sets of business and IT goals. Priorities within these sets will differ depending on a variety of internal and external factors, such as company size, industry and geography. For this research, an industry focus was taken by looking at five sectors: manufacturing and pharmaceuticals, IT professional services, telecommunications and media, government, utilities (such as energy, oil and gas) and healthcare sector, retail and transportation sector. The research was built on an earlier study, in which 20 generic (IT-related) business goals and 28 generic IT goals were defined based on interviews in multiple sectors, and later on published in COBIT 4.0 (see also Chapter 5 in this book on COBIT). The objective of this new research was

- to validate these lists for completeness, consistency and clarity,
- to gain more insight into goals priorities for different sectors and
- to examine the relationship between IT goals and business goals.

Research Box 1.1: Doing Delphi research on defining and linking business goals and IT goals

For the research on defining and linking business goals and IT goals, as discussed in Sect. 1.2.2, the Delphi methodology was used. This method is based on a structured process for collecting and distilling knowledge from a group of experts by means of several feedback rounds. A team of experts was asked to prioritize a list of business and IT goals by using a ranking technique and the averaged results were returned to them. Different rounds were performed in order to achieve consensus between the experts on which were the important goals and how the business goals linked to the IT goals. Another example of Delphi research is discussed in Chapter 2 of this book.

For this research, the ISACA member database was used as a major source to identify subject experts (ISACA is the Information Systems Audit and Control Association, see www.isaca.org). In total 158 business and IT people participated, either managers or auditors, from companies with more than 150 employees, divided over the five sectors. One of the assumptions was that experts, holding a management position or being an auditor, have sufficient knowledge on both IT and business goals.

Figure 1.11 presents the expert team's composition per sector and per geographical area.

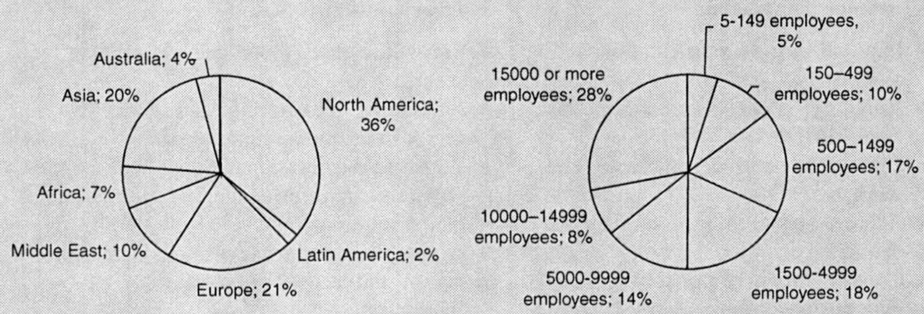

Fig. 1.11 Delphi expert team composition

The outcome of the exercise was an in-depth understanding of business goals, IT goals and how they interrelate. During the research, the original list of IT goals and business goals (as published in COBIT 4.0) has been validated and reviewed multiple times and evolved to a generic list of 17 (IT-related) business goals and 18 IT goals. Figure 1.12 presents the final list of business and IT goals, categorized by their corresponding balanced scorecard (BSC) perspectives (see also Chapter 4 in this book on the IT balanced scorecard).

Both lists of business and IT goals have been prioritized over five different sectors. Figure 1.13 presents the top 10 most important business and IT goals, consolidated over all sectors. Apart from some minor exceptions, the separate lists of the different sectors include the same business goals and IT goals in their individual top 10. This proves that there is a very high degree of consensus that these goals are, generically spoken, the most important IT-related business goals and IT goals.

Although priorities may differ from sector to sector, in general business goals categorized in the Customer and Financial perspective of the BSC do score high in the ranked list, while the Internal and Learning and Growth perspective goals receive lower scores overall. As an example, the customer-oriented business goals "Improve customer orientation and service" and "Establish service continuity and availability" and the financial-oriented business goals "Comply with external laws and regulations" and "Manage

Business Goals	IT Goals
Financial perspective • Manage (IT related) business risks • Provide a good return on investment of (IT enabled) business investments • Improve financial transparency • Comply with external laws and regulations	**Corporate contribution** • Offer transparency and understanding of IT cost, benefits and risks • Provide IT compliance with laws and regulations • Account for and protect all IT assets • Drive commitment and support of executive management • Improve IT's cost-efficiency • Align the IT strategy to the business strategy
Customer perspective • Improve customer orientation and service • Establish service continuity and availability • Offer competitive products and services • Achieve cost optimization of service delivery • Create agility in responding to changing business requirements • Obtain reliable and useful information for strategic decision making	**User orientation** • Make sure that IT services are reliable and secure • Provide service offerings and service levels in line with business requirements • Translate business functional and control requirements in effective and efficient automated solutions • Accomplish proper use of applications, information and technology solutions
Internal perspective • Improve and maintain business process functionality • Improve and maintain operational and staff productivity • Enable and Manage business change • Comply with internal policies • Optimize business process costs	**Operational excellence** • Maintain the security (confidentiality, integrity and availability) of information and processing infrastructure • Deliver projects on time and on budget meeting quality standards • Optimize the IT infrastructure, resources and capabilities • Provide IT agility (in responding to changing business needs) • Seamlessly integrate applications and technology solutions into business processes
Learning and growth perspective • Acquire, develop and maintain skilled and motivated people • Identify, enable and manage product and business innovation	**Future orientation** • Acquire, develop and maintain IT skills that respond to the IT strategy • Acquire knowledge and expertise in emerging technologies for business innovation and optimization • Ensure that IT demonstrates continuous improvement and readiness for future change

Fig. 1.12 Validated lists of business goals and IT goals

Top 10 prioritized list of business goals	Top 10 prioritized list of IT goals
1. Improve customer orientation and service 2. Comply with external laws and regulations 3. Establish service continuity and availability 4. Manage (IT related) business risks 5. Offer competitive products and services 6. Improve and maintain business process functionality 7. Provide a good return on investment of (IT enabled) business investments 8. Acquire, develop and maintain skilled and motivated people 9. Create agility in responding to changing business requirements 10. Obtain reliable and useful information for strategic decision making	1. Align the IT strategy to the business strategy 2. Maintain the security (confidentiality, integrity and availability) of information and processing infrastructure 3. Make sure that IT services are reliable and secure 4. Provide service offerings and service levels in line with business requirements 5. Provide IT compliance with laws and regulations 6. Translate business functional and control requirements in effective and efficient automated solutions 7. Deliver projects on time and on budget meeting quality standards 8. Drive commitment and support of executive management 9. Improve IT's cost-efficiency 10. Account for and protect all IT assets

Fig. 1.13 Top 10 list of business goals and IT goals

IT-related business risks" make up the top four in the generic list and are also systematically ranked high to very high in the individual lists per sector, geography and company size.

For the IT goals list, this trend is confirmed: the IT goals for the related IT BSC perspectives Corporate and User are higher in the list than those for the Learning and Growth perspective. For example, the corporate contribution-related goals "Align the IT strategy to the business strategy" and "Provide IT compliance with laws and regulations" and the user-oriented goals "Make sure that IT services are reliable and secure" and "Provide service offerings and service levels in line with business requirements" are systematically ranked high for the different sectors, geographies and company sizes.

Although in general a relatively high degree of consensus was found regarding the most important (top-10) business and IT goals, a number of sector-specific characteristics were identified. For example, for the IT professional services sector its high dependency on IT skills was confirmed by a higher ranking for the goal "Acquire, develop and maintain IT skills...." Another important asset (differentiator) for the companies operating in this sector is its (knowledge of) advanced technology, which explains the higher reported importance of "Identify, enable and manage product and business innovation." On the contrary, the business goals "Establish service continuity and availability" and "Improve and maintain business process functionality" do score lower, compared to most other sectors. This may be explained due to lower focus (and lower budgets) on their own internal

IT Goals \ Business Goals	1. Improve customer orientation and service	2. Provide compliance with external laws and regulations	3. Establish service continuity and availability	4. Manage (IT related) business risk	5. Offer competitive products and services	6. Improve and maintain business process functionality	7. Provide a good return on investment of (IT related) business investments	8. Acquire, develop and maintain skilled and motivated people	9. Create agility in responding to changing business requirement	10. Obtain reliable and useful information for strategic decision making	11. Achieve cost optimisation and service delivery	12. Optimise business process costs	13. Enable and manage business change	14. Improve and maintain operational and staff productivity	15. Improve financial transparency	16. Provide compliance with internal policies	17. Identify, enable and manage product innovation
1. Align the IT strategy to the business strategy	P	S	S	P	P	P	S	S	P	P	S	S	P	S	S	S	P
2.. Maintain the security (confidentiality, integrety and availability) of information and processing infrastructure	P	P	P	P		S				S						P	
3. Make sure that IT services are available and secure	P	P	P	P	S	S	S		S	S	S	S	S	S		S	
4. Provide service offerings and service levels in line with business requirements	P		P	S	P	P	S		S	S	S	S	S	S		S	S
5. Provide IT compliance with laws and regulations	S	P		P	S		S								S	P	
6. Translate business functional and control requirements in effective and efficient automated solutions	S		S	S	S	P		S	S	S	S	S	S	S		S	S
7. Deliver projects on time and on budget meeting quality standards	S			S	S	S	S		S		S	S	S		S		
8. Drive commitment and support of executive management	S			S	S	S		S	S	S			S			S	S
9. Improve IT's cost-efficiency					S		P				P	P			S		
10. Account for and protect all IT assets		S	S	S			S				S				S		
11. Acquire, develop and maintain IT skills that respond to the IT strategy	S			S				P	S		S		S	S			S
12. Provide IT agility (in responding to changing business needs)	S			S	S	S			P				P				S
13. Offer transparancy and understanding of IT costs, benefits and risks				S			S				S	S			P		
14. Optimise the IT infrastructure, resources and capabilities			S		S		P		S		P	S		S			
15. Accomplish proper use of applications, information and technology solutions	S		S	S	S	S	S		S	S	S	S	S	S		S	
16. Seamlessly integrate applications and technology solutions in business processes	S				S	P	S		S	S	S	S	S	S			S
17. Ensure that IT demonstrates continuous improvement and readiness for future change					S	S		S	P				S				P
18. Acquire knowlegde and expertise in emerging technologies for business innovation and optimisation					S	S		P	S	S			S	S			P

Fig. 1.14 Linking IT goals to business goals

processes while most efforts go to customer services. Another typical example is the retail and transportation sector. This sector is characterized by low profit margins, which explains the higher reported ranking for goals such as "Optimize business process costs." Customer loyalty is also seen as one of the challenges in this sector and initiatives are undertaken to deal with this. This is translated into the reported top four most important business goals, which are all customer oriented. This is also the only sector where the business goal for compliance with external laws and regulations is not in the top three, indicating that compliance is not yet a priority in the retail and transportation sector.

When comparing differences between regions in the world or comparing companies with different sizes fewer variations were identified, which may indicate that sector-related characteristics have a higher impact on setting priorities. Still, some minor but interesting differences were identified. For example, larger organizations tend to pay more attention to business goals such as "Comply with external laws and regulations" and "Manage (IT-related) business risks" compared to smaller organizations. In Europe, the Middle East and Africa, the IT goal "Acquire, develop and maintain IT skills that respond to the IT strategy" appears to be less important compared to other regions in the world.

Another finding is that in general, the level of agreement between the experts for the list of prioritized business goals is lower than the level of agreement for prioritized IT goals. An explanation may be found in the fact that business goals may differ more dependent upon some external or internal factors, such as sector-specific characteristics, company size, geography and others, while IT goals prioritization may follow a more generic pattern and are less influenced by these aspects.

This research also contains detailed findings on how the IT goals can support business goals. Figure 1.14 shows in a matrix how IT goals are related to business goals. From this matrix it becomes (visually) clear that some goals are defined on a higher level compared to others. For example the IT goal "Align the IT strategy to the business strategy" does support all business goals in a primary (P) or a secondary (S) manner, indicating its scope is broadly defined and covers multiple areas of IT responsibilities. On the other hand, the business goal #15 "Improve financial transparency" and the IT goal #13 "Offer transparency and understanding of IT cost, benefits and risks" show only a primary relationship to each other, confirming their similar and narrowly defined scope.

The results of this research provide practical guidance for professionals in the attempt to build up a cascade of business goals and IT goals for their specific organization and in this way obtain a better insight in the business/IT alignment issue. Enterprises can do that efficiently by starting from these generic business and IT goals, selecting what applies to them and updating it for enterprise-specific situations. This will be a good starting point toward implementing Enterprise Governance of IT.

Assignment Box 1.2: Defining and linking business goals and IT goals

Work in groups of three to five people and choose a specific organization or industry sector. Next, run through the following steps:

- Assume that you are the Board or Executive Committee of the organization and define five specific business goals
- Put the business goals aside. Assume you are the IT Management Committee of the same organization, and define five specific IT goals.
- Put the business goals and IT goals in a matrix and try to find correlations on how IT goals support business goals.

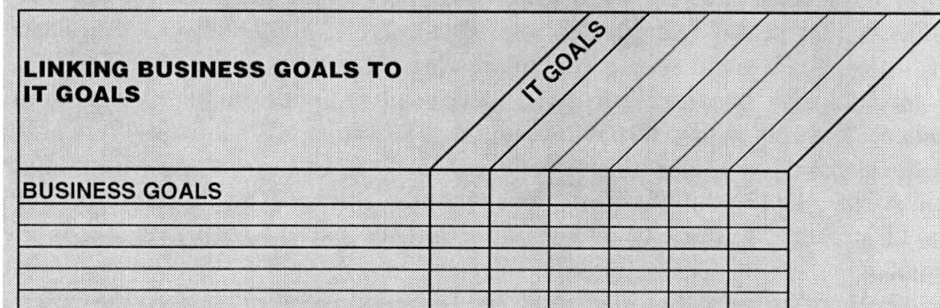

- Discuss and present your conclusions to the group

1.3 Business/IT Alignment and Business Value from IT

A crucial question in the alignment debate is why the notion is so fundamentally important to an organization's success. Much research has been conducted on this issue, particularly with a view to demonstrating the correlation between business/IT alignment and business performance. Studies by Chan et al. and Sabherwal and Chan (2001), for example, confirm the hypothesis that alignment between business and IT strategies improves business performance. Even stronger, from their research it appears that the relative direct impact of strategic alignment on business performance is higher compared to the direct impact of business strategy or IT strategy on business performance. As illustrated in Fig. 1.15, strategic alignment is one of the core drivers in enabling business performance.

Bergeron et al. (2003), on the other hand, argue that such research efforts tend to be too one-sided, because alignment, as defined by Henderson and Venkatram, should also be seen to encompass operational business and IT processes. Still, despite this broader perspective, they too conclude that organizations with high alignment between business and IT strategies on the one hand and business and IT operational processes on the other ultimately achieve

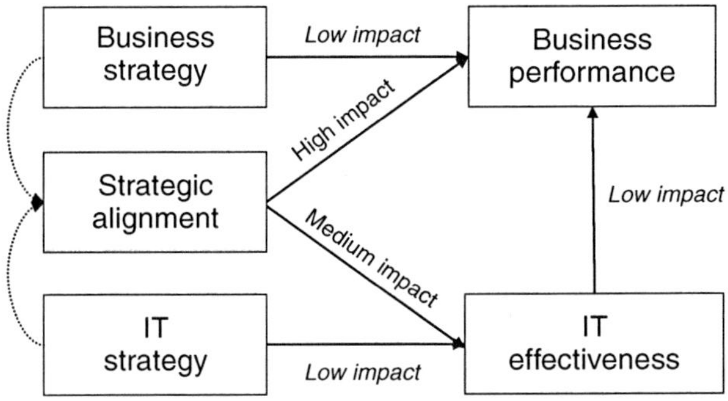

Fig. 1.15 Alignment and business performance
Adapted from: Chan et al. (1997), Business Strategy Orientation, Information Systems Orientation and Strategic Alignment, Information Systems Research, vol. 8, no. 2. Portions reprinted, with permission, from the Institute for Operations Research and the Management Sciences.

better outcomes. Such research findings provide an important addition to the debate initiated by Brynjolfson on the productivity paradox, where no clear correlation could be identified between the amount of investment in IT and business performance.

The above studies suggest that the alignment construct is an important intermediate variable or catalyst for business value creation from IT investments. This is also stressed by ITGI (2008): "The value that IT adds to the business is a function of the degree to which the IT organization is aligned with the business and meets the expectations of the business."

In this textbook, separate chapters are dedicated to international best practices framework COBIT (Chapters 5 and 6) and Val IT (Chapter 7). These frameworks provide a comprehensive model (see Fig. 1.16) to demonstrate how applying governance practices can enable the achievement of IT goals which in turn enable the achievement of business goals and consequently business benefits.

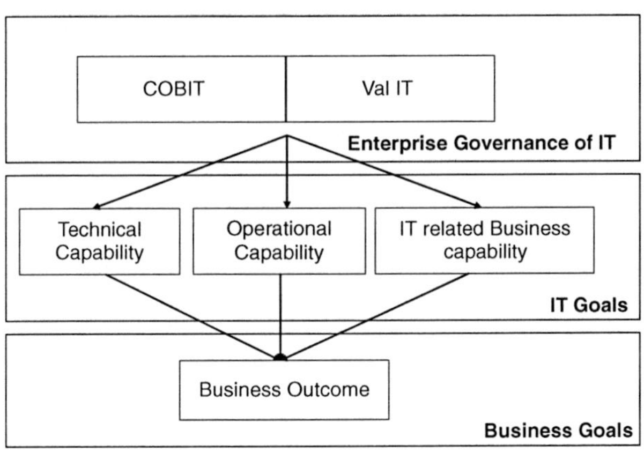

Fig. 1.16 Governance practices and business outcomes

The proposed model states that by applying Enterprise Governance of IT practices as presented in COBIT and Val IT, the likelihood of achieving the IT goals increases. The IT goals are categorized in three domains:

- Technical IT capabilities are about the delivery of IT solutions, e.g., the delivery of a CRM application.
- Operational IT capabilities are about building services around the application, e.g. ensuring continued access to complete customer information.
- IT-related business capabilities are about enabling the business to create value out of the investments in IT and include, e.g., business process redesign, end-user training, etc.

Achieving IT goals in turn increases the likelihood of achieving business goals such as client satisfaction and revenue growth. This model is currently being validated based on empirical data within the IT Alignment and Governance Research Institute of University of Antwerp Management School (www.uams.be/itag) and will provide more insights into how business value (business goals will be used as a proxy for business benefits/value) can be generated from applying governance and alignment practices.

Summary

Enterprise Governance of IT is a relatively new concept in literature and is gaining more and more interest in the academic and practitioner's world. Enterprise Governance of IT addresses the definition and implementation of processes, structures and relational mechanism that enable both business and IT people to execute their responsibilities in support of business/IT alignment and the creation of value from IT-enabled business investments.

Enterprise Governance of IT is an important enabler for business/IT alignment. Business/IT alignment is a complex construct, with important models developed by Henderson and Venkatraman and Maes. These models stress the importance of balancing business and IT strategic and operational issues to obtain alignment. For practitioners in the field, the business/IT alignment concept can be translated into a cascade of business goals and IT goals.

Achieving a high degree of business/IT alignment in turn will enable the achievement of business value from IT, which by itself will not generate value for the business. Value will only be realized when both IT and the business are involved (aligned). For practitioners, both COBIT and Val IT are important international best practice frameworks to realize and implement Enterprise Governance of IT as enablers for business/IT alignment and value creation from IT.

Study Questions

1. Define Enterprise Governance of IT and explain the shift from IT governance toward Enterprise Governance of IT.
2. Review and assess the ISO 38500 principles in relation to the definition of Enterprise Governance of IT.
3. Like Enterprise Governance of IT, governance requirements for other key assets such as financial governance exist. Explain why the Enterprise Governance of IT seems to be more imperative.
4. Explain the difference between IT management and Enterprise Governance of IT.
5. Explain and discuss the two main business/IT alignment questions: how is IT aligned with the business and how is the business aligned with IT.
6. Define and explain what is meant by business/IT alignment principles and give some examples.
7. Explain what is understood by the cascade of business goals/IT goals/IT processes and illustrate with an example.
8. Define business/IT alignment and explain its relationship with achieving business value from IT.
9. Explain and discuss how business/IT alignment can be expressed as a symbiotic combination of business goals and IT goals.

Further Reading

Bergeron, F., Raymond, L., and Rivard, S., 2003, Ideal Patterns of Strategic Alignment and Business Performance, Information & Management, Elsevier, vol. 41, no. 8, pp. 1003–1020.

Broadbent, M., and Weill, P., 1998, Leveraging the New Infrastructure – How Market Leaders Capitalize on Information Technology. Boston, Massachusetts: Harvard Business School Press.

Brynjolfsson, E., and Hitt, L.M., 1998, Beyond the Productivity Paradox, Communications of the ACM, vol. 41, no. 8.

Carr, N.G., 2003, IT Doesn't Matter, Harvard Business Review, vol. 81, no. 5, pp. 41–49.

Chan, Y., Huff, S., Barclay, D.W., and Copeland, D.W., 1997, Business Strategic Orientation, Information Systems Strategic Orientation, and Strategic Alignment, Information Systems Research, vol. 8, no. 2, pp. 125–150.

De Haes, S., 2007, The Impact of IT Governance Practices on Business/IT Alignment in the Belgian Financial Services Sector, Thesis Submitted to Achieve the Degree of PhD in Applied Economics. University of Antwerp, Promotor: Van Grembergen, W.

De Haes, S., and Van Grembergen, W., 2005, IT Governance Structures, Processes and Relational Mechanisms: Achieving IT/Business Alignment in a Major Belgian Financial Group, in Proceedings of Hawaii International Conference on System Sciences (HICSS).

De Haes, S., and Van Grembergen, W., 2006, IT Governance Best Practices in Belgian Organizations, in Proceedings of the Hawaii International Conference on System Sciences (HICSS).

De Haes, S., and Van Grembergen, W., 2008a, Practices in IT Governance and Business/IT Alignment, Information Systems Control Journal, vol. 2.

De Haes, S., and Van Grembergen, W., 2008b, Analyzing the Relationship between IT Governance and Business/IT Alignment Maturity, in Proceedings of the 41st Hawaii International Conference on System Sciences (HICSS).

Evans, B., 2003, Business Technology: IT Is A Must, No Matter How You View It, Information Week, May 19, p. 74.

Henderson, J.C., and Venkatraman, N., 1993, Strategic Alignment: Leveraging Information Technology for Transforming Organizations, IBM Systems Journal, vol. 32, no. 1.

Henderson, J.C., Venkatraman, N., and Oldach, S., 1993, Continuous Strategic Alignment: Exploiting Information Technology Capabilities for Competitive Success. European Management Journal, vol. 11, no. 2, pp. 139–149.

Huizing, A., and De Vries, E., 2007, Information Management: Setting the Scene. Oxford, UK: Elsevier Science.

ITGI, 2003, Board Briefing on IT Governance, Second Edition, from www.itgi.org

ITGI, 2007, COBIT 4.1, from www.itgi.org

ITGI, 2008, Enterprise Value: Governance of IT investments, The Val IT Framework, from www.itgi.org

Maes, R., 1999, Reconsidering Information Management through a Generic Framework, PrimaVera Working Paper 99–15.

Sabherwal, R., and Chan, Y., 2001, Alignment Between Business and IS Strategies: A Study of Prospectors, Analyzers and Defenders, Information Systems Research, vol. 12, no. 1, pp. 11–33.

Thorp, J., 2003, The Information Paradox: Realizing the Business Benefits of Information Technology, McGraw-Hill.

Van Grembergen, W., 2002, Introduction to the Minitrack: IT Governance and its Mechanisms, in proceedings of the 35th Hawaii International Conference on System Sciences (HICSS).

Van Grembergen, W. (Ed.), 2004, Strategies for Information Technology Governance. Hershey, PA: Idea Group Publishing.

Van Grembergen, W., and De Haes, S., 2008, Implementing Information Technology Governance: Models, Practices and Cases, Hershey: IGI Publishing.

Van Grembergen, W., Van Brempt, H., and De Haes, S., 2007, Prioritizing and Linking Business and IT Goals in the Financial Sector, in Proceedings of the 40th Hawaii International Conference on System Sciences (HICSS).

Van Grembergen, W., De Haes, S., and Van Brempt, H., 2007, How Does the Business Drive IT? Identifying, Prioritizing and Linking Business and IT Goals, Information Systems Control, vol. 6.

Weill, P., and Ross, J., 2004, IT Governance: How Top Performers Manage IT Decision Rights for Superior Results. Boston: Harvard Business School Press.

Websites

Information Technology Alignment and Governance Research Institute: www.uams.be/ITAG

ISACA: www.isaca.org

ISO: www.iso.org

IT Governance Institute: www.itgi.org

Chapter 2
Enterprise Governance of IT in Practice

Abstract The previous chapter described what Enterprise Governance of IT is about. However, having developed a high-level model for Enterprise Governance of IT does not imply that governance is actually working in the organization. Conceiving the model for Enterprise Governance of IT is the first step, and deploying it throughout all levels of the organization is the next challenging step. To achieve this, Enterprise Governance of IT can be deployed using a mixture of various structures, processes and relational mechanisms. This chapter provides an overview of best practices that organizations can leverage to implement Enterprise Governance of IT. A lot of case studies are described in this chapter, as each individual governance implementation will be different depending on the organization's size, sector, geography, etc. Finally, detailed discussions are laid out regarding the effectiveness, ease of implementation and importance of each of the presented practices for Enterprise Governance of IT.

2.1 Best Practices for Enterprise Governance of IT

When looking at an organization, it can typically be subdivided into three layers, as shown in Fig. 2.1. It is clear that Enterprise Governance of IT is situated at each of these layers in the organization: at strategic level where the board is involved, at management level within the C-suite and senior management layer and finally at the operational level with operational IT and business management. This implies that all these levels, business as well as IT, need to be involved in the Enterprise Governance of IT process and they have to understand their individual roles and responsibilities within the framework.

To implement Enterprise Governance of IT in practice, an organization requires a holistic set of governance processes, structures and relational mechanisms at each of these layers (see Fig. 2.2).

Enterprise Governance of IT structures include organizational units and roles responsible for making IT decisions and for enabling contacts between business and IT management (decision-making) functions (e.g., steering

W. Van Grembergen, S. De Haes, *Enterprise Governance of Information Technology*, DOI 10.1007/978-0-387-84882-2_2,

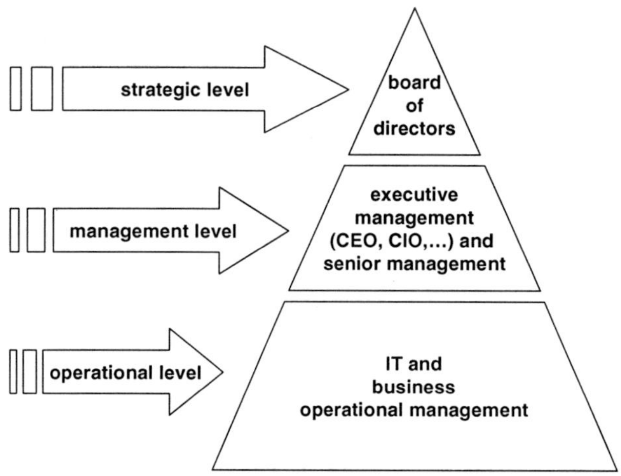

Fig. 2.1 Three layers for Enterprise Governance of IT

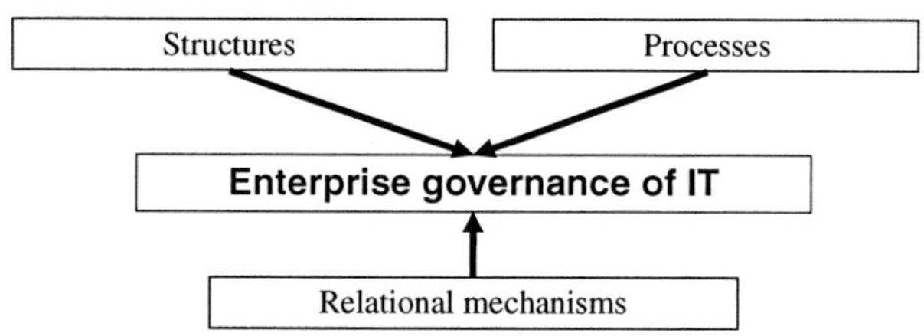

Fig. 2.2 Structures, processes and relational mechanisms for Enterprise Governance of IT

committees). This can be seen as a kind of blueprint of how the Enterprise Governance of IT framework will be structurally organized.

Enterprise Governance of IT processes refer to formalization and institutionalization of strategic IT decision-making or IT monitoring procedures, to ensure that daily behaviors are consistent with policies and provide input back to decisions (e.g., IT balanced scorecard).

The relational mechanisms finally are about the active participation of, and collaborative relationship among, corporate executives, IT management and business management and include announcements, advocates, channels and education efforts. A lot of researchers have stated that relational mechanisms are crucial in the Enterprise Governance of IT framework and paramount for attaining and sustaining business–IT alignment, even when the appropriate structures and processes are in place.

Based on research in the UAMS – ITAG Research Institute, a list of 33 practices for Enterprise Governance of IT were identified and defined, which apply for information–intensive organizations (as most organizations are these days). This set of practices was built based on literature, multiple in-depth case research and experts reviews and is primarily focused on the strategic and management-oriented practices. Reason for the latter focus is that, out of

Research Box 2.1: Exploratory research in the financial services sector

Because research in the domain of Enterprise Governance of IT implementations and its relationship with business/IT alignment is in its early stages and theoretical models are scarcely available, the nature of this type of research is often exploratory rather than hypothesis testing. Indeed, the concept of Enterprise Governance of IT, as it is understood now, only emerged in the late 1990s, and there has been little research material developed on which we can build. The latter is true not only because it is a new research domain, but as denoted by Benbasat and Zmud (1999), "generally, IS researchers have been less successful than their colleagues in other business school disciplines in developing a cumulative research tradition. Without such cumulative results, it becomes difficult, if not impossible, to develop and assess strong theoretical models such that prescriptive actions can confidently be suggested for practice." By exploring this research domain in detail, a basis for future research can be created, by building theoretical models and generating potential hypotheses to be tested.

The choice for doing this exploratory research in the financial services sector is made because, amongst different industries, financial services, together with manufacturing and retailing, is the first industry to use information technologies and as such is already more matured in these domains, making empirical research interesting. Specifically for Enterprise Governance of IT, the latter is confirmed by recent research of the IT Governance Institute, indicating that the financial services sector is leading with 47% in having implemented IT governance (see Fig. 2.3).

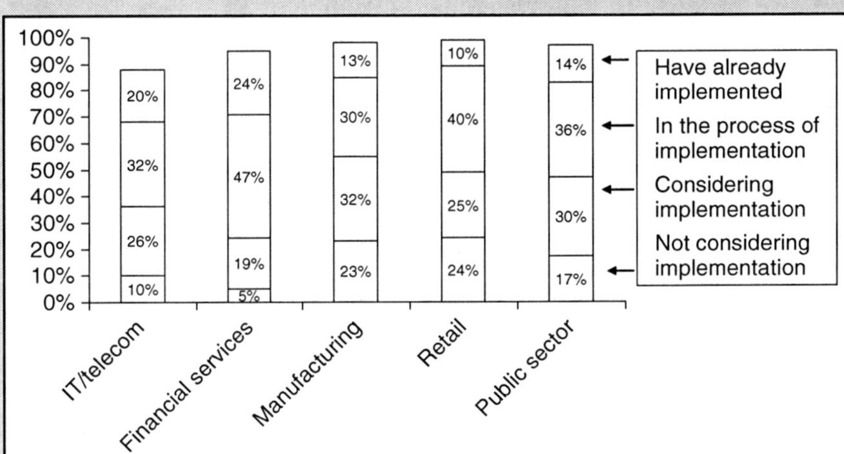

Fig. 2.3 IT governance implementation status by industry
ITGI, 2008b, IT Governance Global Status Report, Report published by ITGI, from www.itgi.org.

in-depth case research it appeared that operational level practices are not the key discriminating factors between good performers and bad performers in terms of business/IT alignment. This does not mean that the operational-oriented practices are less important (typical examples: ITIL, RUP). On the contrary, organizations have to make sure that these operational-oriented practices are sufficiently organized first, even before they can move to higher levels. But the operational-oriented practices by themselves will not generate a higher degree of business/IT alignment; that benefit will only be attained when more mature practices are exploited at management and strategic level as well. It is also clear that many of the Enterprise Governance of IT practices can be leveraged at multiple layers in the organization.

Figure 2.4 identifies and defines 33 practices for Enterprise Governance of IT, 12 structures, 11 processes and 10 relational mechanisms. In the columns at the right, an indication is provided regarding the primary level in the organization where each practice is operating (B = Board, E/S = Executive/Senior Management). In the next section, short cases and an in-depth case are described to illustrate how some of the practices operate in a real environment. After that, an extra section is added analyzing how practitioners perceive the "effectiveness," "ease of implementation" and "importance" of each of those practices. These results are based on exploratory research, mainly focused on the financial services sector. Reason for that industry focus is the assumption that this industry is leading in the adoption of governance practices and that other sectors and industries can learn from it. More information on exploratory research and industry focus is provided in Research Box 2.1.

2.2 Case Studies on Enterprise Governance of IT

To illustrate the practices defined in previous section, short cases are described focusing at respectively structures, processes and relational mechanism for Enterprise Governance of IT. These short cases were studied in the period 2003–2007 and encompass three different industry sectors: insurance, steel and chemicals. After that, a full integrated case is described, addressing structures, processes and relational mechanisms, in a large financial services organization.

2.2.1 Short Case on Structures – Vanbreda (Insurance)

2.2.1.1 Company Introduction

In the 1930s, Bank J. Van Breda & C° was founded in Belgium by Jos and Maurice Van Breda. While they initially focused on bank activities, they evolved over the years into a financial services group with bank and insurance activities. The bank component retained its original name (Bank J. Van Breda & C°),

	Index	Best Practice	Definition	Level	
				B	E/S
Structures	S1	IT strategy committee at level of board of directors	Committee at level of board of directors to ensure IT is regular agenda item and reporting issue for the board of directors	x	
	S2	IT expertise at level of board of directors	Members of the board of directors have expertise and experience regarding the value and risk of IT	x	
	S3	(IT) audit committee at level of board of directors	Independent committee at level of board of directors overviewing (IT) assurance activities	x	
	S4	CIO on executive committee	CIO is a full member of the executive committee		x
	S5	CIO (Chief Information Officer) reporting to CEO (Chief Executive Officer) and/or COO (Chief Operational Officer)	CIO has a direct reporting line to the CEO and/or COO		x
	S6	IT steering committee (IT investment evaluation / prioritization at executive / senior management level)	Steering committee at executive or senior management level responsible for determining business priorities in IT investments.		x
	S7	IT governance function / officer	Function in the organization responsible for promoting, driving and managing IT governance processes		x
	S8	Security/ compliance/risk officer	Function responsible for security, compliance and/or risk, which possibly impacts IT		x
	S9	IT project steering committee	Steering committee composed of business and IT people focusing on prioritizing and managing IT projects		x
	S10	IT security steering committee	Steering committee composed of business and IT people focusing on IT related risks and security issues		x
	S11	Architecture steering committee	Committee composed of business and IT people providing architecture guidelines and advise on their applications.		x
	S12	Integration of governance/alignment tasks in roles & responsibilities	Documented roles & responsibilities include governance/alignment tasks for business and IT people (cf. Weill)	x	x

Fig. 2.4 Thirty-three best practices for Enterprise Governance of IT

Processes	**P1**	Strategic information systems planning	Formal process to define and update the IT strategy	x	x
	P2	IT performance measurement (e.g. IT balanced scorecard)	IT performance measurement in domains of corporate contribution, user orientation, operational excellence and future orientation	x	x
	P3	Portfolio management (incl. business cases, information economics, ROI, payback)	Prioritization process for IT investments and projects in which business and IT is involved (incl. business cases)	x	x
	P4	Charge back arrangements - total cost of ownership (e.g. activity based costing)	Methodology to charge back IT costs to business units, to enable an understanding of the total cost of ownership		x
	P5	Service level agreements	Formal agreements between business and IT about IT development projects or IT operations		x
	P6	IT governance framework COBIT	Process based IT governance and control framework		x
	P7	IT governance assurance and self-assessment	Regular self-assessments or independent assurance activities on the governance and control over IT	x	x
	P8	Project governance/ management methodologies	Processes and methodologies to govern and manage IT projects		x
	P9	IT budget control and reporting	Processes to control and report upon budgets of IT investments and projects	x	x
	P10	Benefits management and reporting	Processes to monitor the planned business benefits during and after implementation of the IT investments / projects.	x	x
	P11	COSO/ERM	Framework for internal control	x	x

Fig. 2.4 (continued)

Relational mechanism	R1	Job-rotation	IT staff working in the business units and business people working in IT		x
	R2	Co-location	Physically locating business and IT people close to each other		x
	R3	Cross-training	Training business people about IT and/or training IT people about business		x
	R4	Knowledge management (on IT governance)	Systems (intranet, …) to share and distribute knowledge about IT governance framework, responsibilities, tasks, etc.	x	x
	R5	Business/IT account management	Bridging the gap between business and IT by means of account managers who act as in-between		x
	R6	Executive/senior management giving the good example	Senior business and IT management acting as "partners"		x
	R7	Informal meetings between business and IT executive/senior management	Informal meetings, with no agenda, where business and IT senior management talk about general activities, directions, etc. (e.g. during informal lunches)		x
	R8	IT leadership	Ability of CIO or similar role to articulate a vision for IT's role in the company and ensure that this vision is clearly understood by managers throughout the organization	x	x
	R9	Corporate internal communication addressing IT on a regular basis	Internal corporate communication regularly addresses general IT issues.	x	x
	R10	IT governance awareness campaigns	Campaigns to explain to business and IT people the need for IT governance	x	x

Fig. 2.4 (continued)

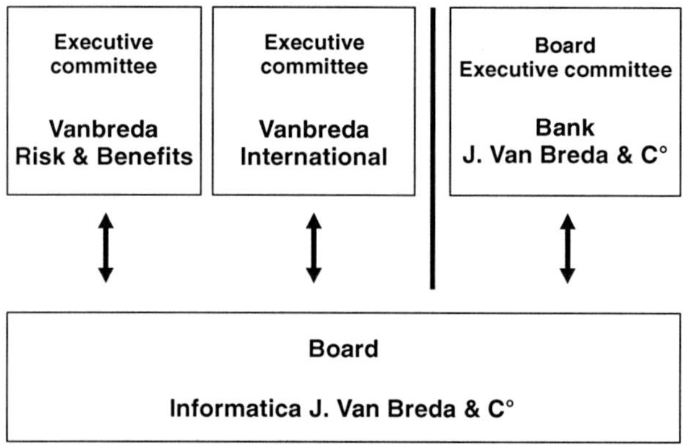

Fig. 2.5 Dependencies between the insurance component and the bank

whereas the insurance component operates these days under the name Vanbreda and currently exists as two companies: Vanbreda Risk & Benefits and Vanbreda International. Another part of the group is Informatica J. Van Breda & C°, the IT servicing company of the aforementioned business divisions. Figure 2.5 illustrates the dependencies between the different Van Breda/Vanbreda companies.

This case description focuses on the Vanbreda insurance branches of which the detailed organizational structure is visualized in Fig. 2.6. Both insurance companies share a number of functional departments, including systems development. They have a combined turnover of €75 million with a headcount of 650. Vanbreda Risk & Benefits focuses on insurance brokerage, risk management and employee benefits within Belgium, whereas Vanbreda International is specialized in the area of international employee benefits. The core business of Vanbreda Risk & Benefits is situated in the areas of insurance brokerage, reinsurance brokerage, consultancy and risk management to enterprises, public authorities, non-profit organizations, and individuals, both domestically and abroad. The core business of Vanbreda

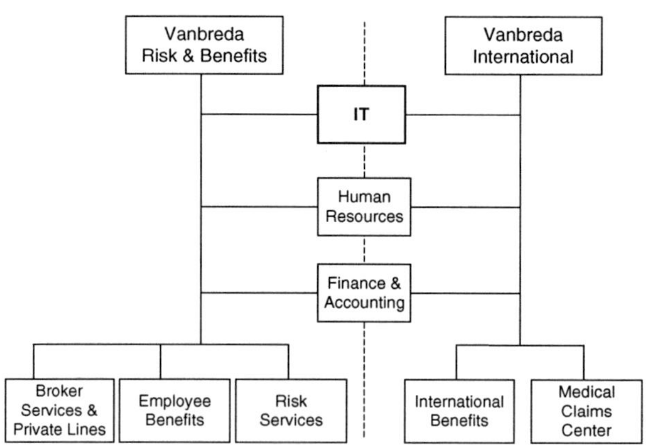

Fig. 2.6 Organization structure of the insurance component

International is the design of health plans for international groups and their claims administration. Vanbreda International is also specialized in giving advice on the most efficient funding arrangements for the social security system of their clients and concentrates on medical and dental coverage, long-term care, pension plans, etc.

2.2.1.2 Context of Enterprise Governance of IT

When asked what is understood by the concept of Enterprise Governance of IT within Vanbreda, the financial director answered: “Enterprise Governance of IT indisputably shows some parallels with corporate governance. It is about setting up the right structures distinguishing between operational and strategic IT aspects. It is important that decisions are being taken at the right level and that one has a ‘helicopter view’ on IT.”

The importance of setting up clear structures became clear to the management of Vanbreda when a major project failed. At that time all IT operations and system development of the group were centralized within Informatica J. Van Breda & C°, partly explaining the project failure because business and IT were drifting apart too much. It was acknowledged that both banking and insurance businesses had the need for specific business applications which led to a new Enterprise Governance of IT structure integrating IT development directly into the business and leaving the operational activities within Informatica J. Van Breda & C°. This is a typical example of the federal IT organization, a model which is wide spread in large organizations. When recently this structure was implemented, IT development staff were transferred away from the single IT organization toward the bank and insurance business entities. By anchoring these IT employees into the business, a better alignment between the business and IT could be achieved. On the other hand, the decision of keeping operations centrally was based on cost efficiency and economic rationality. The entire change is being perceived as a growth process and did not cause substantial problems. The financial director comments: “The whole process is being experienced as a logical evolution.”

2.2.1.3 Structures for Enterprise Governance of IT

As described in previous section, a major characteristic of the IT organization is its federal approach with operations centrally located within Informatica J. Van Breda & C° and systems development within the insurance businesses. Main goal of this structure is to bring IT development closer to the business. Figure 2.7 portrays the organization chart of Informatica J. Van Breda & C°. This chart shows a classical organization of IT operations with production management, systems management, help desk facility, systems architecture and security. Somewhat specific is document management, containing all activities related to archiving, printing and physical mail and voice mail (telephony). Informatica J. Van Breda & C° is a separate company with a turnover of €6.4 million employing 30 people. The turnover can

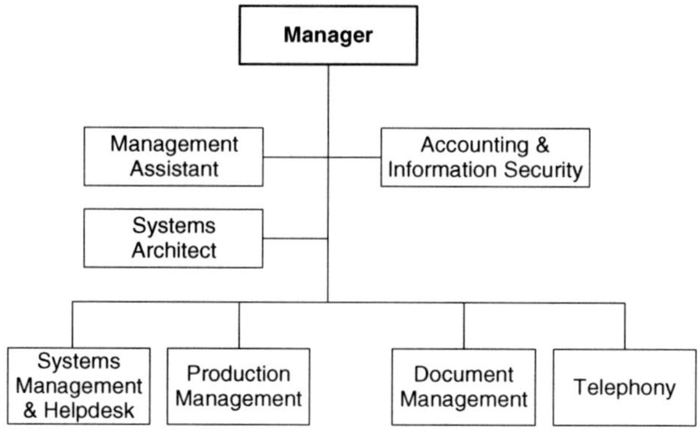

Fig. 2.7 Informatica J. Van Breda & C° organizational structure

be considered as the total IT operations budget of the group. Approximately 60% of this turnover goes to Vanbreda International and Vanbreda Risk & Benefits.

Figure 2.8 shows how the IT Projects and Development department of Vanbreda's insurance business is organized. Within this systems development department, a clear distinction is made between projects and development. The project units form a bridging function, known as account management, between the business and development whereas the development units include the systems architects and the developers. The IT Projects and Development department counts 46 people, of which 40 are developers and 6 are account managers. Their IT budget is about €7.5 million, representing about 10% of the turnover.

Individual function descriptions exist at Vanbreda to define the roles and responsibilities of their employees. These descriptions consist of a function name, objectives, a task description, required skills and the assessors. A typical function description for the IT director is shown in Fig. 2.9. From this description it can be seen that the IT director has complete responsibility over the IT development and implementation activities for the insurance business entities. Currently, this position is taken by a business manager with broad technical expertise, which conforms to the function description and corresponds with the required skills. The related assessors use a competence matrix to monitor

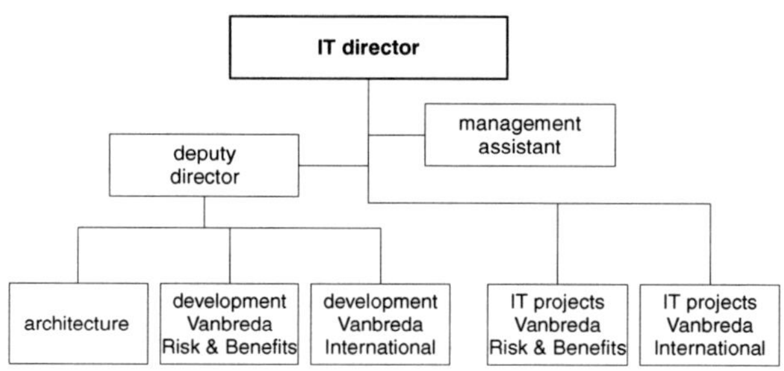

Fig. 2.8 Organizational structure of IT projects and development

Function name:	IT director
Objectives:	He has final responsibility on the IT development for both insurance entities. He is responsible for the continuity and permanent improvement of services. [...]
Task description:	He is responsible for the development of an IT communication strategy that fully supports the business strategy, with an effective and efficient use of specified resources. With strong project organization he needs to deliver high quality applications fast and cost-efficient, respecting the formulated needs and agreed budget and timing. [...] He has to prepare and document strategic IT choices and decisions.
Required skills:	This function requires a broad knowledge of the whole IT area, as well as in-depth knowledge of the different sub domains and good understanding of the business. [...] Furthermore excellent teamwork, communication and leadership skills and focus on efficiency as well as effectiveness and are essential.
Assessment:	This function is to be assessed by the managing director.

Fig. 2.9 Abstract of an individual function description

whether the employee has fulfilled his role and taken up his responsibilities. The competence matrix covers supervisory or management skills, analyzing skills, communicative skills, planning and organizational skills, knowledge, involvement and personal skills.

As shown in Fig. 2.10, Vanbreda establishes a number of committees for steering IT operations and development within the businesses. Each committee has its specific meeting frequency.

The board of Informatica J. Van Breda & C° is co-chaired by the CEOs of the insurance and banking units. In the context of best governance practices the board is extended with an independent member. Other members of the board

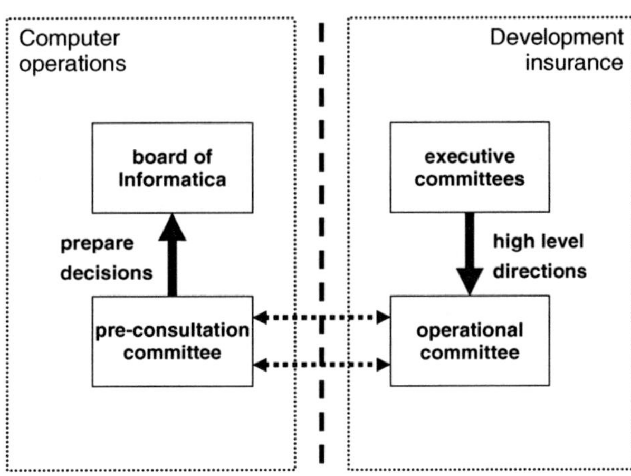

Fig. 2.10 Committees supporting Enterprise Governance of IT

1. Approval and signing of the minutes of the previous Board
2. Overview of the headcount 2004
3. Overview of the projects in 2004
4. SLAs Informatica J. Van Breda & C° (version June 2004)
5. Information Security (version June 2004)

Fig. 2.11 Typical agenda of the board of Informatica J. Van Breda & C°

are the IT manager of Informatica and the ICT Director. This specific composition implies that the board also acts as an executive committee. Typical issues on the agenda are shown in Fig. 2.11 and encompass for example an overview of the IT projects and the approval of established service level agreements between Informatica and the businesses.

The board is supported by a pre-consultation committee having more frequent meetings. This committee has an almost identical composition as the board and is also co-chaired by the CEOs of insurance and the bank. It prepares the board's decisions and discusses operational problems. Whereas the board meets four times a year this committee meets every second week. The development activities of the insurance business are governed by its executive committees, focusing on high-level directions, and an operational committee which prioritizes, selects and tracks projects in line with these directions. The operational committee is composed of the IT director, his deputy and two CEOs representing their insurance entity. Some typical agenda points of the operational committee (Fig. 2.12) such as project priorities, resource allocation and budgeting demonstrate that this committee largely matches with what was defined in the introductory chapter as an IT steering committee.

Figure 2.13 provides a summary of the different committees having IT influence at Vanbreda, their authority and members within IT and the business.

1. Report of previous Operational Committee
2. Tracking of Projects
  2.1. Projects of Vanbreda Risk & Benefits
    – Planning IT development per 1/09/2004
  2.2. Projects of Vanbreda International
    – To be decided: Project E04056 "Translation into English"
    – To be decided: Project E04057 "Translation into English"
    – To be decided: Project E04060 "Split payments"
    – Planning IT development per 1/09/2004
3. Personnel
  – New vacancies Vanbreda International
4. Miscellaneous
  – Budget 2005 project hours Vanbreda Risk & Benefits
  – Budget 2005 project hours Vanbreda International
  – Capacity IT development 2005

Fig. 2.12 Typical agenda of the operational committee

Name	Authority	Composition	
		IT	Business
board of Informatica J. Van Breda & C°	aligning operations to business needs, overview of projects, approval of SLAs	IT directors of insurance and the bank, manager of Informatica	the CEOs
Pre-consultation committee	prepares the board's decisions, discusses operational problems	IT directors of insurance and the bank, manager of Informatica	the CEOs
executive committee Vanbreda Risk & Benefits	providing high level directions	the IT director of the insurance units	all the directors of Vanbreda Risk & Benefits
executive committee Vanbreda International	providing high level directions	the IT director of the insurance units	all the directors of Vanbreda International
operational committee	prioritization, selection and tracking of projects	the IT director and his deputy director of the insurance units	CEOs of both insurance units

Fig. 2.13 Vanbreda committees, authorities and composition

2.2.2 Short Case on Processes – Sidmar/Arcelor (Steel)

2.2.2.1 Company Introduction

Sidmar is a leading international steel producer with headquarters in Ghent, Belgium. The Sidmar company was founded in 1962 as a daughter of the Luxembourgian steel group Arbed. Sidmar produces flat steel with its major clients being car manufacturers. In 2002 Sidmar became part of the Arcelor group due to the merger of Arbed with the Spanish steel group Aceralia and the French Usinor (Fig. 2.14). This steel group is the largest steel producer in the world with a turnover of €26 billion and a workforce of more than 100,000.

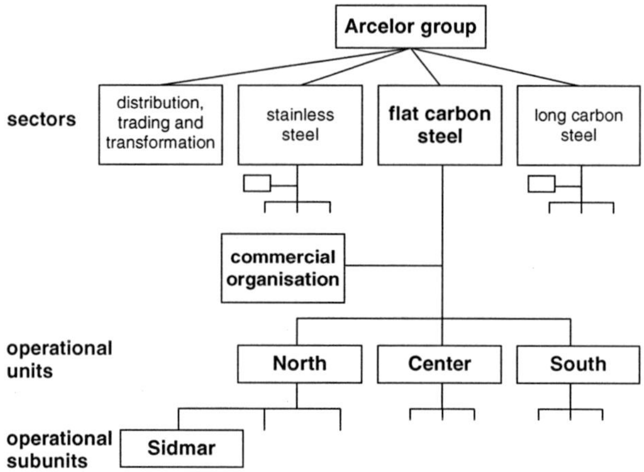

Fig. 2.14 Organization structure of Arcelor

Sidmar employs approximately 5600 people and realizes a turnover of €2 billion. Figure 2.15 displays the organizational structure of Sidmar with a senior vice president responsible for IT.

2.2.2.2 Context of Enterprise Governance of IT

Within Sidmar, the mission and value statement of IT is clear and simple: "Supply and support Sidmar and the Sector Flat products with all needed IT-systems and related services, in order to enable all business processes at all levels (strategic, tactical and operational) to be executed in an integrated and efficient way."

During the last 10 years, the expenditure of the IT department has known a continuous growth. From 1996 to 2001 this growth was rather strong due to a heavy investment program at the Sidmar plant and the delivery of solutions toward the commercial organization of the flat carbon steel sector. Since 2001

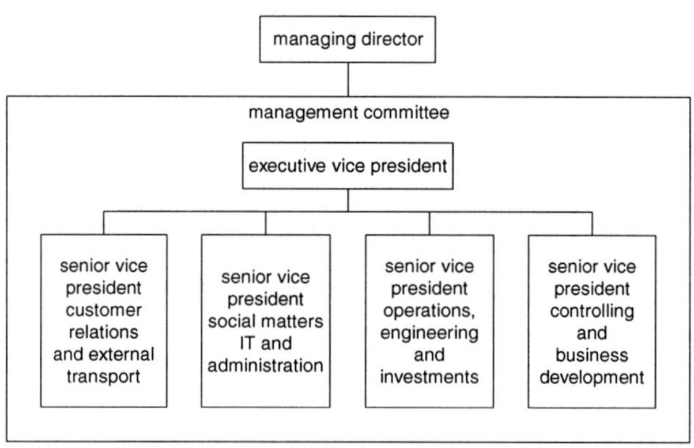

Fig. 2.15 Organization structure of Sidmar

the IT budget is frozen and now that Sidmar is part of Arcelor, the budget is expected to stay under pressure. However, it is the intention that savings on the IT budget will not be at the expense of new projects. A better internal efficiency especially for the infrastructure and maintenance must lead to the optimization of the IT budget.

On business governance level, Sidmar introduced in 2004 a company-wide process-based management system. This is known under the name ICE, standing for Integral Company Excellence. ICE actually brought existing individual components of process management together into one structured whole, covering all levels at Sidmar and describing strategic, tactical, operational and supporting processes. One of the 22 ICE processes is P23: *Management of Information Systems*, under responsibility of the IT department and its director. The process clearly defines Ins and Outs, different sub-processes and its activities, the interdependencies with other processes, measurements (KPIs) and a reporting and evaluation structure.

2.2.2.3 Processes for Enterprise Governance of IT

The IT strategy of Sidmar comes down to supplying and supporting the business with all needed IT systems and related services, in order to enable all business processes to be executed in an integrated and efficient way. As described before, the IT strategy process is completely comprised of formalized ICE processes for Management of Information Systems.

A clear decision-making process for IT projects is in place. This process makes a distinction between small IT projects and enhancements (less than 100 person-days), and large IT projects (more than 100 person-days). All projects originate from ideas generated in the business units. For smaller projects, the decision power and the execution lies in the hands of the individual business unit (IBO), and is covered by their IBO budget. Large projects are always handled by IT and follow a strict decision and prioritization path before the project can be initiated (Fig. 2.16). New opportunities often surface at a fairly low level. In

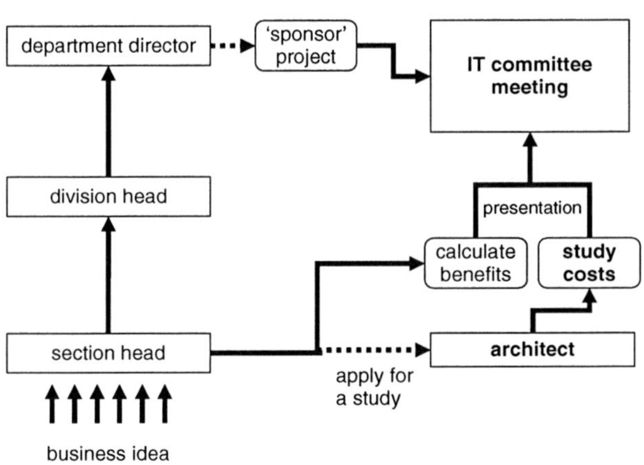

Fig. 2.16 Project initiation process

that case, the section head communicates this idea to his division head who in turn communicates it to the department director. The department director will propose the project in the IT Committee and will act as a sponsor for the project. An architect will be assigned to conduct a feasibility study focusing on the costs and benefits. IT and business people will be involved in this study respectively responsible for the cost estimation and benefits evaluation. The ultimate decision will be taken by the IT committee based on the figures provided by the feasibility study.

The IT Committee prioritizes IT projects on the basis of the size of the projects and four criteria: profitability, competitive advantage, operational urgency and decision support (Fig. 2.17). A decision grid as shown in Fig. 2.18 is used to

	PROJECT CLASS	BASIC CRITERIA			
	NUMBER OF PLANNED MAN DAYS	PROFITA BILITY: PAY BACK TIME (YEARS)	COMPETITIVE ADVANTAGE	OPERATIONAL URGENCY	DECISION SUPPORT
HIGH	> 2000	< 1.5	IMPROVE PERFORMANCE SIGNIFICANTLY ON CUSTOMER KEY BUYING FACTORS FOR STRATEGIC SEGMENTS	DIRECT REACTION ON EXTREME OPERATIONAL RISK, CHANGED LEGAL OR OPERATIONAL ENVIRONMENT, EXTREME MAINTENANCE RISK	HIGH IMPACT SUPPORT FOR KEY DECISION MAKERS
MEDI UM HIGH	1000–2000	1.5–2.5	IMPROVE PERFORMANCE ON CUSTOMER KEY BUYING FACTORS FOR OTHER SEGMENTS	ELIMINATE CRITICAL OPERATIONAL HANDICAPS	OTHER SUPPORT FOR KEY DECISION MAKERS
MEDI UM	500–1000	2.5–4	IMPROVE PERFORMANCE SLIGHTLY ON CUSTOMER KEY BUYING FACTORS	REDUCE WEEK POINTS IN CURRENT OPERATIONS	HIGH IMPACT FOR OTHER MANAGEMENT
MEDI UM LOW	200–500	4–6	IMPROVE PERFORMANCE ON OTHER BUYING FACTORS	AVOID SMALL PROBLEMS IN OPERATIONAL USAGE	ONGOING SUPPORT FOR OTHER MANAGEMENT
LOW	< 200	> 6	NO IMPACT ON COMPETITIVE POSITION	NO URGENCY	NO IMPACT ON MANAGEMENT EFFECTIVENESS

Fig. 2.17 Project class and basic criteria

Profitablity

Project class	L	ML	M	MH	H
H	1	1	2	2	3
MH	1	1	2	3	4
M	1	2	3	3	4
ML	1	2	3	4	5
L	1	2	3	4	5

Competitive advantage

Project class	L	ML	M	MH	H
H	1	1	1	2	3
MH	1	1	2	3	4
M	1	1	2	4	4
ML	1	1	3	4	5
L	1	2	4	5	5

Operational urgency

Project class	L	ML	M	MH	H
H	1	1	1	2	5
MH	1	1	2	3	5
M	1	1	2	3	5
ML	1	1	3	4	5
L	1	2	3	4	5

Decision support

Project class	L	ML	M	MH	H
H	1	1	1	1	1
MH	1	1	1	1	2
M	1	1	1	2	3
ML	1	1	2	3	4
L	1	2	3	4	5

Fig. 2.18 Decision grid

score IT projects. Each project can score up to 5 points per quadrant, so the total score per project varies between 4 and 20 points. (A small project (class L) at the lowest level for all basic criteria will only have a score of 4).

Based on the calculated scores, the projects get a priority class assigned following the set priority classes of Fig. 2.19. Typically projects with a priority class A or B are accepted, while projects with a class C or D are less likely to be implemented. If the project is accepted it will be planned taking into account the available resource capacity. If needed, the IT Committee can decide to bring in new internal and/or external resources. This prioritization method proved to be very effective and both IT and the business are satisfied with this way of working.

As explained earlier, a company-wide process management system is implemented within Sidmar. These 22 processes are also formally measured by means of defined KPIs. For process P23: Management of Information Systems a scorecard is developed. This scorecard is available online and reports indicators

A **5 points on at least one criterion**

Accept, high priority

B **4 points on profitability or 3 points on at least two criteria**

Accept

C **3 points on profitability or total of 7 points**

Accept if resources available

D **3 points on one criterion**

Accept only if subcontractable

E **All other projects**

Decline

Fig. 2.19 Priority classes

such as percentage of support problems solved within the same day against the 85% set objective. This system has recently been set up and the indicators still have to evolve from rather technical toward more customer oriented-parameters.

2.2.3 Short Case on Relational Mechanisms – Huntsman (Chemicals)

2.2.3.1 Company Introduction

Huntsman's roots date back to 1970 with the formation of the Huntsman Container Corporation, which pioneered more than 80 innovative plastic packaging products. The first Huntsman sites were located in California, Ohio and Tennessee and in 1976 the first overseas site was built in England. Nowadays Huntsman has grown to a worldwide supplier of chemicals, polymers, and packaging. Its growth is a result of strategic acquisitions, smart joint ventures and carefully planned internal expansion. Today Huntsman companies account for approximately 11,300 employees active in manufacturing, research and development, sales and administration with 57 operations in 22 countries and with 2004 revenue of $11.5 billion. Figure 2.20 portrays the six Huntsman divisions and appliance industries. This case study focuses on the Polyurethanes and the Advanced Materials divisions.

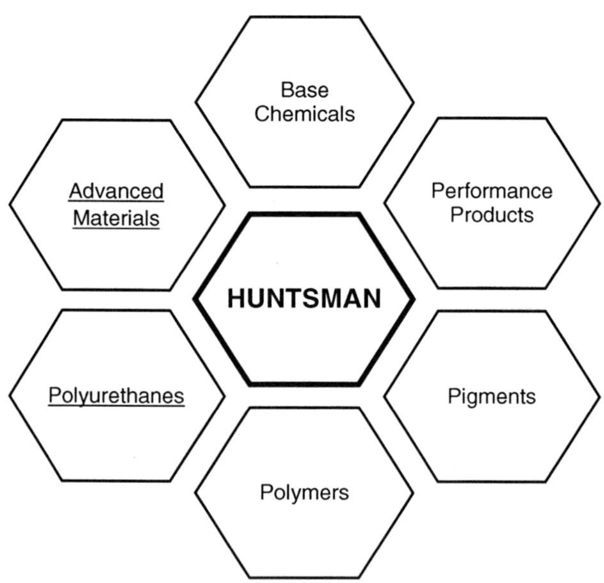

Fig. 2.20 Organizational structure of Huntsman

Huntsman's Polyurethanes provides, for example, seat cushioning for car manufacturers such as BMW and soles for different kinds of specialized sports footwear for Nike, Reebok and Adidas. The Advanced Materials division includes six specialized business units: structural adhesives, electrical insulation materials, printed circuit board technology, structural composites and surface technologies.

2.2.3.2 Context of Enterprise Governance of IT

The history of IT within the Huntsman organization is strongly tied to the substantial growth of the company by means of acquisitions, each bringing in their own IT organization. The need for a more global enterprise-wide IT organization was triggered by the Atlas project. This project was aimed at the globalization of the Polyurethanes business that until then was mainly run on a regional basis. The project implemented single global business processes underpinned by a single global SAP template. During this project, it became clear that there was a great need for having actual views on the status of the entire organization's business and that this kind of information was not readily available to the business (it often took days or even weeks to provide it). A new global IT project and consequently new IT structures had to be developed to meet this urgent demand. The executive vice president comments: "This IT project is doomed for failure if the local entities keep holding on to their legacy systems (mainframe computers, desktops, laptops…). […] We need global embracement of the project in order to be successful."

"The last 5 years, many efforts have been made in order to create single global platforms, to share the 'nuts-and-bolts' of IT," said the executive vice president. In the context of a cost-optimization program, it was a logical step to create one global IT organization, responsible for defining enterprise-wide standards and platforms. Within Huntsman this centralization is called the "global" approach, combining an optimal mix of global synergies and local responsiveness offering the required flexibility.

2.2.3.3 Relational Mechanisms for Enterprise Governance of IT

A major relational problem at Huntsman was that IT is still perceived by some (business) people as "something that has to do with computers, be it desktops, notebooks or other thin-client devices." Clearly, hardware is an essential part of IT but at the same time they represent only a minor part of the entire IT puzzle. The director of global IT Enterprise Business Systems refers to this problem by saying "the IT strategy is not really the business's concern, except when problems arise. There should be an earlier adoption and involvement of IT matters by the business." The goal of IT, explains the director of global IT Enterprise Business Systems, should be "to pro-actively mediate in business issues and in this way to avoid missed opportunities."

Clear communication is acknowledged as being an essential issue in the achievement of good relations between IT and business. A formal document

"Thanks to the recently implemented thin clients, a potentially major production problem could relatively easily be dealt with. On a given Sunday afternoon, Huntsman staff succeeded in solving a production problem after logging in by means of their thin clients at their homes. Only 15 minutes after logging in, Huntsman staff had fixed the problem and the production was restarted. Clearly, losses of great consequence that might have been caused by a longer idle-time were avoided."

Fig. 2.21 Example of a "news story" published in knowledge management system

and slide presentations explaining the IT strategy is distributed at the different management levels. The implemented knowledge management system at Huntsman covers a wide area of subjects including IT issues. The "IT news items," are presented on the same page as the financial results on the corporate intranet. The "IT news items" cover information about running projects, new emerging technologies and "success stories." An example of a typical success story is displayed in Fig. 2.21.

Another supporting mechanism for a better relationship between IT and business is job-rotation. Huntsman offers its employees the possibility to switch between IT and business jobs and vice versa. This possibility is part of every individual's career planning. The career planning depends, among other factors, on the annual performance review, personal preferences, geographical preferences and the match with existing opportunities within the organization. In practice, employees do take the opportunity to widen their knowledge and rotate between different IT and business functions. The relational mechanism of job-rotation contributes to an increased mutual insight in the business and IT.

Assignment Box 2.1: Short cases on Enterprise Governance of IT

Analyze the practices used in each of the three short cases and compare with the relevant 33 Enterprise Governance of IT practices presented in Sect. 2.1. Discuss differences and similarities.

2.2.4 In-Depth Case – KBC (Finance)

2.2.4.1 Company Introduction

KBC is a major Belgian financial services organization that was founded in 1998 after the merger of Kredietbank, Cera Bank and ABB Insurance. These former companies already had a history, before the merger, of more than 100 years. KBC as a merged company is the third largest banking and insurance organization in its home market of Belgium. Comparing market capitalization of other banks in Europe, KBC is ranked number 12 in the Euroland Bank Ranking (Dow Jones Euro Stoxx). The company has focused its international expansion on growth countries in Central Europe (Czech Republic, Hungary, Poland and Slovenia). By the end of 2003, KBC achieved a consolidated net profit of €1,119 million on

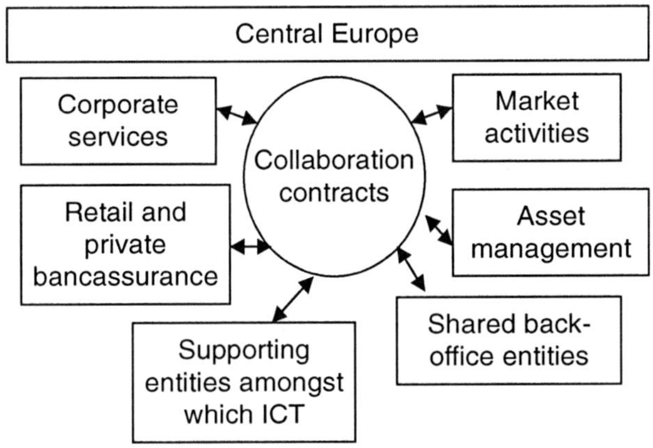

Fig. 2.22 Activity domains of KBC

a gross operating income of €6,498 million. In the same year, KBC employed 49,725 FTE professionals worldwide, of which 2,403 (internal and external) were in the central IT department. Total IT budget for 2003 was €430 million. The decision-making structures of KBC are organized in function of five core activity domains of the business as shown in Fig. 2.22.

Retail and private bankassurance encompasses the activities of the bank branches, agents and brokers, as well as those conducted via electronic channels, that cater for private persons, the self-employed and local businesses (retail bankassurance) and for high-net-worth individuals (private bankassurance). *Corporate services* contain all the banking and assurance activities toward companies. *Asset management* is the business of managing the assets of private persons and institutional investors, as well as the assets of investment funds that are sold primarily via the retail network. *Market activities* refer to activities of the bank's dealing rooms in Belgium and abroad, the market activities of KBC Securities and all the activities engaged in KBC Financial Products, KBC Clearing and KBC Peel Hunt. KBC's businesses on its second home market are grouped under the separate area of activity referred to as *Central Europe*. This encompasses all retail banking and insurance services, corporate services, asset management and market activities in the Czech Republic, Slovakia, Hungary, Poland and Slovenia. These activity domains are supported by shared back-office entities, such as the logistic back-office for payments and securities, and supporting entities, such as bookkeeping and IT. Each of the activity domains has its own management committee. The supporting entities are regarded as being a separate organization that will charge back costs in a non-profit manner. That is why collaboration contracts needed to be established between the activity domains and the supporting entities.

2.2.4.2 Context of Enterprise Governance of IT

To be able to attract new clients and to retain existing clients in the competitive financial market, the business units of KBC are continuously looking for ways to increase the internal and external process efficiency. To be able to meet these business requirements, a flexible IT department is needed offering high-quality services. But as one of the IT governance project managers stated: "Previous years, the management of IT was organized around major projects such as Y2K and the Euro conversion. While working on these projects, however, an enormous backlog grew of other projects to be accomplished. And the questions rose: How to tackle new requests of the business when the current major projects are completed? What if an enormous amount of new projects is initiated? How to give priorities?"

Moreover, the business units of KBC were becoming more aware of what the IT market in general had to offer, which resulted sometimes in the belief that IT services should be best delivered by a third party. The IT governance project manager continues: "IT becomes bigger and bigger, which is reflected in the outline of IT costs for the business. From that, the feeling emerges within the business that there is not much synergy and control achieved within IT. The business requests more and more projects that the IT department cannot immediately respond to and as a result business starts looking for third parties. This way of working can be beneficial in the short-term, but it endangers the coherence and synergies of IT systems on the long-term."

Finally, one of the drivers for the merger in 1998 between Kredietbank, Cera Bank and ABB Assurance was achieving economies of scale in the IT department. According to the member of the Board of Directors: "When the merger was officially completed, one of the first missions for the IT department was to set up a model that would enable the achievement of economies of scale, the set up of a solid IT architecture and the alignment between business and IT."

This context of high business expectations and the awareness that IT is needed to respond to it, together with the need to achieve economies of scale within IT after the merger, prompted the governance project in 2000. The Enterprise Governance of IT project started at a moment that a lot of other important KBC projects were initiated, as the Board of Director's member points out: "An important challenge was that this project was executed in parallel with other major projects such as the fusion of all other KBC departments and the introduction of the Euro. In a way, we were changing tires and axles of the car, while riding."

It was the Executive Committee which initiated the project in 2000 by asking the CIO to develop a business–IT governance model. After this request, the CIO developed an "IT charter" (see infra) clarifying how IT and the business should collaborate in the future. This first proposal from IT created some resistance in the business as they felt that a model was being imposed on them by IT which inhibited flexibility. The former chairman of the Executive Committee therefore requested an audit to evaluate the model. This audit was however never performed, as very quickly, the model was fine-tuned and the department "organization" got involved to assist in implementing the processes behind the IT charter and to act as gatekeeper in certain decisions points (see infra).

From the start on, the goal of the governance project was clearly defined: "set up a governance model for business–IT for the KBC Group for the coming 4–5 years, in a way that the model is resistant to and anticipates organizational changes."

It was believed that this governance model would result in (1) high flexibility for the organization, (2) effective allocation of the IT resources and (3) Economies of scale and specialization through the centralization of IT knowledge.

The goals of the governance project were widely communicated and explained. An internal KBC magazine explaining the project stated: "The business units need to learn to manage IT in a well-thought out manner. They need to make choices and accept the consequences of these choices. The IT department from its side needs to create an environment which enables business to make these well-considered decisions. IT needs to create an insight into the needs of the business, and needs to establish clear agreements and engagements. IT has to define what it can deliver, by when and at which price, in a way that the internal customer knows what his return is for the money spent."

In order to achieve the goals described above, KBC established structures, processes and relational mechanisms, which are described in the following sections. In the very beginning, a project manager was assigned to install the basic processes and structures. Later on, a committee composed of the general directors of the business units, the CIO and the director of "organization" regularly initiated improvement projects, and also now, the model is still growing. For example, in 2004, the IT audit department finalized an IT governance audit, which they initiated themselves, and resulted in some improvement recommendations which were under review at the time that this case study description was finalized (spring 2004).

2.2.4.3 Structures for Enterprise Governance of IT

Effective Enterprise Governance of IT is amongst others determined by the way the IT function is organized and where the IT decision-making authority is located within the organization. Figure 2.23 shows how the IT department is structured and its relation to higher reporting levels and other business

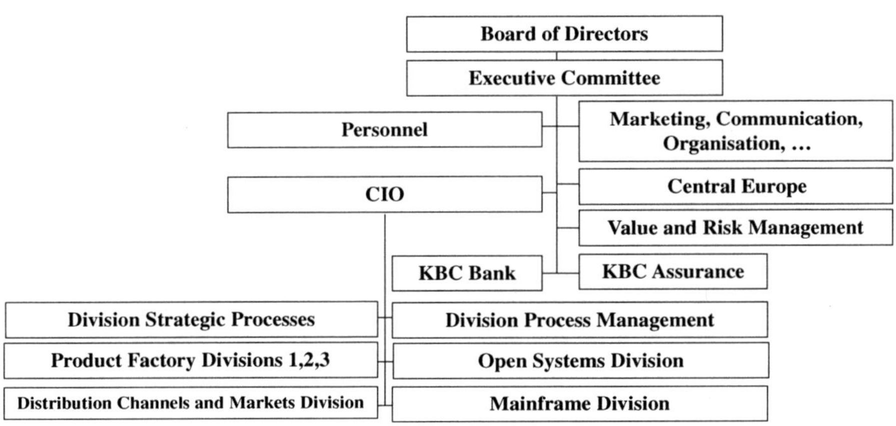

Fig. 2.23 IT organization structure

departments. The IT department is headed by the CIO, who reports directly to the Executive Committee. In this way, the CIO has the same direct reporting line to the Executive Committee as the general directors of the business lines of KBC Bank and KBC Assurance (for example, general director corporate services) and staff functions (for example, marketing, "organization"). The CIO manages a number of IT divisions. The division *Strategic Processes* is responsible for management reporting, chargeback models, education, communication, knowledge management, etc. The division *Process Management* is responsible for the management of IT projects with an impact over several IT divisions, such as Y2K and the Euro conversion. This division also provides advice on architecture, design, testing, tools, etc. There are three product factory divisions, each one responsible for the development in one or more lines of business (for example, product factory 3 in the insurance domain). Finally, there is a division responsible for distribution channels and markets (e.g., bank cards and cash dispensers, B2B–B2C e-commerce) and two divisions, grouped per technology domain (open systems and mainframe) responsible for maintenance and development of the technical infrastructure (databases, networks, operation systems, etc.).

The Board of Directors was composed of 23 members in 2003. This group is constituted of eight managing directors forming together the Executive Committee, 11 representatives of the principal shareholders and four independent directors. In order to permit the Board to fulfill its supervisory task, the Executive Committee reports to it each month on the trend of results and on the progress of major events and projects. Each member of the Executive Committee is responsible for supervising the activities of a number of business units and/or supporting entities such as IT. They meet once a week and address IT issues on a regular basis in terms of decisions on IT budgets and decisions on investment projects (see infra). The CIO, although not part of the Executive Committee, reports directly to one of its members and is frequently invited to the Executive Committee meetings. In this way, a close link between business and IT at a high level in the organization is established.

KBC documents roles and responsibilities as described above and this for all hierarchical levels involved in the governance framework. An intranet site was developed where all roles and responsibilities are explained and can be consulted by both business and IT.

As argued before, Enterprise Governance of IT should be the prime responsibility of the Board of Directors, and IT therefore should be regularly addressed in the Board meetings. A supportive mechanism to obtain this is establishing an IT strategy committee of which the role is defined by ITGI (2003) as follows: "an IT strategy committee has to consider how the Board should become involved in IT governance, how to integrate the Board's role in IT and business strategy, and the extent to which the committee has an ongoing role in IT governance." KBC established such a committee composed of three Board members (who are also member of the Executive Committee), the CIO and directors of the Strategic Processes and Process Management IT divisions. This committee focuses on establishing and reviewing the IT strategy, but does not enable a more thorough and ongoing involvement of the Board in IT governance. This implies that this committee does not comply with the strict definition of an IT strategy committee as proposed by the IT Governance Institute. KBC's Board works at a very high, strategic level and they are consequently not the "steering power" for IT or Enterprise Governance of IT. Nevertheless, it could be argued that the Board maybe not involved as a whole, but still via its members of the Executive Committee who also have a seat in the Board.

KBC also established a number of other committees which enable the involvement of both business and IT in the preparation of new projects, in the development of projects and the maintenance of systems. There is one IT/business steering committee (IBSC) per activity domain that can set up one or more Domain Consultative Body (DCB) for specific functional business domains such as credit loans or securities. These two committees play an important role in the preparation and decisions of new investment projects (large development projects with a major architectural impact, like for example the implementation of SAP) and continuity projects (development projects mostly driven by evolutions in the market or legislation, for example the implementation of specific reporting due to legal requirements) (see Fig. 2.24).

The Program Management Steering Group (PMSG) is responsible for the project management of investment projects and clusters of continuity projects as soon as they are approved. During the lifetime of a system, the Management Operational Systems Committee (MOSC) decides on maintenance projects (small projects under 8 man-weeks, for example, the enhancement of a specific screen) within the strategy and budget approved by the IBSC.

The roles and responsibilities of these committees are described in more detail in the next section which focuses on processes. In each committee, business and IT people are represented as shown in Fig. 2.25, which enables alignment throughout the different stages of an IT project. Some of the roles mentioned (IT architect, business architect, etc.) are explained in detail in the section on relational mechanisms.

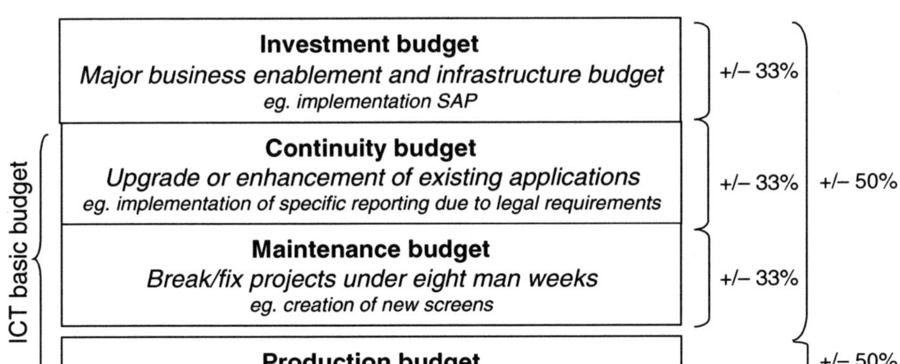

Fig. 2.24 IT budget composition

Committee	Authority	Composition	
		IT representatives	Business representatives
IT business steering committee (IBSC)	Project prioritization Defines the needed budgets	Members of product factory, open systems and mainframe division	Member of executive committee; members of management committee of corresponding activity domain; 'organization'
Domain consultative body (DCB)	Evaluate the business value of new ideas	IT architect; business analyst	Director of involved domain; business architect; process manager
Program Man. Steer. Group (PMSG)	Project management	Involved IT director(s); program manager	sponsor of the project; involved business director(s)
Man. Operational Systems Committee (MOSC)	Decide on maintenance projects	Business analyst; system manager	Director of involved domain; process manager; application manager

Fig. 2.25 Committees representing business–IT

2.2.4.4 Processes for Enterprise Governance of IT

Figure 2.26 illustrates how the above-mentioned committees are involved in the initiation, development and maintenance processes. The process described below does not cover the management of the production budget, as this is still managed as one separate budget for all activity domains. It is the intention to also redistribute this production over the activity domains in the future.

New projects are always initiated by the business, for example by a business architect. This is a role assigned to a business representative, who needs to collect and manage business information that is essential for making business cases of IT projects (see infra). The business architect can initiate continuity or

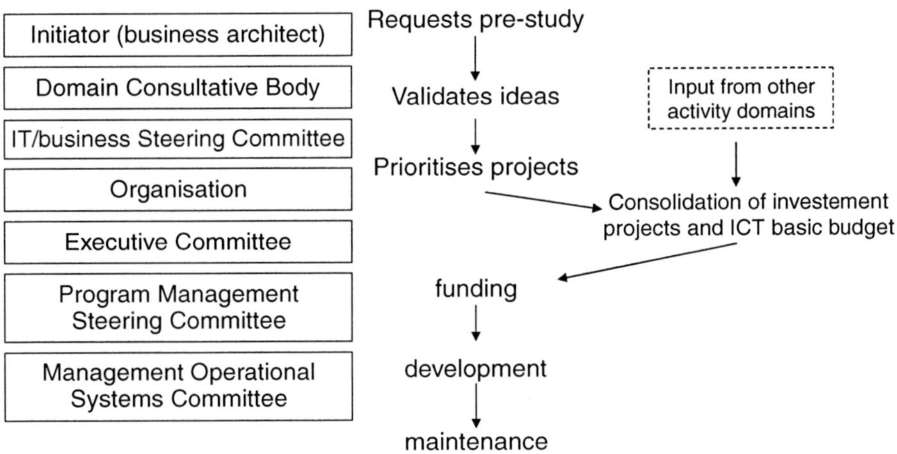

Fig. 2.26 IT project life cycle

investment projects by developing a first idea, and these requests go to the DCB who will evaluate the business value of the new ideas based on the results of a pre-study, that includes the business case, planning, sourcing, identification of synergies and risks, and infrastructure review. To obtain sufficient accuracy, 10–20% of the total cost of a development project is dedicated to this pre-study in which business and IT are involved. The business defines targeted goals, benefits, and costs, while IT focuses more on development costs, architecture, etc. The pre-study results in a kind of service level agreement, offering a fixed-time/fixed-price development project. For every project, a buffer of 10% of development costs is retained in the total price to pay for any cost over-runs.

When the DCB finds the project value-adding it goes to the IBSC of the corresponding activity domain. Every year, this IBSC prioritizes the continuity and investment projects needed for year x + 1 and sets the needed maintenance budget, all within the overall target budget which is set in advance by the Executive Committee. This target defines one overall budget for both maintenance and continuity projects. The IBSC itself has no investment budget. Funding for investment projects always needs to be requested at the Executive Committee, but the IBSC can decide to co-fund an investment project with a part of its continuity budget. When all the IBSCs define what they need in year x + 1, "organization" will aggregate the data before sending it to the Executive Committee. The Executive Committee then approves or amends the IT basic capacity for year x + 1 per activity domain and will decide which investment projects will receive budget. It was noted by one of the interviewees that, when the business case is developed, the decision at IBSC or Executive Committee level is mostly based on budget considerations and less on the content of the complete business case. This situation can be frustrating for business and IT people spending a lot of time in preparing the detailed business cases which go much beyond only financial estimations. On the other hand, by using this process "barriers are embedded that inhibit – partially – the initiation of irrelevant projects, create a natural filter and diminishes the possibility of people asking directly to the Executive Committee for specific funding without a thorough preparation." It could be argued that the model is rather heavy, possibly endangering the organization's ability to quickly jump on new opportunities. However, a member of the board of directors, challenges this argument: "There will always be people who experience the model as being too complex and over-bureaucratic. But we now at least have a model which clearly shows how projects are initiated and decided upon. It is obvious that the business people prefer a very quick time-to-market, but they have to take the impact on the back office into account. If we take unprepared decisions, the danger exists of creating a mess in the back-office, and the cost of cleaning up this mess is much higher than doing a well-considered pre-study in advance."

The Executive Committee prioritizes between the investment projects based on the business case which is complemented with an "information economics" assessment. In essence, information economics is a scoring technique resulting in a weighted total score based on the scores for the ROI and some qualitative criteria (Parker, 1995). The generic information economics method as developed by Benson and Parker is adapted to the own needs of KBC, retaining 10 criteria that are relevant (Fig. 2.27).

Besides the financial criterion of return on investment, non-financial criteria such as "alignment with strategy" are covered. For each criterion, a number of questions are developed. The questions for "competitive advantage and need" for example are "Does the program deliver competitive advantage?" and "Is the program a necessity to remain competitive?" The criterion gets a red color if the average of the underlying questions is lower than 2.4, yellow if the average is between 2.4 and 3.8 and green if the average is above 3.8. There is no overall average calculated over all criteria, so in this way, a kind of traffic light report is generated for each investment project, as visualized in Fig. 2.28.

This scoring is performed by the initiator of the investment project, mostly the business architect. To obtain an objective measurement and a consistent scoring, representatives of "organization" always challenge and overview the scores when they consolidate all investment projects prior to going to the Executive Committee.

For each new agreed investment project or cluster of continuity projects within an activity domain, a Project Management Steering Group (PMSG) is assigned by the IBSC, again composed of business and IT people to ensure

Return on investment	Alignment with strategy	Competitive advantage/need	Necessity (legal, organ.)	Reduces operat. risks
Support management	Project and organis. risks	Support future informat. architecture	Functional uncertainty	Technical uncertainty

Fig. 2.27 Information economics at KBC

Scoring investment files	Return	Alignment to strategy	Competitive advantage	Necessity	Legal necessity	Information architecture	Redcution operational risk	Project & organisational risk	Functional uncertainties	Technical uncertainties
Intrest and liquidity risk project	red	green	green	green	green	green	green	green	red	red
Quantitative credit risk management project	green	green	green	green	green	green	red	red	red	red
Multichannel application project	green	green	green	yellow	yellow	green	green	green	green	green
ERP phase 2 project	red	green	green	green	green	yellow	green	red	red	yellow
...										

Fig. 2.28 Traffic light report for all investment projects

alignment throughout the development process. When a newly developed system goes into production, the further management is transferred to the Management Operational Systems Committee (MOSC), also composed of business and IT people. The goal of the MOSC is to decide on maintenance projects within the strategy and budget approved by the IBSC.

Another process that can be leveraged for achieving more alignment is the use of the Balanced Scorecard (BSC). In KBC, a detailed scorecard is developed for the complete IT department, containing five perspectives: financial and corporate perspective, customer perspective, efficiency perspective, innovativeness and entrepreneurship perspective and staff perspective. The latter proves that KBC pays a lot of attention to the development of its own IT staff. The CIO describes the major advantage of this IT BSC as "a systematic translation of the strategy into critical success factors and metrics, which materializes the strategy." As demonstrated in Chapter 4 of this book, the IT BSC only becomes a real alignment mechanism when causal relationships between metrics, and if possible between scorecards, are defined. There is however no formal causal relationships defined between metrics, nor are there scorecards defined at lower levels in the IT department (e.g., development department) or links developed with a business scorecard. The BSC within KBC is implemented as a measurement tool, but not as a strong alignment or management tool.

Operational costs such as maintenance and user administration are charged back to the business according to Activity Based-Costing (ABC) principles, which provides a methodology to assign direct and indirect costs to real cost drivers. KBC's management found that for operational costs, the real cost drivers were not enough taken into account and that indirect costs were only assigned using arbitrary criteria. For example, in the previous cost model, there was a cost object "workstation," without making any differentiation between PCs or laptops, standard or non-standard. The defined cost also included software and hardware. The only steering factors for the business to reduce its workstation costs were, therefore, reducing the number of workstations. Identifying more clearly the real cost drivers would enable the business to intelligently manage their workstation. The ABC implementation project started at the end of 2002 with four major goals: (1) achieve more cost awareness by end users as well as by the IT department; (2) achieve an optimal allocation of IT costs; (3) set up a mechanism that justifies costs charged back to the business; and (4) achieve more market conformity through benchmarking. During the ABC project, all standard services and products were consolidated in the service catalogue, which creates more cost transparency for the end users and enables them to make well-considered decisions.

2.2.4.5 Relational Mechanisms for Enterprise Governance of IT

One of the important steps KBC took to implement relational mechanisms is the definition of – in their terminology – the IT charter (Fig. 2.29). This IT charter defines mirror roles between business and IT people, and these people need to interact directly. A person can have different roles but some roles are on the other hand divided over several persons. The *business architect* collects and manages information from the business, essential for making the business case of IT projects. He/she is also responsible for managing the business architecture (business functions, processes, . . .) and for analyzing the gap between "as-is" and "to-be" situation of this architecture. The business architect needs to collaborate with the IT architect, who will use all this information to align the IT strategy with business priorities and to analyze where IT can play an enabling role for the business strategy. The *IT architect* is also responsible for ensuring that IT infrastructure responds to the needs of the business infrastructure and for analyzing the "as-is" and "to-be" situation of the IT infrastructure. The *process manager* oversees the process of handling products and services in a specific line of business. This person collaborates with the *business analyst*, a person on IT site who knows the business very well and who prepares input for pre-studies and need's analysis. The *product manager* is the developer of new products and reviews all products and services from a commercial and marketing point of view. The *application manager* is responsible for the functional management of IT for a product, service or channel, which includes involvement in development projects and testing of systems before final delivery. He/she is typically a lead

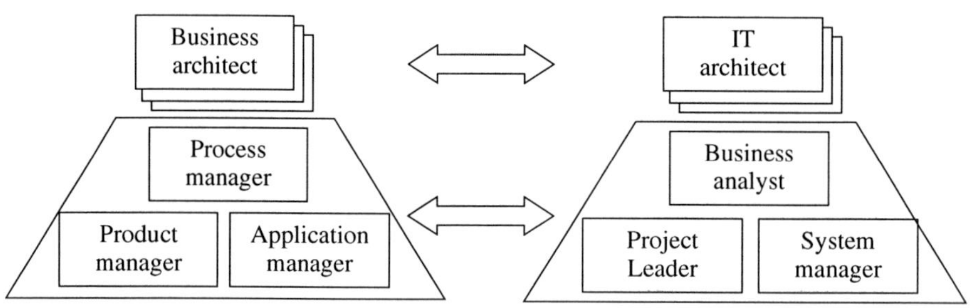

Fig. 2.29 IT charter

user, which implies that this cannot be a full-time role. The application manager acts as a contact point for the system manager, responsible for delivered systems.

While in this IT charter model, IT and business people need to interact directly in the business lines, KBC also organizes account management meetings that establish a bridge between business and IT at the higher level of the different business directions of the Bank and Assurance activities. As explained before, business and IT people are involved in the project initiation and decision-making process via different committees such as IBSC and MOSC. The account management meeting only focuses on the relational aspects between business and IT; it is not project driven, as for example the IBSC and MOSC discusses general ideas and needs, and the ways specific issues can be handled. Per business direction, these account management meetings are composed of the most involved IT division, the service delivery owner (a function within IT), the general director of the business unit and a business architect.

KBC finally also uses other relational mechanisms to manage the "soft" side of the IT–Business relations, such as co-location, language use (for example "partnership" instead of "à-la-carte relationship"), senior IT management giving the good example of collaborating with the business, job-rotation (senior IT people moving to key position in the business), training sessions on business activities, etc. KBC also uses internal magazines to explain the governance model and established a "business–IT governance" site on their intranet, with explanations of the roles and responsibilities, the committees, templates, etc.

In all these ways, KBC tries to achieve an active participation, collaboration and shared understanding between business and IT people in every stage of the project, from a shared understanding of the objectives to collaborative implementation. Yet, as already mentioned, in the beginning the model was experienced as being imposed by IT, although the initial request came from the business. There was indeed a short communication line between the CIO and the Executive Committee, but perhaps a stronger communication was needed toward the general directors of the business departments stating that this new model was requested by the Executive Committee and for the best interest as well of business and IT. Moreover, the model is quite complex, and everyone needs to understand its role in it, and so pro-active training and competence management are very important. The provision of the intranet site is of course very good, but it still remains a pull-technology, while it could be very worthwhile that people are introduced to the governance model via some training. For example, for the use of information economics in business cases, it is important that everyone understands the same things behind the metrics. This is very hard to achieve via a short explanation on the intranet and could be better realized via a more extensive training. Moreover, when the people better understand the "why" of making business cases and information economics assessments, this effort will not be regarded as overhead anymore.

Assignment Box 2.2: In-depth *case study*

Make teams and discuss the Enterprise Governance of IT model of KBC. Evaluate the IT governance maturity based on the model below. Suggest improvements based on the 33 practices presented earlier in this chapter (Fig. 2.4).

IT Governance maturity model

0 Non Existent

Complete lack of any recognizable processes. Organization has not even recognized that there is an issue to be addressed.

1 Initial

There is evidence that the organization has recognized that the issues exist and need to be addressed. There are however no standardized processes but instead there are ad hoc approaches that tend to be applied on an individual or case by case basis. The overall approach to management is chaotic.

2 Repeatable

Processes have developed to the stage where similar procedures are followed different people undertaking the same task. There is no formal training or communication of standard procedures and responsibility is left to the individual. There is a high degree of reliance on the knowledge of individuals and therefore errors are likely.

3 Defined

Procedures have been standardized and documented, and communicated through training. It is however left to the individual to follow these processes, and any deviations would be unlikely to be detected. The procedures themselves are not sophisticated but are the formalization of existing practices.

4 Managed

It is possible to monitor and measure compliance with procedures and to take action where processes appear not to be working effectively. Processes are under constant improvement and provide good practice. Automation and tools are used in a limited or fragmented way.

5 Optimized

Processes have been refined to a level of best practice, based on the results of continuous improvement and maturity modelling with other organizations. It is used in an integrated way to automate the workflow and provide tools to improve quality and effectiveness.

ITGI, 2003, Board Briefing on IT Governance, Second Edition, from www.itgi.org.

2.3 Customizing the Framework for Enterprise Governance of IT

In previous sections, a set of 33 practices for Enterprise Governance of IT was introduced. It is important to recognize that each of the applied processes, structures and relational mechanisms serve specific or multiple goals in the complex alignment challenge. However, dividing the Enterprise Governance of IT framework into smaller pieces, and solving each problem separately, does not always solve the complete problem. A holistic approach toward Enterprise Governance of IT acknowledges its complex and dynamic nature, consisting of a set of interdependent subsystems (processes, structures and relational mechanisms) that deliver a powerful whole. The challenge for organizations is to select an appropriate set of practices, specifically for their own environment. To assist organizations in this challenge, this section evaluates the effectiveness and ease of implementation of each of the 33 Enterprise Governance of IT practices. Also, a minimum baseline is proposed, providing a minimal set of practices each organization should have.

The results reported upon in this section are based on an extensive Dephi-based research. In this type of research, a group of experts in a specific subject area are asked for their opinions in multiple rounds, until the point that they come to a consensus. More information on this research methodology and how it was applied in this context is provided in Research Box 2.2. The overall result from these research steps are shown in Fig. 2.30 and specific visual views on this data set are provided in Figs. 2.31, 2.32 and 2.33. The results for each of the practices will be discussed in the sections below, in the context of one or more of the above-mentioned figures. At the beginning of each paragraph or section when a specific governance practice is discussed, the title of that governance practice will be highlighted in bold.

Research Box 2.2: Delphi research to evaluate Enterprise Governance of IT practices

The Delphi method can be characterized "as a method for structuring a group communication process so that the process is effective in allowing a group of individuals, as a whole, to deal with a complex problem" (Linstone and Turoff, 1975). The Delphi method provides a structured process to solicit expert opinion on a particular subject and enables group interaction without needing a face-to-face meeting. This method is particularly suited as a research methodology for this type research as "the delphi method technique lends itself especially well to exploratory theory building on complex, interdisciplinary issues, often involving a number of new or future trends" (Akkermans et al., 2003). Both Linstone and Turoff and Taylor-Powell stress the importance of selecting the expert panel. "Careful selection of participants is important since the quality and accuracy of responses to a delphi are only as good as the expert quality of the participants who are involved in the process. The number of participants depends upon the purpose of the delphi and the diversity of the targeted population. Ten to 15 people may be adequate for a focused delphi where participants do not vary a great deal" (Taylor-Powell, 2002). Based on these considerations, an expert panel was composed of 29 consultants, senior IT and senior business professionals who are all knowledgeable about organizations operating in the Belgian financial services sector. From this group, 22 experts continued to be involved in the full Delphi research effort (25% drop-off rate). The distribution of the 22 profiles involved in the research is shown in Fig. 2.30.

Profile	Number
Senior business/audit management	6
Senior IT management	8
Senior business/IT consultant	8

Fig. 2.30 Experts involved in the Delphi research

Using the Delphi method, these financial services sector experts needed to complete questionnaires in three consecutive rounds. Similar to the Delphi research work of Keill et al. (2002) on IT project risk, the Delphi research started with a preceded list of structures, processes and relational mechanisms. Instead of having the expert team build a list of possible governance practices from scratch, this research started from a predefined set of structures, processes and relational mechanisms. This list was operationalized based on findings of the literature research and the in-depth exploratory case research of which the results were also presented at the Hawaiian International Conference on System Sciences (HICSS) by De Haes and Van Grembergen in 2005 and 2006. In the first round, the respondents were only asked to provide their feedback on the predefined list practices, giving them the opportunity to make recommendations to add, change, and delete some of the practices. The focus of this first round was on validating the predefined list of practices specifically for the financial services sector, so no other input or feedback was requested at this stage. In the second round, the respondents were asked to rate on a scale of 5, for each of the reviewed governance practices, the "perceived effectiveness" (0 = not effective, 5 = very effective) and the "perceived ease of implementation" (0 = not easy, 5 = very easy). The respondents were also asked to, taken the previous attributes (effectiveness – easy of implementation) and their personal experience into account, to provide the top 10 most important governance practices, which are in their opinion crucial elements or a minimum baseline of an optimal Enterprise Governance of IT mix (the most important practice score 1, the second most important score 2, ..., the 10th most important score 10) (cf. The questionnaire of round 2 in Appendix i). In the third and final round, the respondents were asked to re-evaluate their own scores out of round 2, taken the group averages into account. Goal of this round was primarily to come to a greater consensus in the group. At the end of this round, the degree of consensus between the experts was measured leveraging Kendall's W coefficient, specifically for the question on the minimum baseline. Schmidt (1997) offers an interpretation of Kendall's W (Kendall's coefficient of concordance), indicating that the reached level of consensus in this research of 0.53 can be considered moderate providing a fair degree of confidence in the results. This result together with the fact that the top 10 list of governance practices only slightly differed between round 2 and 3, founded the decision not to start a fourth survey round.

An important challenge in this type research step is that different people often have different understandings of the same concept, also referred to as the "inadequate preoperational explication of constructs threat." Good examples are the use of IT steering committees and IT strategy committees. Although the latter is defined in literature as a committee at the level of the board of directors, many organizations are using the same terminology for a committee operating at executive or management level, which in fact should be catalogued as a steering committee. To address this, short and unambiguous definitions of all the processes, structures and relational mechanisms were provided (based on literature) and the questionnaire was pilot-tested for ambiguities and vagueness by eight people (practitioners and academics) before it was sent out to the experts involved in the research.

2.3.1 Effectiveness and Ease of Implementation

Figure 2.31 addresses the outcome of the rating for "perceived effectiveness" and "perceived ease of implementation" and shows the average score for each governance practice per group of respondents (business/audit (6), consultants (8) and IT (8)), the total average score per governance practice and the total average score per domain of structures, processes and relational mechanisms.

The total averages per governance practice and domain (structures, processes and relational mechanisms) are discussed in the following sections, but drilling down into the data per group of respondents will sometimes help in better understanding or explaining specific results. For example, it is not surprising that the "(IT) audit committee at the level of the board of directors" received the highest scores for "effectiveness" by the business/audit respondents group. Another interesting one is the "architecture steering committee," which apparently the IT respondents groups found less easy to implement compared to the two other respondents (business/audit and consultants) groups. This result might be explained by the fact that likely the IT respondents groups have been more involved in architecture discussions and experienced that architecture issues are hard to address in organizations. In the following sections, the overall results per governance practice will be discussed in more detail.

Figure 2.32 provides the aggregated averages of the ratings for perceived effectiveness and ease of implementation per domain of governance structures, processes and relational mechanisms. In general, it appears that structures and processes are perceived as being equally effective, but that structures are easier to

IT governance practices		Perceived effectiveness					Perceived ease of implementation				
		Business/ Audit	Consult.	IT	Average per practice	Average per domain (S-P-R)	Business/ Audit	Consult.	IT	Average per practice	Average per domain (S-P-R)
S1	IT strategy committee at level of board of directors	3,50	3,88	3,63	**3,67**	**3,57**	3,33	3,88	3,00	**3,40**	**3,39**
S2	IT expertise at level of board of directors	3,17	3,25	3,00	**3,14**		2,17	2,25	2,13	**2,18**	
S3	(IT) audit committee at level of board of directors	3,67	3,00	3,00	**3,22**		3,33	3,38	3,50	**3,40**	
S4	CIO on executive committee	4,00	4,63	4,50	**4,38**		3,67	3,63	3,38	**3,56**	
S5	CIO reporting to CEO and/or COO	4,50	4,25	4,75	**4,50**		4,50	3,88	4,25	**4,21**	
S6	IT steering committee (IT investment evaluation/prioritisation at executive/senior management level)	4,83	4,50	4,75	**4,69**		3,17	3,38	3,50	**3,35**	
S7	IT governance function/officer	3,17	2,63	3,00	**2,93**		3,33	3,13	2,88	**3,11**	
S8	Security/compliance/risk officer	3,33	3,00	3,50	**3,28**		4,17	4,00	4,00	**4,06**	
S9	IT project steering committee	3,83	3,88	4,38	**4,03**		4,17	3,75	4,13	**4,01**	
S10	IT security steering committee	2,83	2,63	3,00	**2,82**		3,83	3,50	3,50	**3,61**	
S11	Architecture steering committee	2,50	3,38	3,25	**3,04**		3,67	3,00	2,75	**3,14**	
S12	Integration of governance/ alignment tasks in roles & responsibilities	3,17	2,88	3,50	**3,18**		2,50	2,63	2,75	**2,63**	

Fig. 2.31 Overall evaluation of practices for Enterprise Governance of IT

P1	Strategic information systems planning	3,83	4,00	3,63	**3,82**	**3,48**	2,83	2,88	2,75	**2,82**	**2,73**
P2	IT performance measurement (e.g. IT balanced scorecard)	4,17	3,88	3,88	**3,97**		2,67	2,63	3,00	**2,76**	
P3	Portfolio management (incl. business cases, information economics, ROI, payback)	4,00	4,13	4,25	**4,13**		3,00	2,50	2,50	**2,67**	
P4	Charge back arrangements– total cost of ownership (e.g. activity based costing)	3,33	3,25	3,25	**3,28**		2,83	2,38	2,00	**2,40**	
P5	Service level agreements	3,67	3,50	3,25	**3,47**		3,50	3,25	2,63	**3,13**	
P6	IT gov. framework COBIT	3,83	2,88	3,38	**3,36**		2,50	2,38	2,38	**2,42**	
P7	IT governance assurance and self-assessment	3,00	2,63	2,75	**2,79**		2,50	2,50	2,63	**2,54**	
P8	Project governance/ management methodologies	4,17	3,88	4,25	**4,10**		2,83	3,00	3,00	**2,94**	
P9	IT budget control and reporting	4,00	4,13	4,25	**4,13**		4,50	3,50	4,00	**4,00**	
P10	Benefits management and reporting	2,67	3,00	2,88	**2,85**		2,83	2,13	2,13	**2,36**	
P11	COSO/ERM	2,67	1,88	2,63	**2,39**		2,00	1,88	2,25	**2,04**	

Fig. 2.31 (continued)

R1	Job-rotation	2,17	2,13	2,75	**2,35**	**3,28**	2,33	2,50	2,25	**2,36**	**3,06**
R2	Co-location	3,00	2,63	2,75	**2,79**		3,67	2,75	2,63	**3,01**	
R3	Cross-training	2,67	2,88	2,75	**2,76**		2,83	2,63	3,00	**2,82**	
R4	Knowledge management (on IT governance)	3,33	3,13	3,25	**3,24**		2,67	2,38	3,00	**2,68**	
R5	Business/IT account management	4,00	3,38	4,00	**3,79**		3,83	3,13	3,13	**3,36**	
R6	Executive/senior management giving the good example	4,00	3,75	3,88	**3,88**		3,17	2,63	2,63	**2,81**	
R7	Informal meetings between business and IT executive/senior management	4,00	3,50	3,88	**3,79**		4,00	3,63	4,00	**3,88**	
R8	IT leadership	4,17	3,63	3,88	**3,89**		2,83	2,50	3,13	**2,82**	
R9	Corporate internal communication addressing IT on a regular basis	3,67	3,25	3,38	**3,43**		3,83	3,63	3,63	**3,69**	
R10	IT governance awareness	3,00	2,63	2,88	**2,83**		3,17	3,00	3,25	**3,14**	

Total average: 3.45 **Total average: 3.07**

Fig. 2.31 (continued)

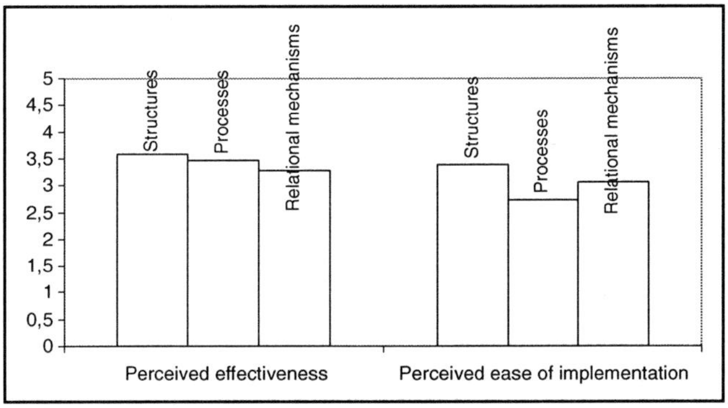

Fig. 2.32 Average effectiveness and ease of implementation

implement compared to processes. This finding is also supported by the personal experiences of the researchers in running an IT Governance Business Game amongst a group of business and IT professionals at the management school. The participants in this game are confronted with a fictitious organization with low business/IT alignment and the assignment is to define governance practices for the organization to improve that situation. Mostly, the participants are very fast in defining structures such as steering committees, but each time it appears to be a much bigger challenge to define supporting Enterprise Governance of IT processes such as portfolio management. Figure 2.32 even shows that relational mechanisms are perceived as being easier to implement compared to governance processes. The latter can probably be explained by the fact that these relational mechanisms sometimes can be informal and less structured, requiring a smaller amount of effort to install them.

Figures 2.33 and 2.34 provide the results for perceived effectiveness and ease of implementation organized per Enterprise Governance of IT practice.

From Fig. 2.33, it appears that the "IT steering committee" is perceived as being the most effective governance structure. This structure is defined as a "steering committee at executive or senior management level responsible for determining business priorities in IT investments." This structure provides a formal platform where business and IT people can directly interact with each other. Out of literature and case research, it was identified that these steering committees are very common in many organizations and play an important role in the portfolio management process. However, it also appeared that each organization has its own organization-specific naming and terminology. The perceived ease of implementation (Fig. 2.33) not surprisingly is also relatively high, with a score 3.35 on a scale of 5 (overall average is 3.07).

The second and third most effective practices are closely related and about having the "CIO reporting to the CEO/COO" or even the "CIO being part of the Executive Committee." These structures prevent that the IT department is only viewed as cost center and provide the CIO the opportunity to demonstrate,

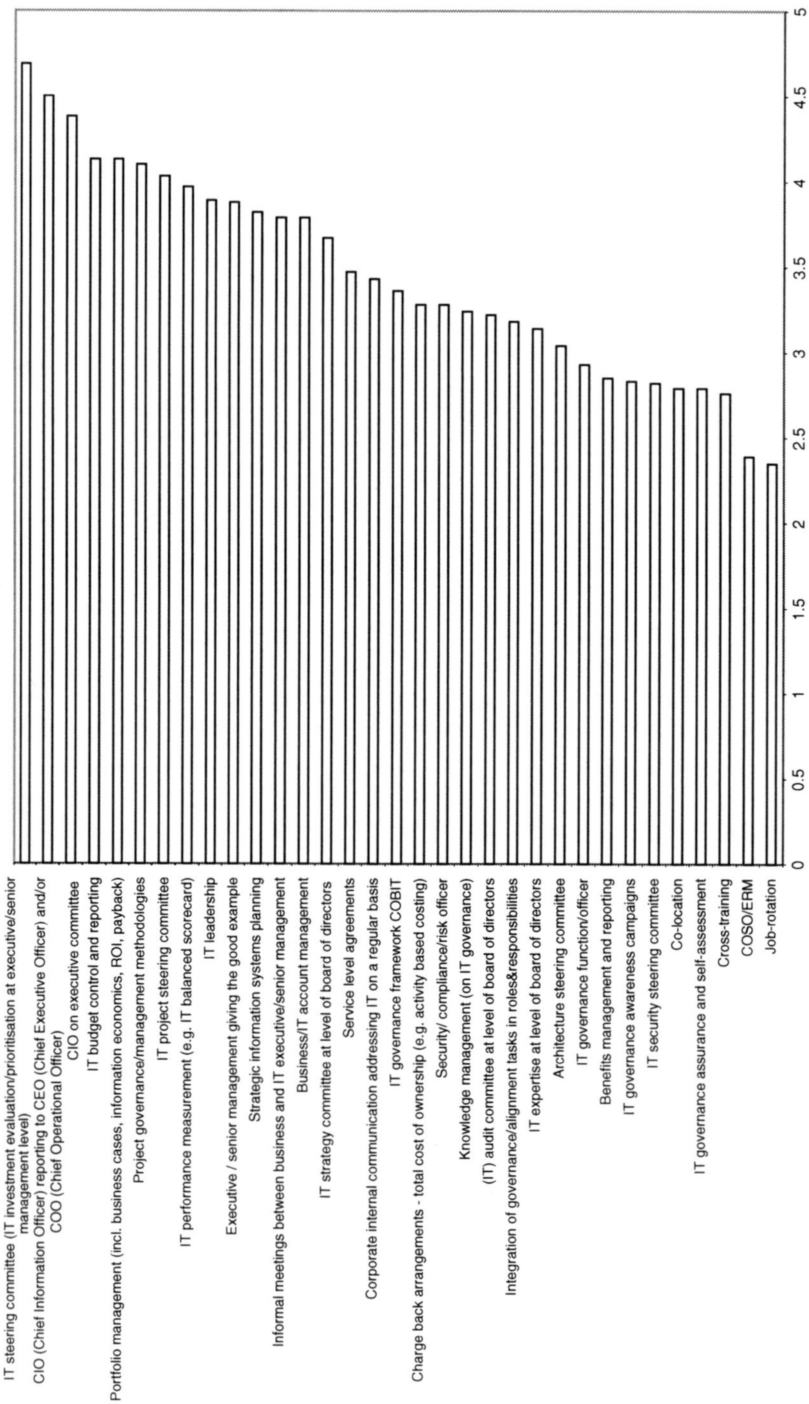

Fig. 2.33 Perceived effectiveness (0=not effective; 5=very effective)

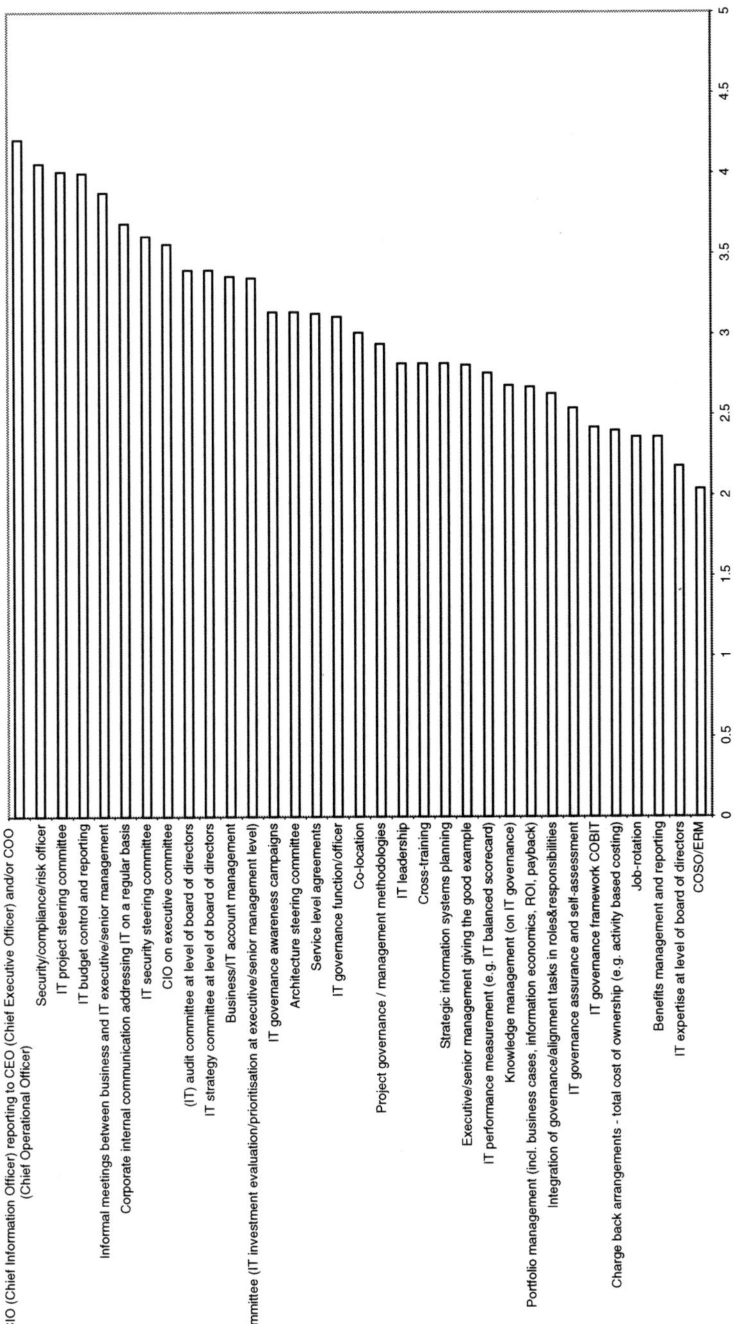

Fig. 2.34 Perceived ease of implementation (0=not easy to implement, 5=very easy to implement)

at executive level, the business value of IT. Consistent with this finding, McKinsey reported in their recent "Annual European Banking IT Cost Benchmark Study" that most top-performing banks indeed have their CIO reporting to COO or CEO. The two structures referred to in the beginning of this paragraph also received high scores regarding ease of implementation, respectively 4.21 and 3.56. This perceived ease of implementation is probably supported by the fact that within the financial services sector, there has been a strong push for many years to bring the CIO on a higher level, because of the high dependency of IT. Using the words of Monnoyer and Willmott (2005): "The IT leader must be part of the executive team to get results and to build the necessary relationships and credibility within the company. CIOs who are perceived to be operating managers – not leaders – rarely sit on the management committee and often report to executives other than the CEO. The solution isn't to clear space at the table for an operating manager; instead companies should search for an IT leader who adds value to the management team." These structures should of course go in close collaboration with the practice ranked ninth in terms of effectiveness, "IT leadership." This relational mechanism is defined as the "ability of CIO or similar role to articulate a vision for IT's role in the company and ensure that this vision is clearly understood by managers throughout the organization." If the CIO is not able to talk in business-oriented terms at executive level, his impact at that level will be small. In terms of ease of implementation, this relational mechanism obtained a score (2.82), which is below the overall average (3.07). This mechanism is indeed highly dependent on the individual competencies of the CIO and not many methods are available to manage it. Moreover, the required skill set of future CIOs is very ambitious: "The CIO role is one of the most demanding jobs in any company and one that usually touches almost every employee in one form or another. CIOs today must have a solid resume, a demonstrated set of accomplishments in both areas of technology and supporting and driving the business to new highs, and be able to communicate strategies and wins effectively" (Smith, 2006). Monnoyer and Willmott define leadership as one of the key success factors to enable structures and processes to be effective: "The problem is that IT governance systems have become a substitute for real leadership. Companies are relying on tightly scripted meetings, analyses, and decision frameworks to unite CIOs and business executives around a common vision for IT. But committee meetings and processes are poor stand-ins for executives who can forge a clear agreement among their peers about IT investment choices and drive the senior-level conversations needed to make tough trade-offs. For several reasons, leadership can achieve what governance systems by themselves cannot" (Monnyer and Willmott, 2005).

Assignment Box 2.3: IT leadership versus Enterprise Governance of IT

Make teams and discuss the following statements:

- IT leadership can be replaced by Enterprise Governance of IT
- Enterprise Governance of IT can be replaced by IT leadership

Another practice that received a rating for effectiveness above 4 is "IT budget control and reporting" (4.13). Monitoring and controlling the IT budget clearly remains high on the agenda in financial services organizations. "IT budget control and reporting" is also perceived as being relatively easy to implement (4.00), maybe because there has been a long tradition in the financial services world to build financial reporting lines. As denoted by ITGI (2007), this governance process supports important objectives such as "Ensure transparency and understanding of IT costs, benefits, strategy, policies and service levels" and "Set and track IT budgets in line with IT strategy and IT investment decisions."

The process "portfolio management," defined as "Prioritization process for IT investments and projects in which business and IT is involved (incl. business cases)," also received a score higher than 4 for perceived effectiveness (4.13). Some important benefits of the portfolio management process are, as reported by ITGI (2008a): "Increase the probability of selecting investments that have the potential to generate the highest return; Increase the likelihood of success of executing selected investments such that they achieve or exceed their potential return; Reduce costs by not doing things they should not be doing and taking early corrective action on or terminating investments that are not delivering to their expected potential; Reduce the risk of failure, especially high-impact failure." The importance of portfolio management processes is also put forward in McKinsey's "Annual European Banking IT Cost Benchmark Study," which concludes that top-performing banks have more mature portfolio management processes compared to other banks (McKinsey, 2006). As mentioned earlier, "portfolio management" is closely related to the "IT steering committee," as these structures play an important role in the "portfolio management" process. Where "steering committees" were perceived as being relatively easy to implement, the "portfolio management" process receives a score lower than average for perceived ease of implementation (2.67). This implies that it appears to be easier to install the structures in the organizations, required to enable the portfolio management process, but that realizing the portfolio management process itself is more difficult. The latter will certainly be true for large and complex financial services organization, with many different business lines and hierarchical levels. In such environment, many processes, procedures, policies, templates, training, etc., need to be developed to ensure that all parties involved in the "portfolio management" process can execute their role. The lower rating for "ease of implementation" can also be explained by the fact that introducing a complex portfolio management process often initiates resistance in the organization and can easily be perceived as being bureaucratic, negatively impacting the time-to-market. This concern was also stated by a board member of the Belgian financial services organization KBC, as described in previous section, "...there will always be people who experience the model as being too complex and over-bureaucratic. But we now at least have a model which clearly shows how projects are initiated and decided upon. It is obvious that the business people prefer a very quick time-to-market, but they have to take the impact on the back office into account. If we take unprepared decisions, the danger exists of creating a mess in the back-office, and the cost of cleaning up this mess is much higher than doing a well-considered pre-study in advance."

"IT project steering committees" and "project governance/management methodologies" also received an effectiveness rating higher than 4 (4.03 and 4.10). These practices can be regarded as structures and processes that come into action after projects are decided by the IT steering committee, focusing on maintaining involvement of business and IT during the execution of a project. Again referring to the KBC case (see previous section): "For each new agreed investment project or cluster of continuity projects within an activity domain, a Project Management Steering Group (PMSG) is assigned by the IT/Business Steering Committee, again composed of business and IT people to ensure alignment throughout the development process." Similar to "IT steering committees," "IT project steering committees" are also perceived as being relatively easy to implement (4.01), however, the related "project governance/management methodologies" received a score below average (2.94). Although a lot of models are available regarding the latter (e.g., Prince II, PMBOK, CMMi, etc.), it is perceived that is not easy to roll out these models in the organization.

The "architecture committee" focused on ensuring business and IT involvement regarding the definition and application of enterprise IT architecture guidelines but received scores for effectiveness below the overall average (3.04). This relatively low score might be surprising, as the concept of the enterprise IT architecture is more and more promoted as a fundamental basis for flexible business process management and business performance. A potential explanation of the low score might be that, although definitions were provided, experts did interpret this structure based on the title as a technological-oriented committee, while the real focus is on building standards and guidelines for building the enterprise IT architecture. This assumption could also explain what the business/audit group, compared to the other respondents group, by far gave the lowest score for effectiveness for this structure. This relatively low score for effectiveness also contradicts with similar research by Cumps et al. (2006) who conclude that "... organizations that have more extensive and mature enterprise architecture management practices have a higher probability of belonging to the group of highly aligned organizations." This contradictory finding should be further explored in future research. Regarding ease of implementation, the "architecture committee" received a score around the average (3.14). The lowest score for ease of implementation was assigned by the IT group respondents, probably people who have already experienced the difficulty of IT architecture issues in a concrete environment. Indeed, it might be that in the group of IT respondents, only recently architecture committee implementations took place, from which the benefits still have to be proven over time. Weill and Ross (2004) also refer to the start up of architecture committees: "At many enterprises, architecture committees get off to a rocky start, usually because the committees are formed to 'impose' technology standards on the enterprise. ... As long as senior management espouses the standardization for business reasons, however, standards gradually gain acceptance."

The "IT security steering committee," also received a score below average for perceived effectiveness (2.82), for which likely, a similar argumentation can be used as in previous discussion on the architecture committee (i.e., perceived as a very technical committee). Regarding ease of implementation, the "IT security steering committee" received a better score (3.61) compared to the "architecture committee." The "IT security steering committee" is being promoted in the context of the BASEL II regulation which addresses the control of operational risk in the finance sector. This regulation is mandatory for the financial services sector and increasingly requires businesses to conduct their operations in a securely managed way. As this regulation mandates organizations to comply, top-management support is more easily attained, for example, to implement such a structure, being promoted in one of the OECD guidelines (2003): "Security assurance requires clear instructions from the top. However, management should effectively incorporate input from all levels of the organization. The roles and responsibilities assumed at all levels in the company – from the Board of Directors to the temporary worker – will vary considerably. There is no magic formula for allocating responsibility in the most effective way. For some organizations, a security committee may be appropriate."

The "IT governance framework COBIT" (Control Objectives for Information and Related Technologies), which is receiving a lot of attention in the post-Sarbanes-Oxley world, received an effectiveness score (3.36) around the overall average (3.45). COBIT is a process-based framework which is promoted by the IT Governance Institute as a solid basis to implement IT governance. However, literature and case research gave indications that there is still a low adoption and little in-depth knowledge of this framework in the field. This low adoption might be an explanation of the low effectiveness scores (people did not yet experience the value), together with the fact that it is perceived as being difficult to implement (2.4). Another explanation for the relatively low score is the fact that COBIT is a very broad process framework and addresses a lot of the other IT governance practices, addressed in this research, as an integral part of its own framework. This implies that COBIT, as a framework, is situated at a much higher level of granularity compared to other more detailed structures and processes. Good examples are the "IT steering committee," the "portfolio management process" and "project management/governance methodologies," all of them receiving a very high effectiveness score in this research, and in COBIT all are an integral part of the "Planning and Organization" processes. This observation is significant information to build up a strong business case for the value of COBIT, demonstrating that it contains a lot of very powerful and effective governance structures, processes and relational mechanisms. Drilling down into the data per respondents group (Fig. 2.30) also reveals that the business/audit group assigned the highest scores for perceived effectiveness. This could be explained by the fact that COBIT initially originated as an audit framework, having gained a large user base and acceptance in the audit community. More information on COBIT is provided in Chapter 5.

An interesting finding to pinpoint is that the Enterprise Governance of IT definition referred to in the beginning of this book stress the prime responsibility of the board of directors, while these results reveal that mechanisms to achieve such as "IT expertise at level of board of directors" are rated relatively low in terms of perceived effectiveness (3.14). This can possibly be explained by the fact that involving the board of directors and making them more IT literate is not easy to achieve, which is confirmed by the second to last score in terms of ease of implementation of "IT expertise at the level of the board of directors" (2.18). The active involvement of the board of directors in a financial services organization is however very important, taking the high dependency on IT into account. In the words of Nolan and McFarlan (2005): "Despite the fact that corporate information assets can account for more than 50% of capital spending, most boards fall into the default mode of applying a set of tacit or explicit rules cobbled together from the best practices of other firms. Few understand the full degree of their operational dependence on computer systems or the extent to which IT plays a role in shaping their firms' strategies." However, the results of this research raise questions on how financial services organizations realize this board involvement in practice. This concern was also raised in the Belgian financial services organization KBC (see previous section), where it was concluded that "the organization's Board works at a very high, strategic level and they are consequently not the 'steering power' for IT or IT governance." Differentiation of the results for the different groups of respondents (business/audit, consultant, IT) (see Fig. 2.30) shows that the consultant groups on average assigned higher scores for effectiveness and ease of implementation, probably indicating that they are promoting this structure in their consulting activities. A potential other structure to achieve board involvement is the "audit committee at the level of board of directors," which received a score of 3.22 in terms of effectiveness and 3.40 for ease of implementation. Establishing an audit committee at the level of the board of directors is a legal requirement for Belgian financial services organization, but the question of course is whether this committee also addresses IT issues on a regular and structured basis.

An interesting result is the relatively high rating of both effectiveness and ease of implementation for "informal meetings between business and IT executive/senior management" (3.79 and 3.88). It demonstrates that a relational mechanism that is perceived as being fairly effective does not always have to be difficult to implement and could have an informal character.

A governance practice that received a very low rating (2.36) for ease of implementation is amongst others "benefits management." "Benefits management" is defined as a "processes to monitor the planned business benefits during and after implementation of the IT investments/projects." In practice, the calculation of the achieved business benefits and/or the re-calculation after implementation is in many cases performed at an ad hoc basis or is even lacking. In the Val IT framework, a publication promoting IT value governance practices, it is stated that organizations in terms of benefits management "traditionally are very bad at this, but if it is not done, effective governance cannot be achieved, value will be eroded and the business will not learn and improve its business case and portfolio management processes" (ITGI, 2008a). In spite of this observation, the "benefits management" process received a relatively low score for perceived effectiveness (2.85). However, this process continues to be promoted by many thought leaders (such as the IT Governance Institute) and consultancy organizations, probably also explaining why the consultants respondents (see Fig. 2.31) assigned the highest effectiveness scores compared to the two other groups of respondents. More information on Val IT is provided in Chapter 7.

The process "COSO/ERM," which is a framework for internal control within an organization, got the lowest score, compared to the other practices, for both effectiveness (2.39) and ease of implementation (2.04). Between the different groups of respondents (see Fig. 2.29), the highest effectiveness score was, not surprisingly, assigned by business/audit. An explanation for the overall low scores might be that the COSO framework goes beyond the scope of IT and probably therefore is perceived as being less relevant for Enterprise Governance of IT.

"Job-rotation" also received low scores for both effectiveness (2.35) and ease of implementation (2.36). In practice, many examples can be found of IT people rotating to business functions (less in the opposite direction). Organizing this type of job-rotation in the context of Enterprise Governance of IT is perceived, by the Delphi expert group, as being less effective and not that easy to realize. However, this contradicts with the findings in the Huntsman case (see previous section): "Another supporting mechanism for a better relationship between IT and business is job-rotation. Huntsman offers its employees the possibility to switch between IT and business jobs and vice versa. This possibility is part of every individual's career planning. ... In practice, employees do take the opportunity to widen their knowledge and rotate between different IT and business functions. The relational mechanism of job-rotation contributes to an increased mutual insight in the business and IT."

A related relation mechanism "Co-location" surprisingly received a relatively low effectiveness score (2.79). The assumption for this relational mechanism is that, by putting both business people and IT people physically close to each other, that this would make communication between business and IT easier. The relatively low score for effectiveness coming out of this Delphi research could be explained by the pervasive availability of modern communication technologies and the fact that this research is on a small geographical area where physical distances are always limited.

2.3.2 Minimum Baseline Practices

Figure 2.35 shows the results of the third question in the Delphi survey (see Research Box 2.2), in which the respondents were asked to identify the crucial

		total times mentioned	total ranking score	total rank
S6	IT steering committee (IT investment evaluation / prioritisation at executive/senior management level)	21	178	1
S4	CIO on executive committee	20	153	2
P3	Portfolio management (incl. business cases, information economics, ROI, payback)	20	142	3
P9	IT budget control and reporting	17	112	4
S1	IT strategy committee at level of board of directors	17	97	5
R8	IT leadership	16	79	6
P1	Strategic information systems planning	13	64	7
S9	IT project steering committee	13	55	8
S5	CIO (Chief Information Officer) reporting to CEO (Chief Executive Officer) and/or COO (Chief Operational Officer)	11	47	9
P8	Project governance / management methodologies	14	45	10

Fig. 2.35 Minimum baseline

elements (in a top ten) of an optimal Enterprise Governance of IT mix. These are the practices that are identified as most important, which can be defined as a kind of minimum baseline for Enterprise Governance of IT. The respondents were asked to build up this top ten, taking the attributes of perceived effectiveness and ease of implementation into account, together with their professional experience of their day-to-day practice. Figure 2.35 shows the final top ten resulting from this ranking exercises, including the number of times a specific practice is mentioned (total times mentioned) and the total ranking score (if a practice was ranked "1," it received ten points).

As could be expected, many of the practices that were rated high in the "perceived effectiveness" figure are recurring here in the minimum baseline. Good examples of the latter are the four practices mentioned first, more specifically "IT steering committee," "CIO on executive committee," "portfolio management" and "IT budget control and reporting." These practices were already discussed in previous paragraphs.

Some new practices appear in the minimum baseline such as "IT strategy committee at the level of board of directors." While it appeared in Fig. 2.34 that it is not easy to build up expertise at the level of the board of directors, this "IT strategy committee" might be a very worthwhile structure to get this expertise to a higher level. Although on its own, this structure did obtain only a little above-average effectiveness score (3.67, see Fig. 2.32), the Delphi group experts did include it as one of the crucial elements in the minimum baseline of practices, stressing its importance in the holistic whole of governance practices.

The IT governance process "Strategic information systems planning" also shows up here. This process was already rated relatively high regarding perceived effectiveness (3.82) and is of course one of the core processes to ensure that business strategic and tactical plan get aligned to IT strategies and tactical plans and vice versa. Or, as stated by ITGI (2007): "IT strategic planning is required to manage and direct all IT resources in line with the business strategy and priorities." Following this argumentation, it is not a surprise that this high-level process is part of the governance minimum baseline. In terms of "ease of implementation," this process received an average rating of 2.82.

The top ten minimum baseline finally not only represents practices at strategic level, but also at management level such as "Project steering committees" and "Project governance/management methodologies." The latter two also scored high in the "perceived effectiveness" ratings (see Fig. 2.33) and were already discussed in previous paragraphs.

2.3.3 *Looking for Highly Effective Practices That Are Easy to Implement*

Figure 2.36 brings it all together, plotting the previous results on two axes. The vertical axis addresses the "perceived effectiveness" while the horizontal axis measures the "perceived ease of implementation." Starting from these quadrants, we are of course interested in the practices that are situated at the top-right level or at least above the horizontal axis. The practices in the grey circle are the ones identified in Fig. 2.35 as being a minimum baseline for Enterprise Governance of IT. They all have "high effectiveness" and are "easy to implement" which demonstrates the consistency in answers of the experts. These minimum baseline practices are to be regarded as a minimal set of governance practices for each organization. They should be supplemented with other practices as required by the specific environment to build up a complete Enterprise Governance of IT framework.

Of course, to complement the minimum baseline, an organization would first consider the other practices that are highly effective and easy to implement. These are the practices in the upper right quadrant (outside the circle) of Fig. 2.35. Some examples are an "IT governance function/officer," "service level agreements" and "co-location." The practices at the top left are highly effective but do require more implementation time. These practices could be important enablers in the overall Enterprise Governance of IT framework, but is should be acknowledged that they do require more implementation time.

Governance practices that are situated at the bottom left of this graphical layout are of course the least interesting practices. In this quadrant, "COSO/ERM" and "job-rotation" are located, which were already discussed before. The value of these practices, in the context of Enterprise Governance of IT, can of course be challenged.

It might have been surprising that the minimum baseline only contained one relational mechanism ("IT leadership"), certainly taking into account what we stated in previous section: "Relational mechanisms are crucial in the IT governance framework and paramount for attaining and sustaining business–IT alignment, even when the appropriate structures and processes are in place."

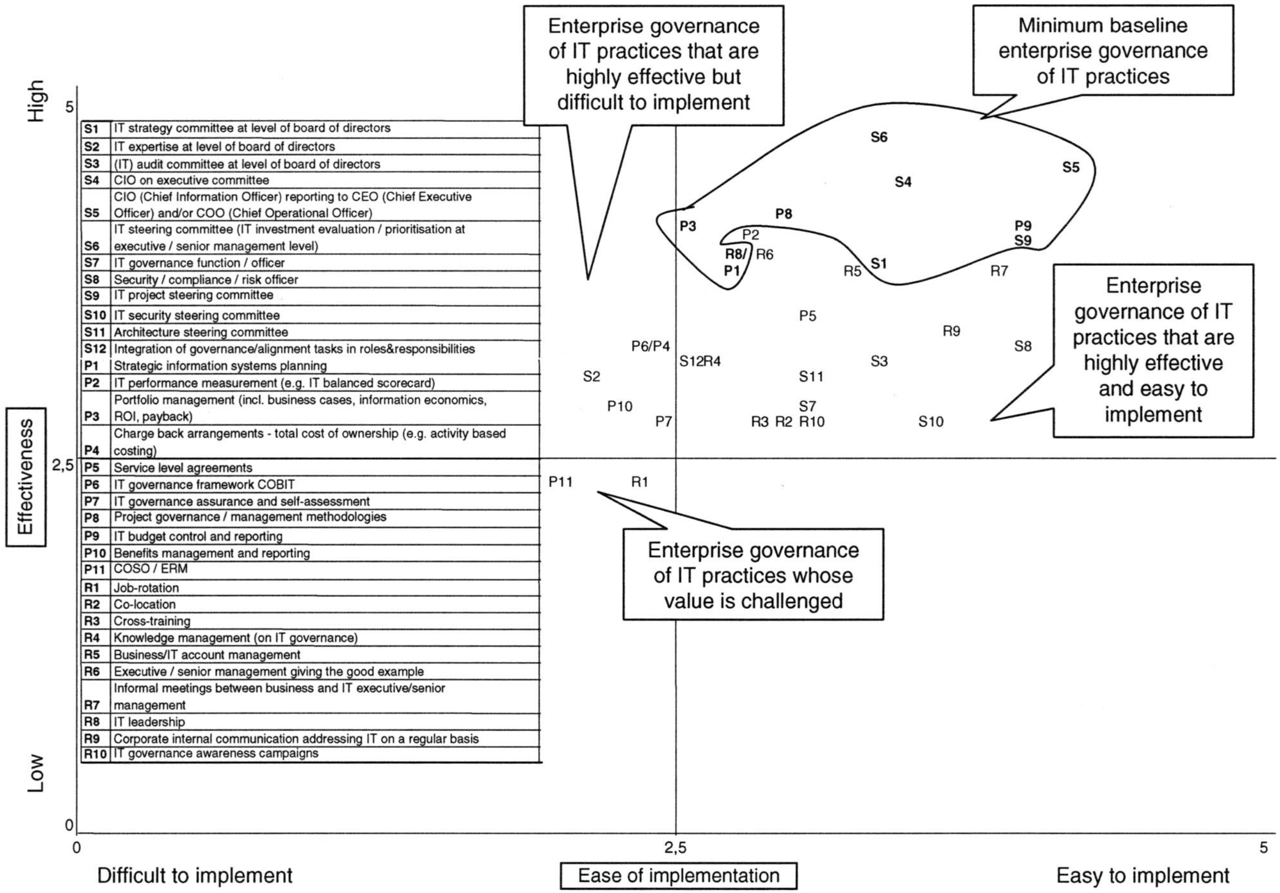

Fig. 2.36 Effectiveness, ease of implementation and minimum baseline

A potential explanation for this might be that there is not that much knowledge available in this domain in organizations. Also in literature, the domain of relational mechanisms is less elaborated, while much research can be found on governance structures and processes.

However, in Fig. 2.36 we now see that very close to minimum baseline practices in the grey circle, some relational mechanisms arise that indeed were not part of the minimum baseline. These mechanisms are "business/IT account management" ("Bridging the gap between business and IT by means of account managers who act as in-between"), "senior management giving the good example" ("Senior business and IT management acting as 'partners'") and "informal meeting between business and IT executive/senior management."

An interesting process that also sits high up in the right upper quadrant is "IT performance management (IT balanced scorecard)," certainly in terms of perceived effectiveness (3.97). The IT balanced scorecard can be used not only as a powerful measurement tool but also as a real management and alignment instrument when cause-and-effect relationships are defined between goals and metrics (see also Chapter 4 on the Balanced Scorecard). In the words of KBC's CIO, the balanced scorecard is "a systematic translation of the strategy into critical success factors and metrics, which materializes the strategy" (see previous section)/Realizing this in-depth application of the balanced scorecard is perceived below average in terms of ease of implementation (2.76). Related measurement/management processes are "service level agreements" between IT and the business. This process received scores for effectiveness (3.47) and ease of implementation (3.13) around the overall average.

The top right quadrant also contains two specific functions/roles that can be used as governance structure. The "security/risk/compliance officer" received a very high score for ease of implementation (4.06), probably because it is often required by regulations in the financial services sector (e.g., BASEL II), but a score close to the overall average (3.28) for effectiveness. The "IT governance officer" received a relatively low score for effectiveness (2.93). This is a surprising result as in practice, this type of function/role is more and more emerging in organizations, not only in the financial services sector. Related to these governance roles is the "integration of governance/alignment tasks in roles/responsibilities." This structure implies that in the job description of business and IT people-specific references are made to their roles on IT governance and alignment. Where it received an average score for effectiveness (3.18), this structure received a score below average for ease of implementation (2.63) (but still in the upright quadrant). Of course, describing these types of roles in job description is relatively easy, but ensuring that these roles are fully understood and executed in day-to-day practice is not easy to realize, requiring amongst others a lot of training and awareness creation. Some relational mechanisms that can support this, such as "cross-training" (training business people about IT activities and vice versa), "corporate internal communication addressing IT on a regular basis" (e.g., internal magazine), "knowledge management on IT governance" (e.g., though intranet) and "IT governance awareness campaigns" however all received a score for effectiveness below or on average.

The top left quadrant contains practices that are relatively effective but rather difficult to implement. This quadrant contains "IT expertise at the level of the board of directors," "IT Governance Framework COBIT," "Benefits management and reporting," "Chargeback arrangements" and "IT governance assurance and self-assessment." Most of these practices have been discussed earlier in this paper, except for the latter two. "Chargeback arrangements" are about the ability to chargeback costs for IT services and development to the appropriate business units. This is an important process to enable the business to fully understand the total cost of ownership for IT operational and development services, but is perceived as not easy to implement. In practice, a methodology based on Activity-Based Costing concepts is often used to realize chargeback processes (cf. the KBC case in previous section). "IT governance assurance and self-assessment" can be a useful instrument to identify potential weaknesses in the existing IT governance framework and to identify improvement projects. It is perceived as relatively difficult to realize, maybe because little guidance/knowledge is available to execute such self-assessments and therefore often require third-party involvement.

Assignment Box 2.4: Effectiveness and ease of implementation of Enterprise Governance of IT practices

Make teams. Discuss the results regarding effectiveness versus ease of implementation for all or some Enterprise Governance of IT practices and try to explain the scores.

Summary

Having developed a high-level model for Enterprise Governance of IT does not imply that governance is actually working in the organization. Conceiving the model for Enterprise Governance of IT is the first step, and deploying it throughout all levels of the organization is the next challenging step. To achieve this, Enterprise Governance of IT can be deployed using a mixture of various structures, processes and relational mechanisms.

It is important to recognize that each of the applied processes, structures and relational mechanisms serve specific or multiple goals in the complex alignment challenge. However, dividing the Enterprise Governance of IT framework into smaller pieces, and solving each problem separately, does not always solve the complete problem. A holistic approach toward Enterprise Governance of IT acknowledges its complex and dynamic nature, consisting of a set of interdependent subsystems (processes, structures and relational mechanisms) that deliver a powerful whole. The challenge for organizations is to select an appropriate set of practices, specifically for their own environment. To assist organizations in this challenge, this chapter evaluated the effectiveness and ease of implementation of each of the 33 Enterprise Governance of IT practices. Also, a minimum baseline is proposed, providing a minimal set of practices each organization should have.

Study Questions

1. Identify the most important structures for Enterprise Governance of IT.
2. Identify the most important processes for Enterprise Governance of IT.
3. Identify the most important relational mechanisms for Enterprise Governance of IT.
4. Identify which governance practices are most relevant for obtaining board involvement.
5. Explain how an organization can select an appropriate set of practices for Enterprise Governance of IT and how the findings of this chapter can be used in this context.
6. Discuss why the financial services sector is an interesting industry for doing research in the domain of Enterprise Governance of IT.
7. Define what an IT steering committee is and explain why it is an important IT governance mechanism.
8. Define what IT portfolio management is and explain why it is an important IT governance mechanism.
9. Define what IT leadership is and explain why it is an important IT governance mechanism.
10. Define what an IT governance awareness campaign is and explain why it is an important IT governance mechanism.

Further Reading

Akkermans, H.A. et al., 2003, The Impact of ERP on Supply Chain Management: Exploratory Findings From a European Delphi Study, European Journal of Operational Research, no. 146, pp. 284–301.

Benbasat I., Zmud R.W., 1999, Emperical research in Information Systems: the practice of relevance, MIS Quarterly, vol. 23, no. 1.

Chiasson, M.W., Davidson, E., 2005, Taking industry seriously in Information Systems research, MIS Quarterly, vol. 29, no. 4, pp. 591–605.

Cook, T.D., and Campbell, D., 1979, Quasi-experimentation: Design and Analysis Issues for Field Settings. Chicago: Rand. Mcnally College Publishing Company.

Cumps, B., Viaene, S., Dedene, G., and Vandenbulcke, J., 2006, An Empirical Study on Business/ICT Alignment in European Organizations, in Proceedings of the Hawaii International Conference on System Sciences (HICSS).

De Haes, S., 2007, The impact of IT Governance Practices on Business/IT Alignment in the Belgian Financial Services Sector, Thesis Submitted to Achieve the Degree op PhD in Applied Economics. University of Antwerp, Promotor: Van Grembergen, W.

De Haes, S., and Van Grembergen, W., 2005, IT Governance Structures, Processes and Relational Mechanisms: Achieving IT/Business Alignment in a Major Belgian Financial Group, in Proceedings of Hawaii International Conference on System Sciences (HICSS).
De Haes, S., and Van Grembergen, W., 2006, IT Governance Best Practices in Belgian Organizations, in Proceedings of the Hawaii International Conference on System Sciences (HICSS).
De Haes, S., and Van Grembergen, W., 2008a, An exploratory Study Into the Design of an IT Governance Minimum Baseline Through Delphi Research, Communications of the AIS, vol. 22.
De Haes, S., and Van Grembergen, W., 2008b, Practices in IT Governance and Business/IT Alignment, Information Systems Control Journal, vol. 2.
De Haes, S., and Van Grembergen, W., 2008c, Analysing the Relationship between IT Governance and Business/IT Alignment maturity, in Proceedings of the 41th Hawaii International Conference on System Sciences (HICSS).
ITGI, 2003, Board Briefing on IT Governance, Second Edition, from www.itgi.org
ITGI, 2007, COBIT 4.1, from www.itgi.org
ITGI, 2008a, Enterprise Value: Governance of IT investments, The Val IT Framework, from www.itgi.org
ITGI, 2008b, IT Governance Global Status Report. Report published by ITGI and PriceWaterhouseCoopers, from www.itgi.org
Keill, M. et al., 2002, Reconciling User and Project Manager Perceptions of IT Project Risk: A Delphi Study, Information Systems Journal, no. 12, pp. 103–119.
Linstone, H.A., and Turoff, M., 1975, The Delphi Method: Techniques and Applications. Reading, Massachusetts: Addison-Wesley Publishing Company, 620p.
McKinsey, 2006, Annual European Banking IT Cost Benchmark Study, Confidential Report.
Monnoyer, E., and Willmott P., 2005, What IT Leaders Do: Companies that Rely on IT Governance Systems Alone Will Come Up Short, McKinsey Quarterly on IT
Nolan, R., and McFarlan, F.W., 2005, Information Technology and the Board of Directors. Harvard Business Review, vol. 83, no. 10, pp. 96–106.
OECD, 2003, Information Security Assurance for Executives, on-line available at http://www.oecd.org/dataoecd/54/22/37019249.pdf
Parker, M., 1995, Strategic transformation and information technology. London: Prentice Hall.
Patel, N.V., 2003, An Emerging Strategy for E-business IT Governance. In Van Grembergen, W. (Ed.), Strategies for Information Technology Governance. Hershey, PA: Idea Group Publishing.
Peterson, R.R., 2004, Information Strategies and Tactics for Information Technology Governance. In Van Grembergen, W. (Ed.), Strategies for Information Technology Governance. Hershey, PA: Idea Group Publishing.
Sambamurthy, V., and Zmud, R.W., 1999, Arrangements for Information Technology Governance: A Theory of Multiple Contingencies, MIS Quarterly, vol. 23, no. 2, pp. 261–290.
Schmidt, R.C., 1997, Managing Delphi Surveys Using Nonparametric Statistical Techniques, Decision Sciences, vol. 28, no. 3.
Siegel, S., 1988, Nonparametric Statistics for the Behavioral Sciences. New York: Mc.Graw-Hill.
Smith G., 2006, Straight to the Top – Becoming a World-class CIO. Hoboken, NJ: John Wiley & Sons.
Taylor-Powell, E., 2002, Quick Tips Collecting Group Data: Delphi Technique, University of Wisconsin, on-line available at http://www.uwex.edu/ces/pdande/resources/pdf/Tipsheet4.pdf
Van Grembergen, W., 2002, Introduction to the Minitrack: IT Governance and its Mechanisms, in Proceedings of the 35th Hawaii International Conference on System Sciences (HICSS).
Van Grembergen, W. (Ed.), 2004, Strategies for Information Technology Governance. Hershey, PA: Idea Group Publishing.

Van Grembergen, W., and De Haes, S., 2008, Implementing Information Technology Governance: Models, Practices and Cases, IGI Publishing.
Van Grembergen, W., Van Brempt, H., and De Haes, S., 2007, Prioritizing and Linking Business and IT Goals in the Financial Sector, in Proceedings of the 40th Hawaii International Conference on System Sciences (HICSS).
Van Grembergen, W., De Haes, S., and Van Brempt, H., 2007, How Does the Business Drive IT? Identifying, Prioritizing and Linking Business and IT Goals, Information Systems Control, vol. 6.
Weill, P., and Ross, J., 2004, IT Governance: How Top Performers Manage IT Decision Rights for Superior Results. Boston: Harvard Business School Press.

Websites

Arcelor/Simar: www.arcelormittal.com/gent/
Huntsman: www.huntsman.com/pu/
Information Technology Alignment and Governance Research Institute: www.uams.be/ITAG
ISACA: www.isaca.org
IT Governance Institute: www.itgi.org
KBC: www.kbc.be
Vanbreda: www.vanbreda.be

Chapter 3
The Impact of Enterprise Governance of IT on Business/IT Alignment

Abstract Previous chapters described what Enterprise Governance of IT is about and how a set of practices can be leveraged to implement Enterprise Governance of IT. In this chapter, the impact of Enterprise Governance of IT implementations on business/IT alignment will be discussed. The first question is how an organization can measure and evaluate its current status of business/IT alignment. This discussion is supplemented with a benchmarking case, where business/IT alignment was measured for the Belgian financial services sector. Next, the impact of Enterprise Governance of IT practices on business/IT alignment is analyzed and illustrated with cases.

3.1 Measuring Business/IT Alignment

There is no universal way to measure business/IT alignment in literature. Many researchers have developed models that attempt to capture the complex alignment construct as complete as possible. Each measurement model has its own approach, and as a result, it is very difficult to compare results of alignment studies. Some potential approaches are discussed below, all having their strengths and weaknesses. In the end, it is important to select the approach that is most suited for the type of activity or research one is trying to do.

3.1.1 The Matching and Moderation Approach

The matching approach looks at the difference in rating between two pairs of related items. When there is a high difference between the ratings of related items, alignment is low, and oppositely, when there is a low difference, alignment is high. Figure 3.1 illustrates the matching approach.

In this type of studies, researchers look for parallelism between business and IT. If the difference in scores between business and IT is high, alignment is low (in Fig. 3.1, difference in scores for low alignment is 5), and oppositely, if the

W. Van Grembergen, S. De Haes, *Enterprise Governance of Information Technology*, DOI 10.1007/978-0-387-84882-2_3,

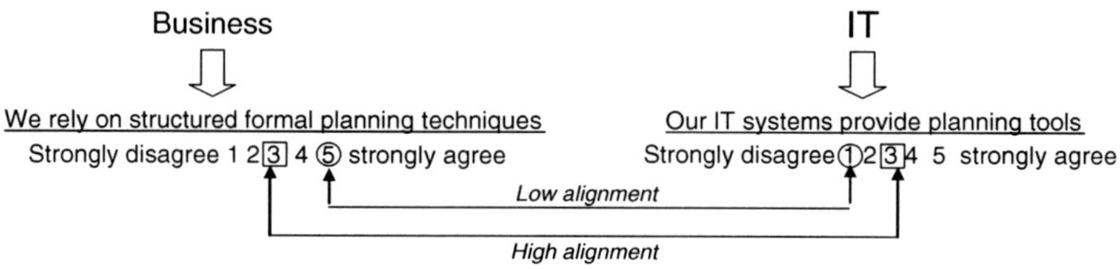

Fig. 3.1 Matching approach

difference between the scores is low, alignment is high (in Fig. 3.1, difference in scores of high alignment is 0). Applying this to a set of questions can lead to an alignment score for the organization. One of the shortcomings of this method is whether the scores necessarily need to be at the same level to indicate high degrees of alignment. Take the example in Fig. 3.1: it is clear that if the business scores 5 on formal planning techniques and IT scores 1 on providing planning tools then alignment is low as IT is not supporting business needs. However, if the business does not rely on structured formal planning techniques (score 1 on left hand side) but IT scores a better rate of 2 or 3 on providing planning tools, maybe IT is outperforming slightly but does that really imply low alignment? However, this method is clearly an intuitive and simple approach to undertake and is therefore often used in practice and research.

A related technique is the moderation approach. In this approach, alignment is viewed as an interaction rather than a parallelism, and in this way is quite different in outcomes compared to the matching approach. It is the combination or synergy between business and IT, rather than the difference, which is important. The moderation approach does not calculate the difference but the product terms. In the example of Fig. 3.1, this implies that the business score of 1 and the IT score of 5 result in an alignment score of 5 and the business score of 3 and the alignment score of 3 in 9. It is clear that this approach differs from the matching approach as two low scores are now seen as "low alignment" where in the matching approach two (equal) low scores result in "high alignment." The basic assumption in the moderation approach is that the interactive relationship (moderation) between business and IT, and not the difference, will impact business performance. For example, two 3's would lead to an alignment score of 9 and two 5's would lead to an alignment score of 25 following the moderation approach. In the matching approach, both scenarios would lead to an alignment score of "0," i.e., high alignment. In the moderation approach, the higher score of 25 (two 5's) is assigned as this represents a higher interaction effect between business and IT which will impact firm importance.

Whichever method is chosen, matching or moderation, it should be clear that both approaches are valuable but that they can lead to different conclusions regarding business/IT alignment in an organization.

3.1.2 The Profile Deviation Approach

Measuring alignment based on the profile deviation approach is based on two steps. First, an "ideal alignment scenario" has to be deducted (from theory) and next, deviations from this ideal state are calculated.

A well-known example here is the study of Sabherwal and Chan. These authors tried to define IT strategies that map best on specific business strategies. Those business strategies were defined based on the Miles and Snow typology, which identifies different types of business strategies: defenders (aiming to reduce costs, maximizing efficiency and effectiveness of production, avoiding organizational change), prospectors (seen as leading innovators, reacting first on signals of change in their market) and analyzers (closely watching competitor's activities and carefully evaluating organizational changes). Figure 3.2 demonstrates which IT strategies align best with specific business strategies, according to their insights. "IT for efficiency" is oriented toward internal and inter-organizational efficiencies and long-term decision-making and maps well on the defender's business strategy. "IT for flexibility" focuses on market flexibility and quick strategic decisions which map on the prospector's business strategy. "IT for comprehensiveness" enables comprehensive decisions and quick responses through knowledge of other organizations which complies with the analyzer's business strategy.

Based on this model, organizations can be classified against each of the categories and the distance against the ideal state can be calculated. It is clear that the value of this type of measurement stands or falls with the validity of the theoretized ideal state model.

A similar approach can be applied leveraging the business goals/IT goals research as introduced in Chapter 1, where "ideal" matches are described between business goals and IT goals. Based on a profile deviation approach, an organization extracts relevant IT goals and business goals out of the provided mapping tables and calculates the percentage of IT goals that are supporting business goals for their specific environment.

Business Strategy / *IT Strategy*	**Defenders**	**Prospectors**	**Analysers**
IT for efficiency	High	Low	Low
IT for flexibility	Low	High	Low
IT for comprehensiveness	Low	Low	High

Fig. 3.2 Mapping IT and business strategies
Based on: Sabherwal, R., and Chan, Y., 2001, Alignment Between Business and IS Strategies: A Study of Prospectors, Analyzers and Defenders, Information Systems Research, vol. 12, no. 1, pp. 11–33.

3.1.3 The Scoring Approach

A typical example of the scoring approach is the information economics method developed by Benson and Parker (1998). This scoring method can be used as an alignment measurement whereby both business and IT people score major IT projects to verify the degree of alignment against a set of business and IT criteria. The method typically departs from the Return On Investment (ROI) of a project and different non-tangibles such as "strategic match of the project" (business evaluation) and "match with the strategic IT architecture" (IT evaluation). In essence, information economics is a scoring technique for projects, resulting in a weighted total score based on the scores for the ROI and the non-tangibles. Typically scores from 0 to 5 are attributed whereby 0 means no contribution, and 5 refers to a high contribution; the values obtain a positive score and the risks a negative score (Fig. 3.3).

A limitation of previous approach is clearly that it is focused only on one major IT project. Alternative scoring instruments are developed by Weill and Broadbent (1998) and Weill and Ross (2004). These researchers developed a "diagnostic to assess alignment" and "governance performance indicator" as

Traditional ROI (+)		
+ value linking (+) + value acceleration (+)	+ value restructuring (+) + innovation (+)	
= Adjusted ROI	***+ Business Value***	***+ IT Value***
	▪ Strategic match (+) ▪ Competitive advantage (+) ▪ Competitive response (+) ▪ Management information (+) ▪ Service and quality (+) ▪ Environmental quality (+) ▪ Empowerment (+) ▪ Cycle time (+) ▪ Mass customization (+)	▪ Strategic IT architecture (+)
	- Business Risk	***- IT Risk***
	▪ Business strategy risk (-) ▪ Business organization risk (-)	▪ IT Strategy risk (-) ▪ Definitional uncertainty (-) ▪ Technical risk (-) ▪ IT service delivery risk (-)
= VALUE (business contribution)		

Fig. 3.3 Information economics
Based on: Van Grembergen, W., and Van Bruggen, R., 1997, Measuring and Improving Corporate Information Technology Through the Balanced Scorecard Technique, in Proceedings of the European Conference on the Evaluation of Information Technology, Delft, The Netherlands.

visualized in Figs. 3.4 and 3.5. This first diagnostic requires the respondents to assess 10 statements that relate to the degree of alignment, on a scale from 1 to 5 (1 = always true, 5 = never true). The average of the assessments on all the 10 statements provides the alignment score.

The governance performance measure is based on the scores regarding perceived governance outcome, i.e., strategic alignment. Respondents have to score on a scale from 1 (not important) to 5 (very important) on how important a particular governance outcome is (Q1), and how well IT governance

	always true				never true
1. Senior management has no vision for the role of IT	1	2	3	4	5
2. The IT group drives IT projects	1	2	3	4	5
3. There is no IT component in the division's strategy	1	2	3	4	5
4. Vital information necessary to make decisions is often missing	1	2	3	4	5
5. Islands of automation exist	1	2	3	4	5
6. Management perceives little value from computing	1	2	3	4	5
7. A "them and us" mentality prevails	1	2	3	4	5
8. IT doesn't help for the hard tasks	1	2	3	4	5
9. It's hard to get financial approval for IT projects	1	2	3	4	5
10. Senior management sees outsourcing as a way to control IT	1	2	3	4	5
	Average:				

Fig. 3.4 Diagnostic to assess alignment
Adapted from: Weill, P., and Broadbent, M., 1998, Leveraging the New Infrastructure: How Market Leaders Capitalize on Information Technology. Boston: Harvard Business School Press. Portions reprinted, with permission, from Harvard Business School Press.

1. How important are the following outcomes of your IT governance, on a scale from 1 (not important) to 5 (very important)?

	Not important 1	2	3	4	Very important 5
Cost-effective use of IT					
Effective use of IT for growth					
Effective use of IT for asset utilisation					
Effective use of IT for business flexibility					

2. What is the influence of the IT governance in your business on the following measures of success, on a scale from 1 (not important) to 5 (very important)?

	Not important 1	2	3	4	Very important 5
Cost-effective use of IT					
Effective use of IT for growth					
Effective use of IT for asset utilisation					
Effective use of IT for business flexibility					

Fig. 3.5 Governance outcome survey
Adapted from: Weill, P., and Ross, J., 2004, IT Governance: How Top Performers Manage IT Decisions Rights for Superior Results. Boston: Harvard Business School Press, 269 blz. Portions reprinted, with permission, from Harvard Business School Press.

$$\frac{(\Sigma_{n=1\text{ to }4}\ (\text{importance of outcome }\{Q1\} * \text{influence of IT governance }\{Q2\})) * 100}{\Sigma_{n=1\text{ to }4}(5 * (\text{importance of outcome}))}$$

Fig. 3.6 Governance performance calculator
Adapted from: Weill, P., and Ross, J., 2004, IT Governance: How Top Performers Manage IT Decisions Rights for Superior Results. Boston: Harvard Business School Press, 269 blz. Portions reprinted, with permission, from Harvard Business School Press.

contributed to meeting that outcome (Q2) (1 = not successful, 2 = very successful) as visualized in Fig. 3.5. The outcomes that are to be scored are cost effective use of IT, effective use of IT for growth, effective use of IT for asset utilization and effective use of IT for business flexibility. In other words, Q1 assesses the importance of a particular outcome and Q2 assesses how well IT governance contributed to meeting the outcome.

Based on the scores a weighted governance performance can be calculated, using the formula of Fig. 3.6. Since not all firms rank the outcomes with the same importance, the answers to the first question are used to weigh the answers to the second question. Then the weighed scores for the four questions are added and divided by the maximum score attainable by that enterprise.

3.1.4 The Maturity Model Approach

Organizations can also use a maturity model to assess the current degree of alignment. This is a method of scoring that enables the organization to grade itself from non-existent (0) to optimized (5). This tool offers an easy-to-understand way to determine the "as-is" and the "to-be" (according to enterprise strategy) position, and enables the organization to benchmark itself against best practices and standard guidelines. In this way, gaps can be identified and specific actions can be defined to move toward the desired level of strategic alignment maturity.

Good examples of strategic alignment maturity models were developed by Luftman and Duffy. Each of these models uses criteria, composed of a variety of attributes, to build different levels of maturity. Luftman defines five maturity levels using the criteria and attributes described in the first two columns of Fig. 3.7. The last two columns indicate the characteristics or values of each attribute to obtain a level 1 or level 5 of the maturity model.

Duffy developed a similar maturity model (Fig. 3.8) which is composed of four maturity levels. Although this maturity model differs from the previous

attribute	characteristics level 1	characteristic level 5
•communications maturity		
• understanding of business by IT	minimum	pervasive
• understanding of IT by business	minimum	pervasive
• inter/intra-organizational learning	casual, ad hoc	strong and structured
• protocol rigidity	command and control	informal
• knowledge sharing	ad hoc	extra-enterprise
• liaison(s) breath/effectiveness	none or ad hoc	extra-enterprise
• competency/value measurements maturity		
• IT metrics	technical	extended to external partners
• business metrics	ad hoc	extended to external partners
• balanced metrics	ad hoc, unlinked	business, partner and IT metrics
• service level agreements	sporadically present	extended to external partners
• benchmarking	not generally practiced	routinely performed with partners
• formal assessments/reviews	none	routinely performed
• continuous improvement	none	routinely performed
• governance maturity		
• business strategic planning	ad hoc	integrated across & external
• IT strategic planning	ad hoc	integrated across & external
• reporting/organization structure	CIO reports to CFO central/decentral	CIO reports to CEO federated
• budgetary/control	cost center, erratic	investment center, profit center
• IT investment management	cost based, erratic	business value
• steering committee(s)	not formal, regular	partnership
• prioritization process	reactive	value added partner

36

attribute	characteristics level 1	characteristic level 5
•partnership maturity		
• business perception of IT value	IT perceived as a cost	IT co-adapts with business
• role of IT in strategic business planning	no seat at business table	co-adaptive with business
• shared goals, risk, rewards/penalties	IT takes risk	risks and rewards shared
• IT program management	ad hoc	continuous improvement
• relationship/trust style	conflict/minimum	valued partnership
• business sponsor/champion	none	at the CEO level
• scope & architecture maturity		
• traditional, enabler/driver	traditional systems	business strategy driver/enabler
• standards articulation	none or ad hoc	inter-enterprise standards
• architectural integration:	no formal integration	evolve with partners
• functional organization		integrated
• enterprise		standard enterprise architecture
• inter-enterprise		with all partners
• architectural transparency, flexibility	none	across the infrastructure
• skills maturity		
• innovation, entrepreneurship	discouraged	the norm
• locus of power	in the business	all executives, including CIO
• management style	command and control	relationship based
• change readiness	resistant to change	high, focused
• career crossover	none	across the enterprise
• education, cross-training	none	across the enterprise
• attract & retain best talent	no program	effective program for hiring & retaining

37

Fig. 3.7 The strategic alignment maturity levels of Luftman
Adapted from: Luftman, J., 2000, Assessing Business-IT Alignment Maturity, Communications of AIS, vol. 4. Portions reprinted, with permission, from Communications of the Association for Information Systems.

Maturity level 1: "Uneasy alliance"	Maturity level 2: "Supplier/consumer relationship"
In this stage, there is a fundamental disconnect between the technology executive and the rest of corporate management. IT responds to business demands with little understanding of how the technology can contribute to value. IT is viewed primarily as something to make the company more efficient. Business units have little understanding of technology and prefer to hold the IT organization accountable for the success and/or failure of any IT related project.	If IT has a strategic plan it is developed in response to the corporate strategy. IT is probably viewed as a cost centre and there is little appreciation for the value that IT contributes to corporate success. In this stage, IT is still not viewed as a strategic tool and IT executives are unlikely to be involved in developing corporate strategy.
Maturity level 3: "Co-dependence/grudging respect"	**Maturity level 4: "United we succeed, divided we fail"**
In this stage, the business is dependent on IT and there are early signs of recognition that it is a strategic tool. CIOs are becoming more knowledgeable about cross-functional business processes because of ERP, CRM, etc. The Internet and interest in e-business forces some level of IT/Business alignment. CEOs begin to recognize that IT is a competitive tool.	In this stage, IT and business are inextricably entwined. Business executives have less time to prove they can deliver. Business cannot continue without IT and IT has little real value if it is not to support the corporate strategy. There is only a single strategy and it incorporates both IT and business. Whether the business is a pure play Internet company, or a "bricks 'n clicks" company, IT and business move in lockstep.

Fig. 3.8 The strategic alignment maturity model of Duffy
Adapted from: Duffy, J., 2002, IT/Business Alignment: Is It an Option or Is It Mandatory? IDC document #26831.

example, it aspires to the same goal, i.e., providing a tool to help management in their journey to align business and IT. This maturity model states that in level one, there is a fundamental disconnect between the technology executive and the rest of corporate management. A maturity level of 4 (the highest level in this model), however, implies that IT and business are inextricably entwined and there is only one single strategy that incorporates both business and IT.

3.2 Business/IT Alignment Benchmark

This section discusses the results of a business/IT alignment benchmark research, based on Luftman's validated maturity model (see previous section and the Research Box 3.1) To do this, 13 Belgian financial services organizations were invited to participate, from which ten committed to participate under the condition that anonymity was guaranteed. Figure 3.9 gives a high-level indication of the profiles of each of those ten organizations. It concerned three mid-sized organizations (between 100 and 1000 employees in Belgium),

Organisation	Number of employees in Belgium	Main activities
A	More than 1000	Banking and Insurance
B	Between 100 and 1000	Banking and Insurance
C	More than 1000	Banking
D	More than 1000	Banking
E	More than 1000	Banking and Insurance
F	More than 1000	Financial transaction services
G	Between 100 and 1000	Banking and Insurance
H	Between 100 and 1000	Banking and Insurance
I	More than 1000	Banking and Insurance
J	More than 1000	Banking and Insurance

Fig. 3.9 Profiles of case organizations

seven large-sized organizations (more than 1000 employees in Belgium) and most of them covered both banking and insurance activities. One organization (D) had both banking and insurance activities, but the research only focused on one, the banking activities. The core business of organization F was not in real banking or insurance activities, but in supporting financial transactions for other financial organizations. More details on the benchmarking research methodology is provided in Research Box 3.1.

Research Box 3.1: Business/IT alignment benchmarking research

The goal of this benchmarking research is to create a reference point of business/IT alignment in Belgian mid to large-size financial services organizations. To achieve this, 13 organizations were contacted, indicating that the creation of this benchmark would be done in a fully anonymous way. Out of 13 organizations 10 committed for participation in the research, most of them re-affirming the importance of the anonymity of the results. In each organization, it was asked that 5–10 senior business and IT managers complete a questionnaire measuring business/IT alignment maturity. This questionnaire was based on an instrument already used in a previous research of Luftman and Cumps, Viaene, Dedene and Vandenbulcke and later validated by Sledgianowski, Luftman and Reilly. The latter validation work resulted in an "assessment instrument based on a model using multiple criteria and multiple levels to represent different degrees of alignment, from less mature to more mature" (Sledgianowski, Luftman and Reilly, 2006). The assessment instrument covers 22 questions in six domains: communication, competency and value measurement, governance, partnership, scope and architecture and skills. Each question has to be rated on a scale of six (from 0 to 5).

Averaging the results over all respondents of one organization provides an alignment maturity score between 0 and 5.

In this type of survey research, the "mortality" threat needs to be taken into account when evaluating internal validity. It could have been the case that only the high performers are willing to participate in the survey, as they are well aware of the importance of IT governance, while the low performers are simply not interested and will not complete the survey. However, the results of the benchmark demonstrated an equal spread between high, low and average performers, providing confidence that we did reach all types of organizations.

Assignment Box 3.1: Business/IT alignment benchmarking

Discuss the Belgian business/IT alignment benchmarking results from Fig. 3.10. Discuss the potential impact of "size of the organization" on the results. Compare with the international results as presented in Fig. 3.11 and try to explain the differences between industries.

In each of these organizations, the researchers managed to have 5–10 business and IT senior managers complete the validated alignment maturity survey. In total 44 senior IT managers and 40 senior business managers across the ten organizations completed the survey. The results are visualized in Fig. 3.10.

Organisation	Total number of respondents	Number of IT respondents	Number of business respondents	Average maturity score by IT	Average maturity score by business	Delta	Total Alignment maturity Score	Deviation from average	
A	9	5	4	2,06	2,14	–0,07	2,10	–0,59	–22%
B	5	3	2	2,27	2,00	0,27	2,16	–0,52	–19%
C	9	3	6	2,59	2,55	0,05	2,56	–0,12	–5%
D	6	3	3	2,98	2,35	0,64	2,67	–0,02	–1%
E	9	5	4	2,69	2,74	–0,05	2,71	0,03	1%
F	8	3	5	3,15	2,46	0,69	2,72	0,04	1%
G	10	5	5	2,75	2,73	0,03	2,74	0,06	2%
H	9	6	2	2,89	2,95	–0,06	2,91	0,22	8%
I	8	5	4	3,23	2,97	0,26	3,11	0,43	16%
J	11	6	5	3,09	3,26	–0,17	3,17	0,48	18%
	Total	Total	Total				**Average**		
	84	**44**	**40**				**2,69**		

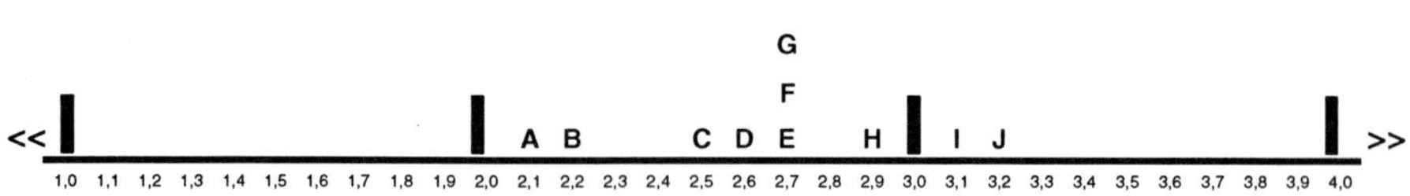

Fig. 3.10 Business/IT alignment maturity benchmark

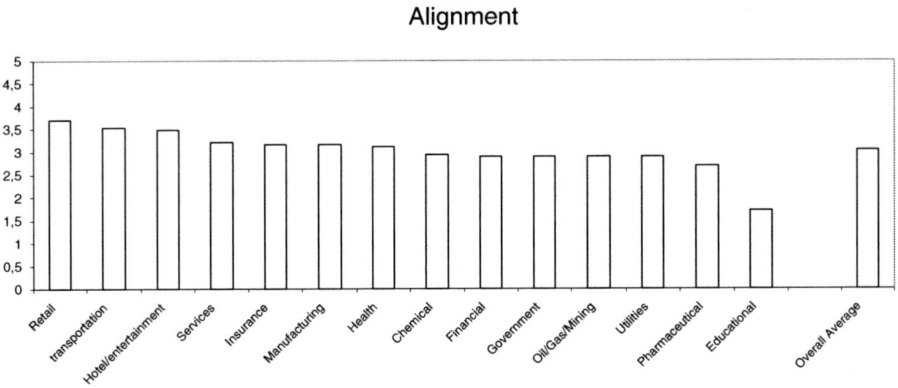

Fig. 3.11 Worldwide business/IT alignment benchmark
Based on: Luftman, J., Kempaiah, R., 2007, An Update on Business/IT Alignment: A Line Has Been Drawn. MISQ Executive, vol. 6, no. 3.

The total business/IT alignment maturity average is 2.69 on a scale of five, with six organizations (C, D, E, F, G, H) being relatively very close to the overall average. Comparing the maturity scores assigned by business and IT per organization reveals that for most organizations the difference between the business and IT rating is not large. This refers to convergent validity, providing relative confidence into the measurement tool, as it shows that two totally independent groups (business and IT) within one single organization are coming up with very similar appreciations for the business/IT alignment maturity. Assuming that this sample of ten organizations is representative for the Belgian financial services sector, conclusion is that the average business/IT alignment maturity in the whole Belgian financial services sector is 2.69. Such a maturity score only becomes meaningful when it can be compared against a target or against results, for example, in other sectors. An interesting consideration here is what the desired target or to-be situation would be for the financial services sector. There is no literature available in this domain, but taken the high dependency on IT into account, one could argue that at least a maturity level 3 would be required, which implies standardized and documented processes and procedures. There is also not much data available to compare this result against other sectors. However, reference can be made to the study of Luftman who created a benchmark within 197 mainly global organizations, coming to the conclusion that most organizations are (in 2007) around level 3 (3.04, see Fig. 3.11). This would imply that the Belgian financial services sector on average performs close to the overall average. On the other hand, the benchmark in Fig. 3.10 is only focused on the financial services sector for which one could expect an above-average alignment maturity compared to other industries, such as manufacturing, because of the high dependency on IT and the strong impact of regulations. The latter is, however, not confirmed in the full data set of Luftman (see Fig. 3.11), where the financial services sector obtained an average score of 2.9 against the overall average of 3.04.

3.3 The Relationship Between Enterprise Governance of IT and Business/IT Alignment

As discussed in the first chapter, the ultimate outcome of Enterprise Governance of IT is business/IT alignment. In this section, the impact of Enterprise Governance of IT on business/IT alignment is discussed, based on results of extreme case research. More background on the extreme case research methodology is provided in Research Box 3.2. Also, two short cases are described, giving an overview of how Enterprise Governance of IT is implemented in a poorly aligned and a highly aligned organization.

3.3.1 Extreme Cases on Business/IT Alignment

The extreme cases research focused on organizations A, B, I and J as presented in Fig. 3.10. In each of these organizations, interviews/workshops took place to define the maturity of each of the 33 governance practices used (cf. Chapter 2), on a scale from 0 to 5. During each workshop, it was ensured that at least one senior representative from the business and one senior representative from IT was present who had a view on how IT governance was addressed in their environment. The profiles of the interviewees in each of these organizations are visualized in Fig. 3.12. In organization A, a separate interview was done after the workshop with the Director Organization Department, which was

Organization	Interviewees
A	Adjunct director Organization Department Service delivery manager Director Organization Department
B	CEO Change Manager
I	Head IT Governance Head IT Development Head Project Management Office
J	CIO Head Accounting

Fig. 3.12 Interviewees in case studies

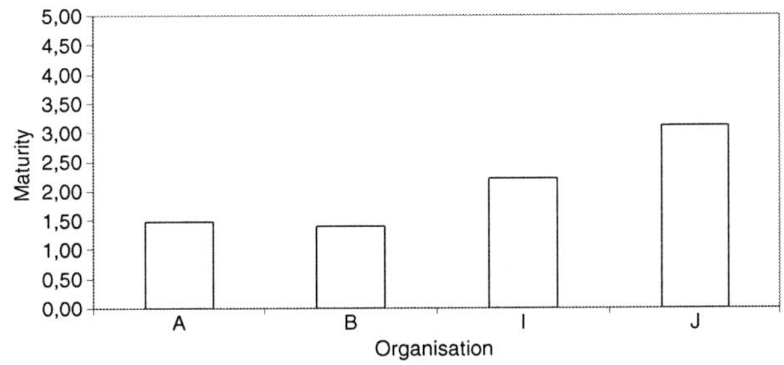

Fig. 3.13 Average maturity of Enterprise Governance of IT practices in extreme cases

recommended during the workshop by the two initial interviewees, to get a full view on the IT governance practices.

The maturity levels for each of the governance practices, as assigned by the interviewees, are provided in the following sections. The average maturity over all governance practices for organization A is 1.50, for organization B 1.37, for organization I 2.21 and for organization J 3.11, as visualized in Fig. 3.13. This difference between governance practices maturity already provides a high-level indication that might lead to a better understanding of the gap in business/IT alignment maturity between organizations A–B and I–J.

Figure 3.14 shows that all extreme cases, the poorly as well as the highly aligned organizations, did have a lot of practices in place (i.e., above maturity level 0). However, calculating the average maturity over all governance practices per organization (see also Fig. 3.13) reveals that the average practices maturity is clearly lower in the poorly aligned organizations (A, B) compared to the highly aligned organizations (I, J). This outcome indicates that organizations with a higher degree of business/IT alignment maturity seem to have more mature Enterprise Governance of IT practices. It also suggests the other direction of the relationship: organizations with more mature Enterprise Governance of IT practices are likely to obtain a higher degree of business/IT alignment maturity. Moreover, it appears that the average governance practices maturity in the poorly aligned organizations is clearly below maturity level 2. This finding suggests that at least a maturity level of 2 is required to positively influence business/IT alignment, implying that at least repeatable structures and processes should be in place, leading to "similar procedures being followed by different people undertaking the same task" (see the generic maturity model of Fig. 3.15). This result is supported by the work of Cumps et al. (2006) who conclude in their research: "Typically, what we see is that organizations with high alignment scores have more mature structures, practices and processes in place for measuring and managing their ICT investments. So building routines into your structures, practices and processes rather than ad-hoc management of ICT investments contributes to an organization's alignment capability."

	A	B	I	J
S1	0	0	0	0
S2	4	1	0	1
S3	3	3	3	3
S4	2	5	2	0
S5	2	5	4	5
S6	2	2	4	4
S7	2	0	4	4
S8	2	3	4	5
S9	2	2	4	4
S10	0	0	0	4
S11	0	0	1	3
S12	2	1	2	5
P1	1	2	1	4
P2	1	2	4	4
P3	1	2	4	4
P4	0	0	2	5
P5	0	0	2	4
P6	0	0	1	4
P7	1	0	1	1
P8	2	3	3	4
P9	1	2	4	5
P10	0	1	1	3
P11	0	0	0	0
R1	1	0	1	2
R2	5	2	3	3
R3	2	0	2	1
R4	3	3	4	4
R5	2	0	0	4
R6	2	2	5	5
R7	2	0	0	0
R8	1	4	4	4
R9	2	0	2	3
R10	1	1	1	1
	1,48	**1,39**	**2,21**	**3,12**

Fig. 3.14 Maturity of Enterprise Governance of IT practices in extreme cases

Research Box 3.2: Extreme case research

When the business/IT alignment benchmark (see Sect. 3.2) was created, some organizations were selected for further case study investigation. When selecting an organization for a case study, researchers often use information-oriented sampling, during which specific cases are deliberately selected based on pre-defined criteria, as opposed to random sampling. This is because the typical or average case is often not the richest in information. Extreme or atypical cases often reveal more information because they activate more basic mechanisms. Extreme cases research is particularly useful "to obtain information on unusual cases, which can be especially problematic or especially good in a more closely defined sense" (Flyvbjerg, 2006). Or in other words: "since all high-performing organizations are extreme cases, so one must study extreme cases to understand excellence.... Study of extreme cases can help researchers counteract over-generalization, narrow focus on averages, and static theories about systems in equilibrium. Extreme cases help to expose a world filled with individuality, complexity, variety, and change" (Starbuck, 2004). Based on these considerations, the two organizations with the highest alignment maturity and the two organizations with the lowest alignment maturity were retained for further analysis. Having four case organizations was found to be sufficient to allow for in-depth cross-case analysis, as also argued by Eisenhardt (1989): "With fewer than 4 cases, it is often difficult to generate theory with much complexity.... With more than 10 cases, it quickly becomes difficult to cope with the complexity and volume of the data."

Within each of those extreme cases, an interview/workshop was organized (2–3 hours meeting) with a senior IT and senior business manager to investigate what the maturity was of the used individual IT governance practices within the case organization. These interviews were structured according to the list of 33 management and strategic level governance practices as defined earlier (Chapter 2).

For each of the practices, the interviewees were asked to assign a maturity score from 0 to 5, based on a generic maturity model as proposed by the IT Governance Institute (Fig. 3.15). At the beginning of each interview, the

- **0 Non-existent.**
  Complete lack of any recognisable processes. The enterprise has not even recognised that there is an issue to be addressed.
- **1 Initial/Ad Hoc.**
  There is evidence that the enterprise has recognised that the issues exist and need to be addressed. There are, however, no standardised processes; instead there are ad hoc approaches that tend to be applied on an individual or case-by-case basis. The overall approach to management is disorganised.
- **2 Repeatable but Intuitive.**
  Processes have developed to the stage where similar procedures are followed by different people undertaking the same task. There is no formal training or communication of standard procedures, and responsibility is left to the individual. There is a high degree of reliance on the knowledge of individuals and, therefore, errors are likely.
- **3 Defined Process.**
  Procedures have been standardised and documented, and communicated through training. It is mandated that these processes should be followed; however, it is unlikely that deviations will be detected. The procedures themselves are not sophisticated but are the formalisation of existing practices.
- **4 Managed and Measurable.**
  Management monitors and measures compliance with procedures and to take action where processes appear not to be working effectively. Processes are under constant improvement and provide good practice. Automation and tools are used in a limited or fragmented way.
- **5 Optimised.**
  Processes have been refined to a level of good practice, based on the results of continuous improvement and maturity modelling with other enterprises. IT is used in an integrated way to automate the workflow, providing tools to improve quality and effectiveness, making the enterprise quick to adapt.

Fig. 3.15 Generic maturity model
IT Governance Institute, 2007, COBIT, online available at www.itgi.org.

researcher explained this maturity model, to ensure common understanding of the scales. After that, it was up to the interviewees to assign maturity scores for each of the Enterprise Governance of IT practices, during which process the researcher only acted as observer and independent referee to ensure that no organization was structurally over- or underestimated itself compared to the other organizations.

For each of the assigned scores, evidence was captured during the interviews by taking notes and tape-recording the interviews. These data were supplemented with data captured during telephone and e-mail conversations after the interviews and extra internal documentation that was shared (PowerPoint presentations, notes, minutes, etc.). This approach allowed the researcher to build up a short narrative for each of the assigned scores, as rationale. This approach is consistent with generally accepted assurance practices as applied by auditors in real-life organization to obtain an objective and accurate view on how practices are effectively applied. All data received from the different sources were organized in a structured way to allow for cross-case analysis.

When comparing the averages of Enterprise Governance of IT practices maturity per domain of structures, processes and relational mechanisms, it again appears that in general the highly aligned organizations have more mature governance structures and processes, as shown in Fig. 3.16. This figure also shows that processes on average were less mature compared to structures, indicating that it is probably more difficult to implement processes compared to structures (see also discussion on this in Sect. 2.3.1).

Whereas in the literature, the importance of relational mechanisms is stressed (see Chapter 1) this importance was not clearly demonstrated in this research. Figure 3.17 plots the average maturity of structures, processes and relational mechanisms on a scale per extreme case. Based on previous discussions that highly aligned organizations on average have more mature governance practices, we would expect a clearly increasing curve for structures, processes and relational mechanisms. However, the relational mechanisms chart is not consistent with the expectation.

A possible explanation might be that the structures and processes applied in organization I and J, which were already working on Enterprise Governance of

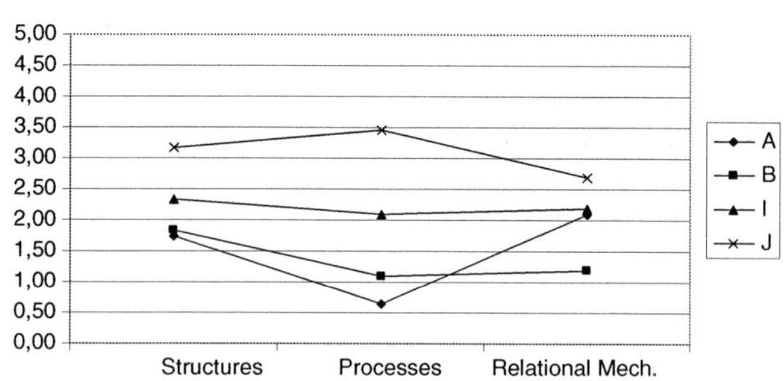

Fig. 3.16 Average maturity of structures, processes and relational mechanisms in extreme cases (1)

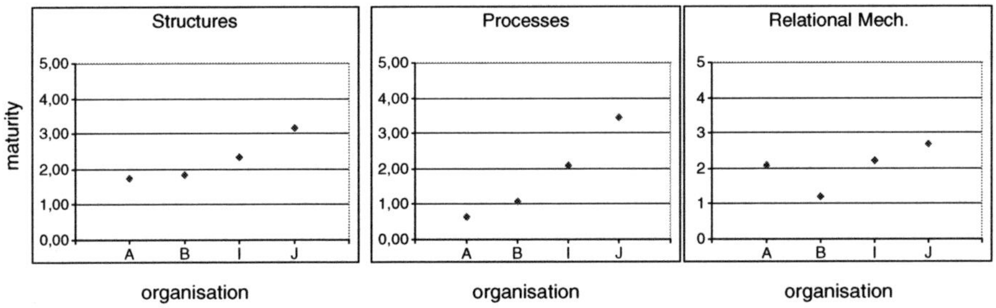

Fig. 3.17 Average maturity of structures, processes and relational mechanisms in extreme cases (2)

IT for more than 5 years, were already thoroughly embedded in day-to-day practice and became part of the organization's culture. This could explain that there was less need to manage the relational aspects of Enterprise Governance of IT. Organizations A and B were rather in the phase of starting up their governance efforts, during which issues such as motivating people, creating awareness, etc., all relational aspects, are relatively more important.

Referring back to Fig. 3.14, it appears that some governance practices are not used by any of the organizations. The first example is the "IT strategy committee at the level of the board of directors." This practice is promoted as a structure to ensure that the board gets involved in a structured way in IT issues. During the interviews, organizations B, I and J indicated that the level of board involvement is not feasible and probably not required. The representatives of the shareholders at that level are concerned with the core financial services activities and less worried about (operational) IT issues. Exception was organization A, where the board of directors was composed of the family owners (instead of shareholders), them being much closer to the operational activities. "COSO," a generic framework for internal control, was neither used by any of the organizations for IT governance purposes. Many interviewees were not aware of the contents of this framework, and where some other interviewees indicated they assumed it was used in the internal audit department, no specific links were identified toward Enterprise Governance of IT or business/IT alignment.

In trying to identify what the real differentiating factors are, it is useful to extract those practices that are clearly more mature in the high performers compared to the low performers (at least 1 level maturity difference) and attain a maturity level equal to or above two in the high performers (because we assume that practices with a maturity equal or less than 1 will not impact the outcome, cf. previous discussion). This extracting exercise results in the following list:

- IT steering committee,
- IT governance function,
- Security/risk/compliancy officer,
- IT project steering committee,

- IT performance measurement,
- Portfolio management,
- Chargeback arrangements,
- Service level agreements,
- IT budget control and reporting,
- Knowledge management,
- Executive/senior management giving the good example.

Comparing this to the minimum baseline in Sect. 2.3.2, it can be seen that only four practices can be mapped:

- IT steering committee
- IT project steering committee
- portfolio management
- IT budget control and reporting

In relation to the other six minimum baseline practices from Sect. 2.3.2, the top performers also attained a maturity level of 2 for "CIO reporting to the CEO/COO," "IT leadership" and "project governance/management methodologies," again demonstrating the importance of these practices. This argumentation provides confidence that 7 out of the 10 earlier defined minimum baseline practices are crucial for IT governance:

- IT steering committee
- IT project steering committee
- Portfolio management
- IT budget control and reporting
- CIO reporting to the CEO/COO
- IT leadership
- Project governance/management methodologies

This list will be referred to as key minimum baseline in the remainder of this book, covering the discriminating factors between the low and high performers in this research. All these key minimum baseline practices are part of the "high effectiveness/high easiness to implement" quadrant (see Fig. 3.18). Recommendation from these findings is that the best approach to implement Enterprise Governance of IT is to start with setting up the seven key minimum baseline practices: "IT steering committees," "IT project steering committees," a structure to have the "CIO reporting to the CEO/COO" and rolling out a "portfolio management process," "IT budget control and reporting process," "project management methodologies" and "establishing IT leadership." This core set of practices should be supplemented with other key practices. For this, the remaining three minimum baseline practices can be considered (as defined in Sect. 2.3.2 ("IT strategy committee," "CIO on executive committee" and "strategic information systems planning") together with the practices that can be found in the upper right quadrant of Fig. 3.18, being highly effective and easy to implement.

Fig. 3.18 Key minimum baseline

3.3.2 Short Case – Enterprise Governance of IT in a Poorly Aligned Organization

Organization A (cf. Fig. 3.10) is a large-sized family-owned organization, active in both the banking and the insurance business domains. The attention and focus for Enterprise Governance of IT only recently emerged, with concrete initiatives to formalize existing practices and enhance the current governance framework starting from 2005. The maturity of each of the governance practices, including a corresponding rationale or justification, is provided in Fig. 3.20 and some highlights are discussed in the paragraphs below. The total average maturity of all the governance practices is 1.50, with structures at level 1.75, processes at 0.64 and relational mechanisms at 2.1 (see Fig. 3.19).

The average maturity of all governance structures was rated 1.75. Specific attention goes to "IT expertise at the level of board of directors," which obtained a maturity level 4. Although there is no "IT strategy committee" in this organization (maturity level 0), the IT expertise at board level is scored relatively high. A potential explanation is the fact that this is a family-owned business, with the family members in the board being actively involved and very close to the business operations. Most of the other governance structures obtained a maturity score of 2, indicating that these structures are repeatable but still intuitive. There is no "IT security committee" or "architecture committee" in this organization (maturity level 0).

The Enterprise Governance of IT processes obtained an average maturity of 0.64. Five out of 10 governance processes were rated initial/ad hoc (maturity level 1), which can be explained by the fact that this organization was only starting up many of the Enterprise Governance of IT initiatives. Some processes are not applied at all, more specifically "service level agreements," "benefits management," "COBIT" and "chargeback arrangements." Only one process received a maturity level 2, which is "project management." Recently, PRINCE2 was introduced as project management methodology

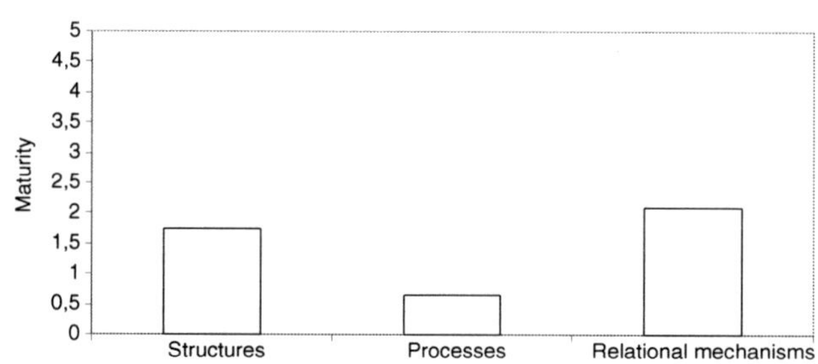

Fig. 3.19 Average maturity of Enterprise Governance of IT practices in organization A

and at the time of the interviews, trainings were organized to educate the involved people in this methodology.

Finally, relational mechanisms received an average maturity of 2.1, which is relatively high compared to the structures and relational mechanisms. This focus on the relational aspect can be explained by the fact that organization A

		Maturity						Rationale
S1	IT strategy committee at level of board of directors	**0**	1	2	3	4	5	No IT strategy committee. A family owned business, representatives of the family (not shareholders) compose the board, which operates very close to the operational activities (meets weekly).
S2	IT expertise at level of board of directors	0	1	2	3	**4**	5	Specific members of the board are closely involved in deciding on major IT projects (>150 person days) and follow-up of operational issues such as the management of specific incidents.
S3	(IT) audit committee at level of board of directors	0	1	2	**3**	4	5	There is a formal audit committee. IT is part of the yearly audit planning; examples of 2006: penetration testing, Internet banking, IT outsourcing.
S4	CIO on executive committee	0	1	**2**	3	4	5	The CIO is full member of the Executive Committee of the Banking branch. The CIO is not member of Executive Committee of Insurance branch, but IT delivers services to Insurance branch as well.
S5	CIO reporting to CEO and/or COO	0	1	**2**	3	4	5	Within executive committee of the banking branch, CIO reports to the CEO. No reporting line from the CIO to the CEO of the insurance branch.
S6	IT steering committee (IT investment evaluation/prioritization at executive/senior management level)	0	1	**2**	3	4	5	Two types of IT steering committees exist: 1. One IT steering committee composed of the director of the Banking branch, the director of the Insurance branch, the CIO and the head of the department "Organization" (see S7). This group is responsible for macro planning, classifying projects into mandatory, quick wins and new projects with impact. (Mandatory and quick wins are always done, new projects prioritized within remaining budget/resources availability). 2. Multiple IT steering meetings per business domain (savings, loans, bookkeeping, etc.): monthly meetings composed of business analysts, domain managers and directors branches. Monthly meeting takes macro planning to a next level of detail identifying priorities for different domains (including costs, resources,...). These structures are only recently defined, therefore maturity level 2.

Fig. 3.20 Maturity of Practices in Organization A (assigned scores are in bold)

S7	IT governance function/officer	0	1	**2**	3	4	5	No explicit IT governance officer or function. The department "Organization" plays an important role in making the link between business and IT (function since 2005). Head of this department supports and designs many IT governance processes.
S8	Security/compliance/risk officer	0	1	**2**	3	4	5	IT security officer is a new function, as a staff function reporting to CIO. There is a risk and compliance cell at the level of the group, but link with IT not structurally addressed.
S9	IT project steering committee	0	1	**2**	3	4	5	When a project is started, a project steering committee is created, composed of process owner (business), product owner (business), IT project leader and business analyst (from department "Organization," responsible for the general coordination, meetings, problem solving, testing, implementation). Project steering committee reports to IT steering committee This meeting joins regularly with fixed agenda, templates, etc., but is only initiated recently (<1/2 year).
S10	IT security steering committee	**0**	1	2	3	4	5	No specific steering committee addressing (IT) security.
S11	Architecture steering committee	**0**	1	2	3	4	5	No specific steering committee addressing architecture.
S12	Integration of governance/alignment tasks in roles & responsibilities	0	1	**2**	3	4	5	For specific functions, alignment roles are defined in job descriptions, such as the product/process manager. But these are again fairly new functions/roles, therefore maturity level 2.
P1	Strategic information systems planning	0	**1**	2	3	4	5	Business goals are defined by the board of directors and business units for 3 year period. IT issues are part of this 3 year planning, as well as projects for the department "Organization." This process is based on an excel that is reviewed each year.

Fig. 3.20 (Continued)

P2	IT performance measurement (e.g. IT balanced scorecard)	0	**1**	2	3	4	5	No balanced scorecard, some operational oriented metrics are defined and reported on ad hoc basis. For specific projects, e.g. Internet banking, regular reporting to the board is done, because of the sensitivity of the project.
P3	Portfolio management (incl. business cases, information economics, ROI, payback)	0	**1**	2	3	4	5	Project fiches are prepared per business domain, briefly describing the business need for a specific project. IT steering committee (executive committee level) makes a high-level prioritization, classifying projects into mandatory, quick wins and new project with impact. Mandatory and quick wins are always done, new projects prioritized within remaining budget/resource availability. This process is documented, but very recently defined. No in-depth business case analyses are done covering cost and benefits analysis. IT steering committees per business domain (savings, loans, bookkeeping, etc.) take agreed business cases to a next level of detail (identifying costs, resources,...). If after detailing, the business case appears to be not valid anymore, it should be escalated to the IT steering group at executive level, but criteria for escalation are not clear.
P4	Chargeback arrangements –total cost of ownership (e.g. activity-based costing)	**0**	1	2	3	4	5	Not present, result is that the business is not aware of the total cost of ownership for e.g. high availability.
P5	Service level agreements	**0**	1	2	3	4	5	No "internal SLA" defined between IT and business.
P6	IT governance framework COBIT	**0**	1	2	3	4	5	Not applied, high-level training done previous years to raise awareness.
P7	IT governance assurance and self-assessment	0	**1**	2	3	4	5	No formal approach to regularly assess IT governance performance. There has been an external audit addressing some IT governance issues. Results from previous external audit initiated many improvement projects. An IT governance audit is planned for 2008.

Fig. 3.20 (Continued)

P8	Project governance/ management methodologies	0	1	**2**	3	4	5	Recently, Prince 2 is adopted. Training is running.
P9	IT budget control and reporting	0	**1**	2	3	4	5	As part of the 3 year planning, IT budgets (for projects) are calculated for the upcoming years. Yearly budgets are forecasted for systems/operations as well (based on historical data). No post-calculation is done and no control on compliance against the budget.
P10	Benefits management and reporting	**0**	1	2	3	4	5	Not present.
P11	COSO/ERM	**0**	1	2	3	4	5	Not used in context of governance/alignment.
R1	Job-rotation	0	**1**	2	3	4	5	Ad-hoc examples exist of job-rotation from business to IT and vice versa. But no formal approach to do this from governance perspective.
R2	Co-location	0	1	2	3	4	**5**	Most business and IT people are centralized in main headquarters.
R3	Cross-training	0	1	**2**	3	4	5	IT is invited to basic business training that are organized for the commercial bank agents. Attendance for IT development people was "forced" in 2006. Attendance of IT operational people is ad hoc.
R4	Knowledge management (on IT governance)	0	1	2	**3**	4	5	Two intranet platforms, one is a library of templates, policies, etc., the other about how the business operates. Both are actively used by business and IT and there is a strong focus on keeping these platforms up to date. This is already operating more than 5 years in the organization.
R5	Business/IT account management	0	1	**2**	3	4	5	The department "Organization" exists for about 1 year and acts as in-between for business and IT. Role of this department is still evolving and not yet really matured out.
R6	Executive/senior management giving the good example	0	1	**2**	3	4	5	While in the past, there was more a "business versus IT" attitude, in the recent years a lot of efforts are made in making more transparent what the responsibilities of the business and the responsibilities of IT are.
R7	Informal meetings between	0	1	**2**	3	4	5	Specific meeting: everyone with management responsibilities in the organization (business and IT) meet every 3 months, to discuss/communicate high-level strategic issues. Informal approach with food and drinks.

Fig. 3.20 (Continued)

R8	IT leadership	0	**1**	2	3	4	5	The current CIO is very recently appointed, previous CIO was only 6 months on board. Because of the recent appointment of the current CIO, and the recent changes, this "IT leadership" attribute still needs to be proven.
R9	Corporate internal communication on addressing IT on a regular basis	0	1	**2**	3	4	5	During the general meetings for all employees, IT issues are addressed on a regular basis. Taking the recent strong evolution into account on new structures etc., there have been specific efforts from the board to organize meetings for IT to discuss emerging issues/concerns.
R10	IT governance awareness campaigns	0	**1**	2	3	4	5	No structured IT governance awareness campaigns, although the department "Organization" undertook specific actions on an ad-hoc basis.

Fig. 3.20 (Continued)

was really starting up governance initiatives and recognized that proper business change management was required to make these governance initiatives successful. For that reason, most of the relational mechanisms received a maturity score of 2 or higher (Fig. 3.20).

3.3.3 Short Case – Enterprise Governance of IT in a Highly Aligned Organization

Organization J is a large-sized financial services organization, active in both the banking and insurance business domains. Enterprise Governance of IT has been on the agenda for many years, initiated in the beginning of 2000, with the CIO acting as the major sponsor. The maturity of each of the governance practices, including a corresponding rationale, is provided in Fig. 3.22. The total average maturity of all the governance practices is 3.11, with the IT governance structures at 3.17, the processes at 3.45 and the relational mechanisms at 2.7 (see Fig. 3.21).

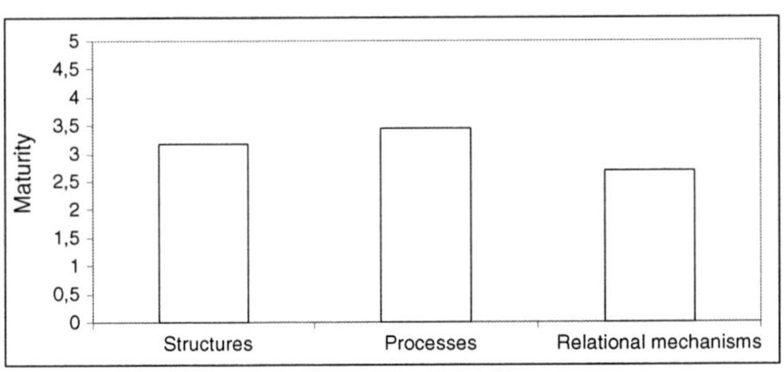

Fig. 3.21 Average maturity of Enterprise Governance of IT practices in organization J

		Maturity						Rationale
S1	IT strategy committee at level of board of directors	**0**	1	2	3	4	5	No IT strategy committee. There is an ad-hoc attention toward IT at the level of the board, e.g. when new IT strategy is presented to the board by the CIO (normally once a year).
S2	IT expertise at level of board of directors	0	**1**	2	3	4	5	No structured approach to assign "IT experts" at that level. IT expertise at board level is ad-hoc, dependent on the personal background of the individuals.
S3	(IT) audit committee at level of board of directors	0	1	2	**3**	4	5	There is a formal audit committee. IT is part of the yearly audit plan, in the same way as other departments/processes are addressed.
S4	CIO on executive committee	**0**	1	2	3	4	5	The CIO is not member of the Executive Committee.
S5	CIO reporting to CEO and/or COO	0	1	2	3	4	**5**	The CIO reports to the COO.
S6	IT steering committee (IT investment evaluation/prioritization at executive/senior management level)	0	1	2	3	**4**	5	Two types of IT steering committees: 1. IT steering committees at level of each of the main business activities (e.g. retail banking). These steering committees are composed of a member of the Executive Committee, the Director of the respective activity domain, business architect and IT directors (CIO or N-1). Meets every 3 months with agenda and minutes. Supported by a support team. 2. IT steering committees for specific business domains (trade, finance). Composed of directors business domain, directors IT, work preparation managers, ICT representatives as required These are mature structures, exist since 2002. Some are legally required, as IT is a separate legal entity.

Fig. 3.22 Maturity of practices in organization J

S7	IT governance function/officer	0	1	2	3	**4**	5	There is not a separate officer, but a steering committee exists specifically focused on the business domain governance. This committee makes the necessary preparations when e.g. a new IT steering committee at the level of a business activity (higher level) needs to be created. There is a department "Organization" responsible for design and implementing business/IT processes.
S8	Security/compliance/risk officer	0	1	2	3	4	**5**	IT security officer exists. Risk and compliance officers in IT and business exist.
S9	IT project steering committee	0	1	2	3	**4**	5	When a group of projects is started, a program management steering committee is created, composed of the required business stakeholders, IT representatives, program manager and business owner. Meeting is chaired by program leader (IT or business role) and joins every month. For specific projects in the program: project steering committees are created with representatives at lower level.
S10	IT security steering committee	0	1	2	3	**4**	5	A committee exists in which all the risk managers of all the business domains meet. This committee acts as an advisory board (no decision authority) providing a discussion forum and attempting to obtain business buy-in risk and security related matters.
S11	Architecture steering committee	0	1	2	**3**	4	5	An ICT architecture meeting exists, focusing on ICT architecture and a business architecture meeting exists focusing on business architecture. Per business domain, the IT steering committee for that domain is responsible for the IT/business architecture.
S12	Integration of governance/alignment tasks in roles&responsibilities	0	1	2	3	4	**5**	Mirror roles are defined at multiple business and IT levels, for which the alignment roles are clearly documented and described. Examples are process manager, business architect, IT architect, etc.

Fig. 3.22 (Continued)

P1	Strategic information systems planning	0	1	2	3	**4**	5	This is part of the formal 4 year planning process of the business, of which IT is part. Every year, the 4 year planning is reviewed and updated. This creates the framework in which the projects are prioritized. This is a very formal process, and runs parallel/similar to the project prioritization process.
P2	IT performance measurement (e.g. IT balanced scorecard)	0	1	2	3	**4**	5	There is no dashboard at aggregated level, focus is on ensuring quality and measuring performance in each process step and at each activity domain. Some high-level benchmark metrics (e.g. total cost IT, total cost per IT employee) is reported to executive committee. Very formal project status reports measure different aspects of project performance, this is automated process. Metrics are also discussed at account meetings with main business domains (quality issues, performance issues...) (not project driven).
P3	Portfolio management (incl. business cases, information economics, ROI, payback)	0	1	2	3	**4**	5	Business initiates a first idea, the business domain IT steering committee will evaluate the value of the new ideas based on the results of a pre-study, that includes the business case, planning, sourcing, identification of synergies and risks, and infrastructure review. 10–20% of the total cost of a development project is dedicated to this pre-study, resulting in a fixed time/price project proposal (10% deviation margin) Value-adding proposal go to the IT steering committees at business activity level (group of domains). This committee prioritizes the projects needed for year x+1 and sets the needed maintenance budget. When all the IT steering committees defined what they need in year x+1, "Organization" will aggregate the data before sending them to the Executive Committee. Funding for large investment projects always to be decided by Executive

Fig. 3.22 (Continued)

P4	Chargeback arrangements – total cost of ownership (e.g. activity-based costing)	0	1	2	3	4	**5**	Since 2002, detailed charged back system applied based on activity-based costing, charging 100% of development and operations cost back to the business/IT. These chargeback arrangements are also discussed during the account management meetings. Challenge is the accuracy of the model, this is reviewed each year.
P5	Service level agreements	0	1	2	3	**4**	5	There are good SLAs with all the different business lines for development and operation, but no overall SLM process overviewing all the individual SLAs.
P6	IT governance framework COBIT	0	1	2	3	**4**	5	In the context of BASEL2, 80% of COBIT compliance COBIT processes also mapped on existing processes; Large degree of compliance found, but few "improvements projects" derived from this exercise. This led to better structured/documented processes, also enabled using same language between e.g. audit and IT. Resulted in 28 documented processes.
P7	IT governance assurance and self-assessment	0	**1**	2	3	4	5	No formal approach, but is part of operational risk assessment. This covers a set of 7 of the 28 IT processes. Governance aspects are part of this assessment. At this moment, the first review round is being set up.
P8	Project governance/management methodologies	0	1	2	3	**4**	5	An organization specific PM methodology is used. This is applied in projects (templates, procedures). For smaller projects, more degrees of freedom.
P9	IT budget control and reporting	0	1	2	3	4	**5**	Very mature process because of the legal structure of IT being a separate organization.
P10	Benefits management and reporting	0	1	2	**3**	4	5	At the level of the business case, metrics are defined that are to be used to measure the business benefits after the fact. However, not always measured, but certainly done for major projects such as SAP implementation.
P11	COSO/ERM	**0**	1	2	3	4	5	Not used in context of governance/alignment.

Fig. 3.22 (Continued)

R1	Job-rotation	0	1	**2**	3	4	5	Is part of talent management (goal: have people experience different domains). More from IT to business, less from business to IT. So it is a well funded option to do this, but not orchestrated. Good example: function of process owners often held by former IT'ers.
R2	Co-location	0	1	2	**3**	4	5	IT is physically located close to the important business function (not all). For specific projects, specific teams are physically put close to each other.
R3	Cross-training	0	**1**	2	3	4	5	Not done in structured approach. Ad-hoc approach for specific projects or in specific business domains.
R4	Knowledge management (on IT governance)	0	1	2	3	**4**	5	Detailed intranet solution providing templates, job descriptions, ... This is the only place where everything is stored, so actively used by business and IT.
R5	Business/IT account management	0	1	2	3	**4**	5	Mirror roles at different levels in business and IT (project driven) Account management meetings, each 3 months, per major business domain; Not project driven, about general IT and business issues to be discussed.
R6	Executive/senior management giving the good example	0	1	2	3	4	**5**	It took a time to convince everyone of the value of the governance structures. But at this time, e.g. senior management always attends the appropriate steering committees and takes it very seriously.
R7	Informal meetings between business and IT executive/senior management	**0**	1	2	3	4	5	Not present, there are enough formal (and informal because business and IT are close to each other) ways to meet.
R8	IT leadership	0	1	2	3	**4**	5	Access of CIO to all business levels is very easy, from board to operational management, so trust is very high.
R9	Corporate internal communication addressing IT on a regular basis	0	1	2	**3**	4	5	In the internal "newsline" (for business), IT is addressed evenly as other departments (balanced mix). Also IT governance theme was addressed there.
R10	IT governance awareness campaigns	0	**1**	2	3	4	5	IT governance awareness campaigns very thoroughly done previous years, as part of the IT governance framework roll-out. At this moment not done anymore, the processes are embedded in the organization.

Fig. 3.22 (Continued)

The Enterprise Governance of IT structures obtained an average maturity of 3.17. The "CIO was reporting to the COO" but "not a member of the executive committee." There was no "IT strategy committee" and the "IT expertise at board level" is dependent on the personal background of the individuals (maturity level 1). Maturity level 4 was assigned for "IT steering committees" (at multiple level), "IT governance function/officer," "IT project steering committee" and an "IT security committee." "Security/risk/compliance officer" obtained maturity level 5, as well as "integration of governance/alignment tasks in documented roles and responsibilities." The "architecture committee" was rated a maturity level 3.

The average maturity of governance processes was rated at 3.45, having a maturity level 4 for 6 out of 11 processes ("strategic information systems planning," "IT performance management," "portfolio management," "service level agreements," "COBIT" and "project management methodologies"). "Chargeback arrangements" and the related process "IT budget control and reporting" was fully applied, obtaining a maturity level of 5. "IT governance self-assessment" is rarely done (maturity level 1) and "benefits management" received maturity level 3.

Finally, the relational mechanisms reached an average maturity of 2.7. An elaborate "knowledge management system" received maturity level 4, as well as "business/IT account management." As the CIO had very easy access to all business levels, "IT leadership" was also rated maturity level 4. Related to the latter, "executive management giving the good example" obtained maturity level 5. "Cross-training" was ad hoc, and where there formerly was more attention for "awareness campaigns" (when the Enterprise Governance of IT project was started), this now was rated maturity level 1. "Co-location" and "corporate internal communication addressing IT" obtained maturity level 3. "Job-rotation" was part of the organization's talent management and reached maturity level 2.

Assignment Box 3.2: Comparing Enterprise Governance in highly and poorly aligned organizations

Make teams and compare the case description of organization A and organization J. Develop a program for bringing the low performer up level.

Summary

There is no universal way to measure business/IT alignment in literature. Many researchers have developed models that attempt to capture the complex alignment construct as complete as possible. Each measurement model has its own approach, and as a result, it is very difficult to compare results of alignment studies. Some potential approaches are described in this chapter, all having their strengths and weaknesses. In the end, it is important to select the approach that is most suited for the type of activity or research one is trying to do.

This chapter also reported on the results of a business/IT alignment benchmark research, based on Luftman's maturity model. To do this, 13 Belgian financial services organizations were invited to participate, of which ten committed to participate under the condition that anonymity was guaranteed. Assuming that this sample of ten organizations is representative for the Belgian financial services sector, conclusion is that the average business/IT alignment maturity in the whole Belgian financial services sector is 2.69. Based on some benchmarking data and the fact that the finance sector is highly regulated, an alignment maturity score around 3 is at least expected.

Comparing the use of Enterprise Governance of IT practices in the extreme cases of this benchmark, it appeared that seven practices are crucial enablers for business/IT alignment:

- IT steering committee
- IT project steering committee
- Portfolio management
- IT budget control and reporting
- CIO reporting to the CEO/COO
- IT leadership
- Project governance/management methodologies

Recommendation from these findings is that the best approach to implement Enterprise Governance of IT is to start with setting up the seven key minimum baseline practices: "IT steering committees," "IT project steering committees," a structure to have the "CIO reporting to the CEO/COO" and rolling out a "portfolio management process," "IT budget control and reporting process," "project management methodologies" and "establishing IT leadership." This core set of practices should be supplemented with other key practices. For this, the remaining three minimum baseline practices can be considered (as defined in Sect. 2.3.2 ("IT strategy committee," "CIO on executive committee" and "strategic information systems planning") together with the practices that are rated as being highly effective and easy to implement.

Study Questions

1. Discuss how business/IT alignment can be measured and determine which is the most practical approach.
2. Explain how information economics can be used in the IT portfolio management process.
3. Explain how business/IT alignment can be measured through Luftman's model.
4. Explain the relationship between Enterprise Governance of IT and business/IT alignment.
5. What are the key Enterprise Governance of IT practices to enable business/IT alignment?

Further Reading

Cumps, B., 2007, Business-ICT Alignment Practices and Determinants, Thesis Submitted to Achieve the Degree op PhD in Applied Economics. University of Leuven, Promotor: Viaene, S.

Cumps, B., Viaene, S., Dedene, G., and Vandenbulcke, J., 2006, An Empirical Study on Business/ICT Alignment in European Organizations, in Proceedings of the Hawaii International Conference on System Sciences (HICSS).

Duffy, J., 2002, IT/Business Alignment: Is it an Option or is it Mandatory? IDC Document #26831.

De Haes, S., 2007, The Impact of IT Governance Practices on Business/IT Alignment in the Belgian Financial Services Sector, Thesis Submitted to Achieve the Degree op PhD in Applied Economics. University of Antwerp, Promotor: Van Grembergen, W.

De Haes, S., and Van Grembergen, W., 2005, IT Governance Structures, Processes and Relational Mechanisms: Achieving IT/Business Alignment in a Major Belgian Financial Group, in Proceedings of Hawaii International Conference on System Sciences (HICSS).

De Haes, S., and Van Grembergen, W., 2006, IT Governance Best Practices in Belgian Organizations, in Proceedings of the Hawaii International Conference on System Sciences (HICSS).

De Haes, S., and Van Grembergen, W., 2008a, Practices in IT Governance and Business/IT Alignment, Information Systems Control Journal, vol. 2.

De Haes, S., and Van Grembergen, W., 2008b, Analysing the Relationship between IT Governance and Business/IT Alignment maturity, in Proceedings of the 41th Hawaii International Conference on System Sciences (HICSS).

Eisenhardt, K.M., 1989, Building Theories from Case Study Research, Academy of Management Review, vol. 14, no. 4, pp. 532–550.

Flyvbjerg, B., 2006, Five Misunderstandings About Case Study Research, Qualitative Inquiry, vol. 12, no. 2, pp. 219–245.

ITGI, 2007, IT Assurance Guide, from www.itgi.org

Luftman, J., 2000, Assessing Business-IT alignment Maturity, Communications of AIS, vol.4.

Luftman, J., and Kempaiah, R., 2007, An Update on Business/IT Alignment: A Line has been Drawn, MISQ Executive, vol. 6, no. 3.

Miles, R.E., and Snow, C.C., 1978, Organizational Strategy, Structure and Process. New York: McGraw-Hill.

Parker, M., Benson, R., and Trainor, H., 1988, Information Economics: Linking Business Performance to Information Technology. London: Prentice Hall.

Sabherwal, R., and Chan, Y., 2001, Alignment Between Business and IS Strategies: A Study of Prospectors, Analyzers and Defenders, Information Systems Research, vol. 12, no. 1, pp. 11–33.

Sledgianowski D., J. Luftman, R.R. Reilly, 2006, Development and Validation of an Instrument to Measure Maturity of IT Business Strategic Alignment Mechanisms, Information Resources Management Journal, vol. 19, no. 3, 18–33.

Starbuck, B., 2004, Learning from Extreme Case, Stern School of Business, online available at http://www.lums.lancs.ac.uk/events/research/3061/

Van Grembergen, W., 2002, Introduction to the Minitrack: IT Governance and its Mechanisms, in Proceedings of the 35th Hawaii International Conference on System Sciences (HICSS).

Van Grembergen, W. (Ed.), 2004, Strategies for Information Technology Governance. Hershey, PA: Idea Group Publishing.

Van Grembergen W. and Van Bruggen R., 1997, Measuring and Improving Corporate Information Technology Through the Balanced Scorecard Technique, in Proceedings of the European Conference on the Evaluation of Information Technology, Delft, The Netherlands.

Van Grembergen, W., and De Haes, S., 2008, Implementing Information Technology Governance: Models, Practices and Cases, IGI Publishing.

Van Grembergen, W., Van Brempt, H., and De Haes, S., 2007, Prioritizing and Linking Business and IT Goals in the Financial Sector, in Proceedings of the 40th Hawaii International Conference on System Sciences (HICSS).
Van Grembergen, W., De Haes, S., and Van Brempt, H., 2007, How Does the Business Drive IT? Identifying, Prioritizing and Linking Business and IT Goals, Information Systems Control, vol. 6.
Weill, P., and Broadbent, M., 1998, Leveraging the New Infrastructure: How Market Leaders Capitalize on Information Technology. Boston: Harvard Business School Press.
Weill, P., and Ross, J., 2004, IT Governance: How Top Performers Manage IT Decision Rights for Superior Results. Boston: Harvard Business School Press.
Yin, 2002, Case Study Research: Design and Methods, Third Edition, (Applied Social Research Methods), Sage Publications Inc.

Websites

Information Technology Alignment and Governance Research Institute: www.uams.be/ITAG
IT Governance Institute: www.itgi.org
ISACA: www.isaca.org
bITa Center: www.bita-center.com

Chapter 4
The IT Balanced Scorecard as a Framework for Enterprise Governance of IT

Abstract The balanced scorecard (BSC) is a performance management system that enables businesses to drive strategies based on measurement and follow-up. The BSC is initially developed at enterprise level by Kaplan and Norton. The BSC can however easily be applied to information technology (IT) investments, projects or departments as an IT performance management and alignment instrument. This chapter discusses how the IT BSC can be used as an instrument for Enterprise Governance of IT and also includes a detailed case study.

4.1 Introduction

The IT BSC is becoming a popular tool with its concepts widely supported and dispersed by international consultant groups such as Gartner, IDC and others. As a result of this interest, many real-life applications have been developed and are supported by software tools. Recent research of the IT Governance Institute (www.itgi.org) on "Measuring and demonstrating the value of IT" demonstrated that about 30% of the IT managers use the IT BSC as an instrument to measure and manage the performance of IT investments, projects and departments (see Figs. 4.1 and 4.2).

4.2 IT BSC Core Concepts

In the early 1990s, Kaplan and Norton introduced the BSC at enterprise level. Their fundamental premise is that the evaluation of a firm should not be restricted to a traditional financial evaluation but should be supplemented with objectives and measures concerning customer satisfaction, internal processes and the ability to innovate. Results achieved within these additional perspective

W. Van Grembergen, S. De Haes, *Enterprise Governance of Information Technology*, DOI 10.1007/978-0-387-84882-2_4,

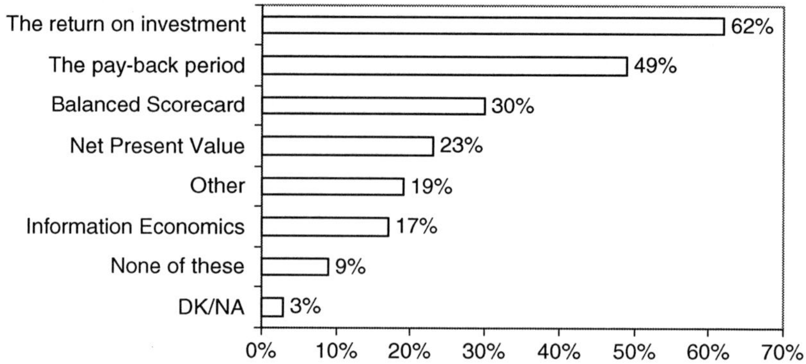

Fig. 4.1 Use of performance measurement techniques for IT projects and investments
Van Grembergen, W., and De Haes, S., 2005b, Measuring and Demonstrating the Value of IT, in IT Governance Domain Practices and Competencies (series of IT Governance Institute).

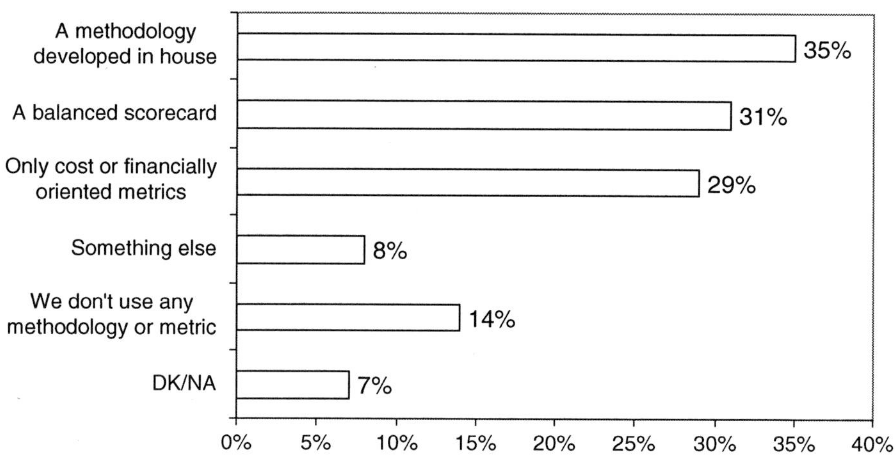

Fig. 4.2 Measurement techniques for the IT department
Van Grembergen, W., and De Haes, S., 2005b, Measuring and Demonstrating the Value of IT, in IT Governance Domain Practices and Competencies (series of IT Governance Institute).

areas should assure future financial results and drive the organization toward its strategic goals while keeping all four perspectives in balance. For each of the four perspectives of the business BSC, Kaplan and Nolon propose a three-layered structure, as shown in Fig. 4.3:

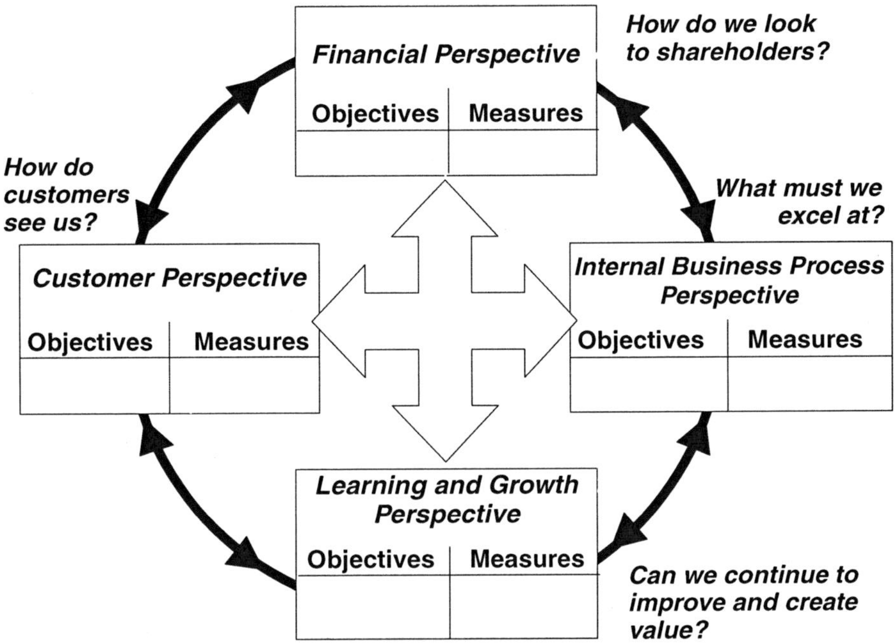

Fig. 4.3 Generic business balanced scorecard
Adapted from: Kaplan, R., and Norton, D., 1996, The Balanced Scorecard: Translating Vision into Action. Boston: Harvard Business School Press. Portions reprinted, with permission, from Harvard Business School Press.

1. Mission (e.g., to become the customers' most preferred supplier)
2. Objectives (e.g., to provide the customers with new products)
3. Measures (e.g., percentage of turnover generated by new products)

The BSC can be applied to the IT function, its processes and projects. To achieve that, the focus of the four perspectives of the business BSC need to be translated, as shown in Fig. 4.4. The User Orientation perspective represents the user (internal or external) evaluation of IT. The Operational Excellence perspective represents the IT processes employed to develop and deliver the applications. The Future Orientation perspective represents the human and technology resources needed by IT to deliver its services over time. The Business Contribution perspective captures the business value created from the IT investments.

Again, each of these perspectives has to be translated into corresponding goals and metrics that assess the current situation. These assessments need to be repeated periodically and aligned with pre-established goals and benchmarks. Example metrics for the four perspectives are provided in Fig. 4.5.

To leverage the IT BSC as a management and alignment instrument, it should be enhanced with cause-and-effect relationships between measures. These relationships are articulated by two types of measures: outcome

USER ORIENTATION **How do the users view the IT department?**	**CORPORATE CONTRIBUTION** **How does management view the IT department?**
Mission to be the preferred supplier of information systems	Mission to obtain a reasonable business contribution of IT investments
Objectives ▪ preferred IT supplier ▪ partnership with users ▪ user satisfaction	Objectives ▪ control of IT expenses ▪ business value of the IT function ▪ business value of new IT projects
OPERATIONAL EXCELLENCE **How effective and efficient are the IT processes?**	**FUTURE ORIENTATION** **How well is IT positioned to answer future challenges?**
Mission to deliver effective and efficient deliver IT applications and services	Mission to develop opportunities to answer future challenges
Objectives ▪ efficient software development ▪ efficient computer operations ▪ efficient help desk function	Objectives ▪ training and education of IT staff ▪ expertise of IT staff ▪ research into emerging information technologies

Fig. 4.4 Generic IT balanced scorecard

measures (or lag indicators) and performance drivers (or lead indicators). A well-developed scorecard should contain a good mix of these two metrics. Outcome measures without performance drivers do not communicate how they are to be achieved. And performance drivers without outcome measures may lead to significant investment without a measurement indicating whether the chosen strategy is effective. A good example of a cause-and-effect relationship defined throughout the whole scorecard is shown in Fig. 4.6; more and better education of IT staff (future perspective) is an enabler (performance driver) for a better quality of developed systems (operational excellence perspective) that in turn is an enabler for increased user satisfaction (user perspective) that eventually must lead to a higher business value of IT (business contribution perspective).

The proposed IT BSC links with the business, mainly through the business contribution perspective. The relationship between IT and business can be more explicitly expressed through a cascade of scorecards. In Fig. 4.7 the relationship between IT scorecards and the business scorecard is illustrated. The IT Development BSC and the IT Operational BSC both are enablers of the IT Strategic BSC that in turn is the enabler of the Business BSC. This cascade of scorecards becomes a linked set of measures that will be instrumental in aligning

Corporate contribution

- Control of IT expenses
  - percentage over or under IT budget
  - allocation to different budget items
  - IT budget as a percentage of turnover
  - IT expenses per staff member
- Business value of the IT function
  - percentage of the development capacity engaged in strategic projects
  - relationship between new developments/infrastructure investments/replacement investments
- Business value of new IT projects
  - financial evaluation based on ROI, NPV, IRR, PB
  - business evaluation based on information economics

User orientation

- Preferred IT supplier
  - percentage of applications managed by IT
  - percentage of applications delivered by IT
- Partnership with users
  - index of user involvement in generating strat. applications
  - index of user involvement in developing new applications
- User satisfaction
  - index of user friendliness of applications
  - index of user satisfaction

Operational excellence

- Efficient software development
  - average days late in delivering software
  - average unexpected budget increase
  - percentage of projects performed within SLA
  - percentage of maintenance activities
- Efficient computer operations
  - percentage unavailability of network
  - response times per category of users
  - percentage of jobs done within time
- Efficient help desk function
  - average answer time of help desk
  - percentage of questions answered within time

Future orientation

- Training and education of staff
  - number of educational days per person
  - education budget as a % of total IT budget
- Expertise of the IT staff
  - number of years of IT experience per staff member
  - age pyramid of the IT staff
- Research into emerging technologies
  - % of budget spent on IT research

Fig. 4.5 Example metrics for IT balanced scorecard

Fig. 4.6 Cause-and-effect relationships within the IT strategic balanced scorecard

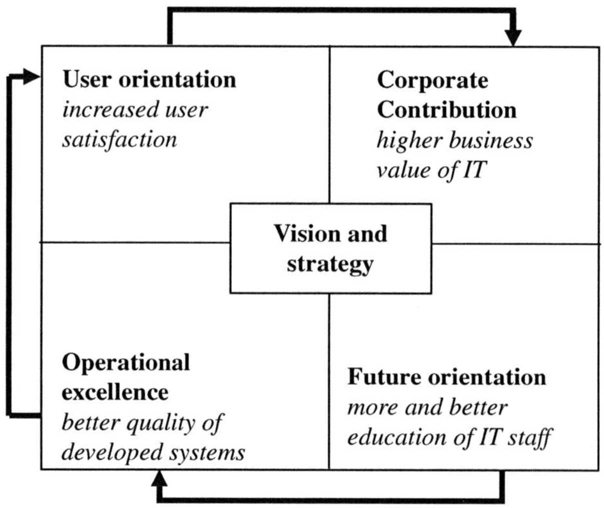

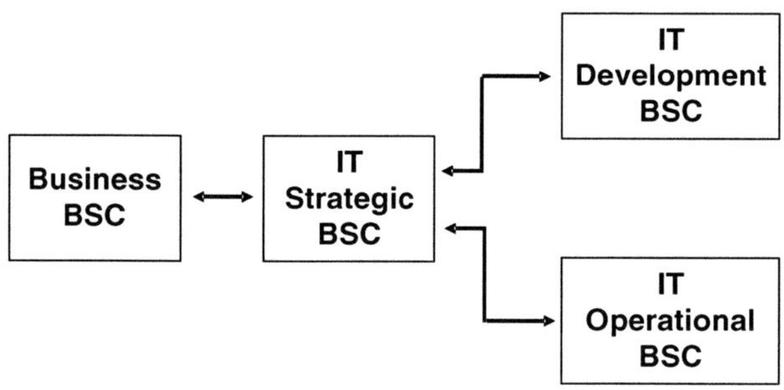

Fig. 4.7 Cascade of balanced scorecards

IT and business strategy and that will help to determine how business value is created through IT.

4.3 Maturity Model for IT BSC Implementation

To drive the development of the IT BSC, one could leverage a maturity model for an IT BSC, as shown in Fig. 4.8. It enables the organization to identify the as-is and to-be situation of the IT BSC in its organization, to analyze the gaps between as-is and to-be and to translate those gaps into pragmatic improvement projects.

Level 1 Initial

There is evidence that the organization has recognized there is a need for a *measurement system* for its information technology division. There are ad hoc approaches to measure IT with respect to the two main IT processes, i.e. operations and systems development. This measurement process is often an individual effort in response to specific issues.

Level 2 Repeatable

Management is aware of the concept of the *IT balanced scorecard* and has communicated its intent to define appropriate measures. Measures are collected and presented to management in a scorecard. Linkages between outcome measures and performance drivers are generally defined but are not yet precise, documented or integrated into strategic and operational planning processes. Processes for scorecard training and review are informal and there is no compliance process in place.

Level 3 Defined

Management has standardized, documented and communicated the IT BSC through formal training. The scorecard process has been structured and *linked to business planning cycle*. The need for compliance has been communicated but compliance is inconsistent. Management understands and accepts the need to integrate the IT BSC within the alignment process of business and IT. Efforts are underway to change the alignment process accordingly.

Level 4 Managed

The IT BSC is fully integrated into the strategic and operational planning and review systems of the business and IT. Linkages between outcome measures and performance drivers are systematically reviewed and revised based upon the analysis of results. There is a full understanding of the issues at all levels of the organization that is supported by formal training. Long-term stretch targets and priorities for IT investment projects are set and linked to the IT scorecard. A business scorecard and *a cascade of IT scorecards* are in place and are communicated to all employees. Individual objectives of IT employees are connected with the scorecards and incentive systems are linked to the IT BSC measures. The compliance process is well established and levels of compliance are high.

Level 5 Optimized

The IT BSC is fully aligned with the business strategic management framework and vision is frequently reviewed, updated and improved. Internal and external experts are engaged to ensure industry best practices are developed and adopted. The *measurements* and results are part of management reporting and *are systematically acted upon* by senior and IT management. Monitoring, self-assessment and communication are pervasive within the organization and there is optimal use of technology to support measurement, analysis, communication and training.

Fig. 4.8 Maturity model for IT balanced scorecard implementation

4.4 In-Depth Case – IT BSC at a Major Canadian Financial Group

In this section, the development and implementation of an IT BSC within the Information Services Division (ISD) of a Canadian tri-company financial group consisting of Great-West Life, London Life and Investors Group (hereafter named The Group) is described and discussed. This case description is developed in the period 2002–2003. The research methodology for developing this case is described in Research Box 4.1.

Research Box 4.1: Developing a single case study on the IT balanced scorecard

Case research is particularly appropriate for research within the IT area because researchers in this field often lag behind practitioners in discovering and explaining new methods and techniques. This is certainly true for the balanced scorecard and its application to IT. The Balanced Scorecard is becoming a popular technique with its concepts supported and dispersed by consultants. A single case design is appropriate when "the investigator has access to a situation previously inaccessible to scientific observation" (Yin, 2002). Like Benbasat et al. (1987) we believe "that the case research strategy is well suited to capturing the knowledge of practitioners and developing theories from it."

A case study research approach was used to study the phenomenon of the IT BSC and its development and implementation in a single organization. In this case research, the researcher's role was purely the role of observers who were interested in investigating how the IT BSC concepts, they and other researchers developed in earlier publications, were applied by practitioners and how the experience and knowledge of practitioners could help to improve the earlier proposed IT BSC frameworks.

The research took place in two phases. In both research periods, the data was collected through in-depth interviews with the CIO by means of multiple e-mail conversations and also through some casual face-to-face conversations when the authors met during international conferences on IT performance measurement. During the second research period, additional in-depth interviews were conducted with the project manager of the IT balanced scorecard project. Also six individuals who have key roles and accountabilities for scorecard deliverables at the organization were interviewed (including the Vice President Information Services, the Financial Control Director, the Operations & Technical Support Technology Services Director, the Mainframe Technical Support Manager, the Career Centers Director and the Project Management Career Center Leader). These interviews were done by means of e-mail and telephone conversations and an intensive workshop at the headquarters of the company. Data from other sources such as internal reports and slides from the CIO's presentations for his management were used to develop and complete an understanding of the case company, its processes, its technology, its IT organization and its development and implementation of the IT BSC.

4.4.1 Company Introduction

The Great-West Life Assurance Company, London Life and Investors Group are members of the Power Financial Corporation group of companies, with London Life as a wholly owned subsidiary of The Great-West Life Assurance Company. In 2001, MacKenzie financial was also acquired by the Power Financial Corporation Group, but as the IT balanced scorecard project does not cover this company, MacKenzie's organization and IT division will not be taken into account in this article.

The Great-West Life Assurance Company is an international corporation offering life insurance, health insurance, retirement savings, specialty reinsurance and general insurance, primarily in Canada and the United States. Great-West serves the financial security needs of more than 13 million people in Canada and the United States. Great-West has more than \$86.9 billion (all figures in this article are in Canadian dollars) in assets under administration and \$477 billion of life insurance in force. Founded in Winnipeg in 1891, Great-West is now a leading life and health insurer in the Canadian market in terms of market share.

London Life was founded in Ontario in 1874 and has the leading market share of individual life insurance in Canada. London Life markets life insurance, disability insurance and retirement savings and investment products through its exclusive sales force. The company is a supplier of reinsurance primarily in the US and Europe and is a 39% participant in a joint venture life insurance company Shin Fu in Taiwan. London Life has more than \$30 billion assets under administration and \$142.6 billion of life insurance in force.

Investors Group, with its corporate headquarters in Winnipeg, was founded more than 70 years ago. Investors Group is Canada's leading provider of mutual funds, offering a wide spectrum of funds, including those created through strategic partnerships with some of the best known Canadian and international investment management firms. It also offers a wide range of insurance and mortgage options and currently has \$17.1 billion of life insurance coverage in force through three different carriers, and administers with more than \$7.6 billion of primarily residential mortgages. Investors Group manages assets of \$40.5 billion.

The trend in financial services industry consolidation was a motivating factor behind the acquisition of London Life by Great-West Life and the merger of the IT divisions of the three companies in November 1997. At that time, the tri-company IT expenditures had exceeded \$200 million. The ability to reduce these costs and to achieve true synergies and economies of scale within the IT operations was clearly a driver and opportunity for the companies to realize. The merger enabled single system solutions across all three companies to be explored and implemented as well as single operational processes. Forming a tri-company shared services organization positioned management to

- achieve world-class status as an information services group,
- maximize purchasing power and operating efficiency,

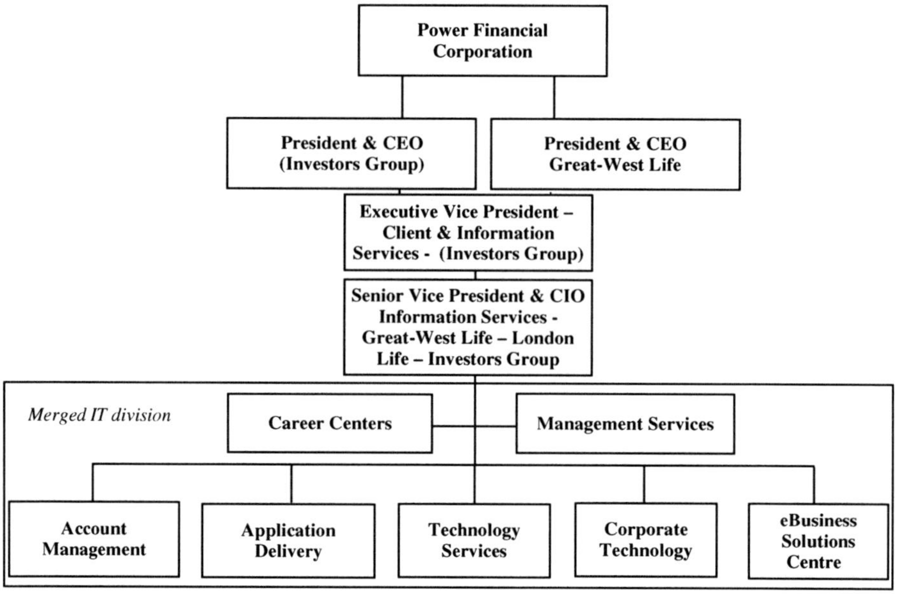

Fig. 4.9 Organization chart

- leverage technology investments,
- optimize technical infrastructure and application support costs.

Figure 4.9 depicts the current IT organizational structure of the merged IT division, which employed 812 full-time/part-time employees in 2002. Also the position of the IT division relative to the higher reporting levels is indicated. *Application Delivery* and *Technology Services* are respectively the traditional IT department's Systems Development and Operations of the combined organizations. Application Delivery is separated from account management and people management in order to focus on continuous improvement of delivery performance. *Account Management* is the linkage with the clients/users. This component ensures effective communication and translation of business needs into IT processes and educates users on the IT corporate agendas. Account Management employs IT generalists who provide IT insights into business strategy and decision-making. *Career Centers* are focused on the professional development of IT people and ensure attention to people issues in order to reduce turnover of talented IT employees. *Corporate Technology* enables the development of a common architecture and provides technology directions. The *e-Business Solution Center* works on the introduction of new technologies that enable e-Business solutions for The Group. *Management Services* focuses on running IT as a business and ensures effective financial management and management reporting including IT scorecard reporting.

4.4.2 IT BSC Project and Its Organization

Before the merger, the CIO of Great-West Life (who is the present CIO of the merged IT division) began focusing on the scorecard as a (potentially) effective measurement tool. His objective was to ensure that IT was fairly evaluated. In his own words: "Through the balanced scorecard I would know what was important to the business and I would not fall victim to the early termination syndrome. Or at least I would have a better chance of survival."

However, once the three companies came together through the acquisition and merger of the IT groups, the stakes were raised considerably. Now, the IT division had exposures on multiple fronts with stakeholders who were concerned about the perceived loss of control over their vital IT services. This prompted an executive request for a formal measure of factors to measure IT success. The response of the merged IT division was to formalize the criteria into a new and extended IT scorecard based on the experiences gained within Great-West Life.

Senior management of all the three companies questioned the benefits of huge investments in IT and how more value might be achieved through better alignment of business strategy and IT strategy. Within The Group the specific concerns for the different stakeholders were (Fig. 4.10):

The concepts of the balanced scorecard and its application to information technology were discovered through an Internet search primarily through the website of the IT Governance Institute (www.itgi.org). Departing from this website, relevant publications on the IT balanced scorecard from academics and practitioners were identified and consulted. It was believed that the scorecard could provide an answer to the key questions of the different stakeholders.

The formal development of the IT balanced scorecard began in 1998 and from the start the objectives were clearly stated:

- Align IT plans and activities with business goals and needs
- Align employees' efforts toward IT objectives
- Establish measures for evaluating the effectiveness of the IT organization
- Stimulate and sustain improved IT performance
- Achieve balanced results across stakeholder groups

At the beginning of the implementation period (December 1999), the scorecard effort was not yet approached as a formal project and as a result, progress had been somewhat limited. In 2000 the formality of the project was increased and the CIO (Information Services Executive) was appointed as sponsor. In 2001, a project manager/analyst was formally assigned to the IT balanced scorecard project.

4.4.3 Building the IT BSC

It was recognized by the CIO that building an IT BSC was meaningful under two conditions which required (a) a clearly articulated business strategy and (b) the new Information Services Division moving from a commodity service

Stakeholders	Key questions
Board of directors Executive management Committee	Does IT support the achievement of business objectives? What value does the expenditure on IT deliver? Are IT costs being managed effectively? Are IT risks being identified and managed? Are targeted inter-company IT synergies being achieved?
Business unit executives	Are IT's services delivered at a competitive cost? Does IT deliver on its service level commitments? Do IT investments positively affect business productivity or the customer experience? Does IT contribute to the achievement of our business strategies?
Corporate compliance internal audit	Are the organization's assets and operations protected? Are the key business and technology risks being managed? Are proper processes, practices and controls in place?
IT Organization	Are we developing the professional competencies needed for successful service delivery? Are we creating a positive workplace environment? Do we effectively measure and reward individual and team performance? Do we capture organizational knowledge to continuously improve performance? Can we attract/retain the talent we need to support the business?

Fig. 4.10 IT concerns of the different stakeholders

provider to a strategic partner. The newly constructed ISD is viewed as a strategic partner. During several meetings between IT and executive management, the vision, strategy, measures of success and value of IT were jointly created. Typically, pure business objectives were used as the standard to assess IT. The vision and strategy of ISD were defined as

- ISD is a single IT organization focused on developing world-class capabilities to serve the distinct customer needs of its three sponsoring companies.
- ISD operates as a separate professional services business on a full recovery, non-profit basis.
- ISD supports the achievement of company strategies and goals through the industry consolidation period.
- ISD becomes the "supplier of choice" of information services.
- ISD establishes a forward-looking enterprise architecture strategy which enables the use of technology as a competitive edge in the financial service market place.
- ISD becomes the "employer of choice" for career-oriented IT professionals in the markets in which ISD and The Group operate.

These issues go to the heart of the relationship between IT and the business and will be reflected in the IT strategic balanced scorecard as is illustrated in Figs. 4.11 and 4.12. Figure 4.11 shows the perspective questions and mission statements for the four quadrants: corporate contribution, customer orientation, operational excellence and future orientation. Figure 4.12 displays the objectives for each perspective.

4.4.3.1 Corporate Contribution Perspective

The corporate contribution perspective evaluates the performance of the IT organization from the viewpoint of executive management, the Board of Directors and the shareholders, and provides answers to the key questions of these stakeholders concerning IT governance (cf. Fig. 4.10). The key issues, as depicted by Fig. 4.12, are business/IT alignment, value delivery, cost management, risk management and inter-company synergy achievement. Benchmarks have been used where an objective standard was available or could be determined in most cases from external sources.

The main measurement challenges are with the areas of business/IT alignment and the value delivery. Currently, *business/IT alignment* is measured by the approval of the IT operational plan and budget. Although not a discrete measure of alignment, the approval process within the Group is particularly thorough and as a result is accepted by business executives as a good indicator. All aspects of development, operations and governance/support services are examined and challenged to ensure they are essential to achieving business objectives or supporting the enabling IT strategy.

In the *value delivery* area, the performance of a specific IT services group delivering to a specific business unit (e.g., "group insurance" services) is measured.

Customer orientation	**Corporate contribution**
Perspective question How should IT appear to business unit executives to be considered effective in delivering its services? *Mission* To be the supplier of choice for all information services, either directly or indirectly through supplier relationships.	*Perspective question* How should IT appear to the company executive and its corporate functions to be considered a significant contributor to company success? *Mission* To enable and contribute to the achievement of business objectives through effective delivery of value added information services.
Operational Excellence	**Future orientation**
Perspective question At which services and processes must IT excel to satisfy the stakeholders and customers? *Mission* To deliver timely and effective IT services at targeted service levels and costs.	*Perspective question* How will IT develop the ability to deliver effectively and to continuously learn and improve its performance? *Mission* To develop the internal capabilities to continuously improve performance through innovation, learning and personal organizational growth.

Fig. 4.11 Perspective questions and mission statements of the IT strategic scorecard

For each business unit, specific metrics are and/or will be defined. The ultimate responsibility for achieving and measuring the business value of IT rests with the business and is reflected in the business results of the individual lines of business in different ways, depending on the nature of value being sought.

Cost management is a traditional financial objective and is in the first place measured through the attainment of expense and recovery targets. The expenses refer to the costs that the IT organization has made for the business, and the

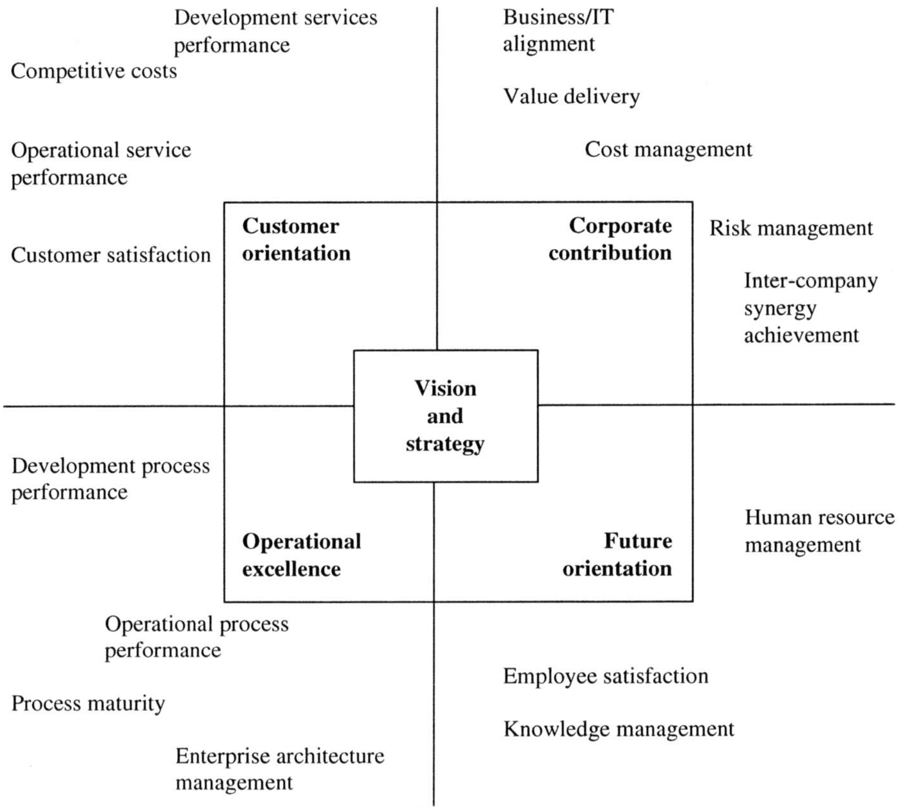

Fig. 4.12 IT strategic scorecard framework

recovery refers to the allocation of costs to IT services and the internal charge back to the business. All IT costs are fully loaded (no profit margin) and recovered from the lines of business on a fair and equitable basis as agreed to by the companies' CFOs. Comparisons with similar industries will be drawn to benchmark these metrics. Next to this, IT unit costs (e.g., application development) will be measured and compared to the "top-performing levels" benchmark provided by Compass.

The development of the *risk management* metrics is the priority for the upcoming year. At this moment, the results of the internal audits are used and benchmarked against criteria provided by OSFI, the Canadian federal regulator in the financial services sector. The execution of the Security Initiative and the delivery of a Disaster Recovery Assessment need to be accomplished in the upcoming year. This will enable the business to get an insight on how well they are prepared to respond to different disaster scenarios.

Synergy achievement is measured through the achievement of single system solutions, targeted cost reductions and the integration of the IT organizations.

This measure is very crucial in the context of the merger of the three IT organizations in the sense that it enables a post-evaluation of this merger and demonstrates to management whether the new IT organization is effective and efficient. The selection of single system solutions was a cooperative effort between business leaders and IT staff, resulting in a "Target State Architecture" depicting the target applications architecture. The synergy targets were heavily influenced by the consulting firm (Bain & Co.) that was used to assist in evaluating the London Life acquisition and the tri-company IT merger potential. The consultants suggested specific dollar reduction targets for technology services (IT operations) and application delivery services (IT development) largely based on norms they had developed from their previous merger and acquisition work. The approval of the Target State Architecture plan and the attainment of the targeted integration cost reductions will be measured.

The IT organization integration metric refers to the synergies within the IT organization, e.g., is there one single service desk for the three companies or are there three different ones? (Fig. 4.13).

Objective	Measures	Benchmarks
Business/IT alignment	- Operational plan/budget approval	- Not applicable
Value delivery	- Measured in business unit performance	- Not applicable
Cost management	- Attainment of expense and recovery targets - Attainment of unit cost targets	- Industry expenditure comparisons - Compass operational "top performance" levels
Risk management	- Results of internal audits - Execution of Security Initiative - Delivery of disaster recovery assessment	- OSFI sound business practices - Not applicable - Not applicable
Inter-company synergy achievement	- Single system solutions - Target state architecture approval - Attainment of targeted integration cost reductions - IT organization integration	- Merger & Acquisition guidelines - Not applicable - Not applicable - Not applicable

Fig. 4.13 Corporate contribution perspective

4.4.3.2 Customer Orientation Perspective

The customer orientation perspective evaluates the performance of IT from the viewpoint of internal business users (customers of IT) and, by extension, the customers of the business units. It provides answers to the key questions of these stakeholders concerning IT service quality (cf. Fig. 4.10). As shown in Fig. 4.12, the issues this perspective focuses on are competitive costs, development services performance, operational services performance and customer satisfaction.

In the *customer satisfaction* area, the IT BSC of the merged IT organization is relying on annual interviews with key business managers. It is the intent to set up one generic survey, which can be re-used, with relevant questions that cover the topics mentioned in Fig. 4.12.

Insight into the *competitive costs* area can demonstrate to the business how cost competitive the IT organization is compared to other (e.g., external) parties. This insight is realized by measuring the attainment of IT unit cost targets and the blended labor rate. This rate model provides an overall single rate for any IT professional who is appointed to the business. The competitive costs measures are benchmarked against Compass's operational "Top-Performing level" and against the offerings of commercial IT service vendors (market comparisons).

Development services performance measures are project oriented using attributes such as goal attainment, sponsor satisfaction and project governance (i.e., the way the project is managed). These data are mostly captured by interviews with key managers. The most effective time to establish the basis for these (project) development measures is at the point where business cases are being prepared and projects are evaluated. Each IT project initiative will be evaluated by the IS Executive Committee in which IT and business managers determine – based on the business drivers, budget and state architecture compliance – which projects need to be executed. When a project is approved, the project manager defines clear targets for cost, schedule, quality, scope and governance. The quantitative data (e.g., budget) are reported throughout the life cycle of the project. After completion of the project, the quantitative and qualitative data are evaluated during the major project review and the main success drivers, delivery issues and lessons learned are documented.

In terms of *Operational service performance,* IT management measures achievement against targeted service levels. For each operational unit (e.g., data center), average response time, service availability and resolution time for incidents are rolled-up to these service performance metrics in the strategic balanced scorecard. The results are benchmarked against the performance of competitors (Fig. 4.14).

4.4.3.3 Operational Excellence Perspective

The operational excellence scorecard provides the performance of IT from the viewpoint of IT management (process owners and service delivery managers)

Objective	Measures	Benchmarks
Customer satisfaction	- Business unit survey ratings: - Cost transparency and levels - Service quality and responsiveness - Value of IT advise and support - Contribution to business objectives	- Not applicable
Competitive costs	- Attainment of unit cost targets - Blended labor rates	- Compass operational "Top Level Performing" levels - Market comparisons
Development services performance	- Major project success scores - Recorded goal attainment - Sponsor satisfaction ratings - Project governance rating	- Not applicable
Operational services performance	- Attainment of targeted service levels	- Competitor comparisons

Fig. 4.14 Customer orientation perspective

and the audit and regulatory bodies. The operational excellence perspective copes with the key questions of these stakeholders and provides answers to questions of maturity, productivity and reliability of IT processes (cf. Fig. 4.10). The issues that are of focus here, as displayed in Fig. 11, are development process performance, operational process performance, process maturity and enterprise architecture management.

In relation to *development process performance*, function point-based measures of productivity, quality and delivery rate such as number of faults per 100 installed function points and delivery rate of function points per month, are defined. Benchmark data on industry performance will be gathered from a third party (e.g., Compass). In the operational process performance area, measures of productivity, responsiveness, change management effectiveness and incident occurrence level are benchmarked against selected Compass studies (e.g., on data centers, client server, etc.).

The *process maturity* is assessed using the COBIT (Control Objectives for IT and related Technology) framework and maturity models (ITGI, 2000). The Group has identified 15 out of the 34 priority processes that should have a maturity assessment in 2003 and the other processes will be measured later (Fig. 4.15).

Objective	Measures	Benchmarks
Development process performance	- Function point measures of: - Productivity - Quality - Delivery rate	- to be determined
Operational process performance	- Benchmark based measures of: - Productivity - Responsiveness - Change management effectiveness - Incident occurrence levels	- Selected Compass benchmark studies
Process maturity	- Assessed level of maturity and compliance in priority processes within: - Planning and organization - Acquisition and implementation - Delivery and support - Monitoring	- To be defined
Enterprise architecture management	- Major project architecture approval - Product acquisition compliance to technology standards - "State of the infrastructure" assessment	- Not applicable

Fig. 4.15 Operational excellence perspective

Enterprise architecture management deals with the IT responsibility to define an enterprise architecture which supports long-term business strategy and objectives and to act as a steward on behalf of business executives to protect the integrity of that architecture. Major project architecture approval measures the compliance of net new systems as they are proposed, developed and implemented. Product acquisition compliance technology standards measure the adherence to detailed technology standards which are at the heart of minimizing technology diversity and maximizing inter-company technology synergies. The "State of the Infrastructure" assessment measures the degree to which IT has been able to maintain a robust and reliable infrastructure as required to deliver effectively to business needs. It does so by comparing each platform area against risk-based criteria for potential impact to business continuity, security and/or compliance.

4.4.3.4 Future Orientation Perspective

The future orientation perspective shows the performance of IT from the viewpoint of the IT organization itself: process owners, practitioners and support professionals. The future orientation perspective provides answers to stakeholder questions regarding IT's readiness for future challenges (cf. Fig. 4.10). The issues focused on, as depicted in Fig. 4.12, are human resources management, employee satisfaction and knowledge management. The metrics that will appear in the future orientation quadrant of the IT strategic balanced scorecard are in many cases the aggregated results of measures used in the unit scorecards (e.g., career center).

Human resource management is an objective that is tracked by comparing measures as described in Fig. 4.12 against predefined targets: the staff complement by skill type (number of people with a certain profile, e.g., systems analyst), staff turnover, staff "billable" ratio (i.e., hours billed/total hours salary paid; if this ratio can be increased, the IT organization can charge lower rates to the business for the IT-assigned people) and professional development days per staff member.

Employee satisfaction is measured by using surveys with questions relating to compensation, work climate, feedback, personal growth, and vision and purpose. Benchmark data of North American technology dependent companies are provided by a third party.

In the *knowledge management* area, the delivery of internal process improvements to the "Cybrary" is very important. The "Cybrary" refers to the intranet that all employees can access for seeking and sharing knowledge. To measure improvements, metrics (e.g., number of hits per day on the Cybrary) still need to be developed. Closely linked to this, knowledge management is also measured by the implementation of the "lessons learned" sharing process. Here too, specific metrics still need to be developed (Fig. 4.16).

Objective	Measures	Benchmarks
Human resource management	- Results against targets: - Staff complement by skill type - Staff turnover - Staff 'billable' ratio - Professional development days per staff member	 - Not applicable - Market comparison - Industry standard - Industry standard
Employee satisfaction	- Employee satisfaction survey scores in: - Compensation - Work climate - Feedback - Personal growth - Vision and purpose	- North American technology dependent companies
Knowledge management	- Delivery of internal process improvements to "Cybrary" - Implementation of ''lessons learned'' sharing process	- Not applicable - Not applicable

Fig. 4.16 Future orientation perspective

4.4.4 Maturity of the Developed IT BSC

At the beginning of the project, the IT BSC was primarily focused on the operational level of the IT department. It was acknowledged from the beginning that this could not be the end result. Therefore, actions were started to go beyond the operational IT BSC and to measure the true value of IT at the business level. The Vice President Information Services emphasized: "The Balanced Scorecard gives a balanced view of the total value delivery of IT to the business. It provides a snapshot of where your IS organization is at a certain point in time. Most executives, like me, do not have the time to drill down into the large amount of information."

The organization established two ways to demonstrate the business value, one at service delivery level and one at the IT strategy level. As will be illustrated

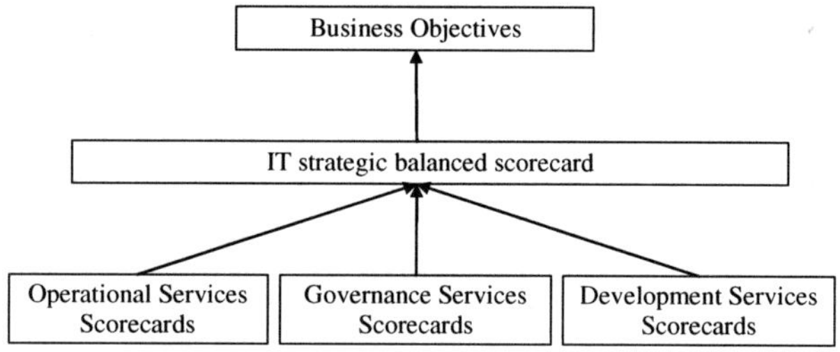

Fig. 4.17 Cascade of scorecards

hereafter, the goal is to evolve to an IT strategic BSC that shows how the business objectives are enabled by IT.

A cascade of balanced scorecards has been established to create a link between the scorecards at the unit level and the overall business objectives (see Fig. 4.17). A link between the IT BSC and the Business BSC is not yet implemented as there is currently no formal Business BSC for the Group. The scorecards at the unit level are classified into three groups: operational services scorecards (e.g., IT service desk scorecard), governance services scorecards (e.g., career centre scorecard), and development services scorecards (e.g., application development scorecard). The measures of these unit scorecards are *rolled-up* or *aggregated* in the IT strategic balanced scorecard. This, in turn is fed into and evaluated against the business objectives. In this way, the service (and value) delivered by IT is directly measured against the objectives of the overall business. Further, on an annual basis, the IT strategic BSC is reviewed by business and IT management and the result is fed back into the next annual planning cycle. This planning cycle defines what the business needs are and what IT must do to accomplish those needs.

For example, from the IT service desk scorecard (i.e., a unit scorecard, which is situated in the operational services scorecard group), metrics such as average speed of answer, overall resolution rate at initial call and call abandonment rate (all three customer orientation metrics) are *rolled-up* to service level performance metrics in the IT strategic balanced scorecard. Other metrics of this unit scorecard such as expense management (corporate contribution perspective), client satisfaction (customer orientation perspective), process maturity of incident management (operational excellence perspective) and staff turnover (future orientation perspective), will *aggregate* as part of the IT strategic scorecard. The overall view of the IT strategic balanced scorecard is then fed into and evaluated against the defined business objectives.

The second way to demonstrate business value is situated within the IT strategic balanced scorecard. The cause-and-effect relationships between performance drivers and outcome measures of the four quadrants are established as indicated in Fig. 4.18. These connections help to understand how

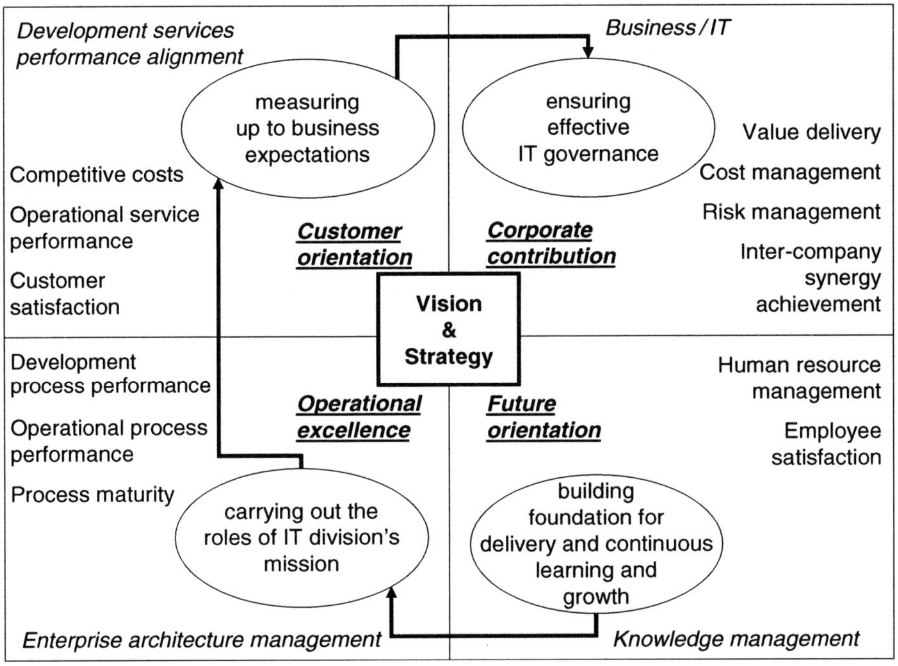

Fig. 4.18 IT strategic scorecard objectives and cause-and-effect

the contribution of IT toward the business will be realized: building the foundation for delivery and continuous learning and growth (future orientation perspective) is an enabler for carrying out the roles of the IT division's mission (operational excellence perspective) that is in turn an enabler for measuring up to business expectations (customer expectations perspective) that eventually must lead to ensuring effective IT governance (corporate contribution perspective). The construction of cause-and-effect relationships is a critical issue in the further development of the IT strategic BSC. These relationships have not yet been explicitly defined although they are implicit in the existing scorecard, e.g., the *Professional development days per staff member* measure can be identified as a performance driver for the outcome measures *Development process performance.*

The Corporate contribution perspective of Fig. 4.18 is an enabler (performance driver) of the (generic) business objectives of the financial group with its specific measures such as *Business/IT alignment*, *Value delivery*, *Cost management*, *Risk management* and *Inter-company synergy achievement*. The CIO and its executive management are aware that an explicit articulation of these relationships has to be done and that it may help to improve the IT strategic BSC and its link with the business objectives, later on with the implementation of a Business BSC.

Assignment Box 4.1: Cause-and-effect relationship

A major point in developing an IT balanced scorecard is identifying the cause-and-effect relationships across the whole scorecard. In the case study, these relationships are not described. Identify what you think are outcome measures and what their corresponding performance drivers are.

Assignment Box 4.2: Cascade of scorecards

At the case company there are, besides the IT strategic balanced scorecard, also scorecards implemented at unit level. The measures of these unit scorecards are rolled-up or aggregated in the IT strategic balanced scorecard. Develop a generic scorecard for the IT development department.

Assignment Box 4.3: Maturity of the IT BSC

Assess the maturity of the IT BSC implementation of the presented case study. Suggest improvements for the IT BSC implementation.

Summary

Kaplan and Norton introduced the balanced scorecard (BSC) at an enterprise level. Their fundamental premise is that the evaluation of a firm should not be restricted to a traditional financial evaluation but should be supplemented with measures concerning customer satisfaction, internal processes and the ability to innovate. Results achieved within these additional perspective areas should assure future financial results and drive the organization toward its strategic goals while keeping all four perspectives in balance. For each of the four perspectives they propose a three layered structure: (1) mission (e.g., to become the customers' most preferred supplier), (2) objectives (e.g., to provide the customers with new products) and (3) measures (e.g., percentage of turnover generated by new products).

The balanced scorecard can be applied to the IT function and its processes. To achieve this the focus of the four perspectives of the business BSC need to be translated. The User Orientation perspective represents the user (internal or external) evaluation of IT. The Operational Excellence perspective represents the IT processes employed to develop and deliver the applications. The Future Orientation perspective represents the human and technology resources needed by IT to deliver its services over time. The Business Contribution perspective captures the business value created from the IT investments.

To leverage the IT BSC as a management and alignment instrument, it should be enhanced with cause-and-effect relationships between measures. These relationships are articulated by two types of measures: outcome measures (or lag indicators) and performance drivers (or lead indicators). A well-developed scorecard should contain a good mix of these two metrics.

The proposed IT BSC links with the business, mainly through the business contribution perspective. The relationship between IT and business can be more explicitly expressed through a cascade of scorecards. This cascade of scorecards becomes a linked set of measures that will be instrumental in aligning IT and business strategy and that will help to determine how business value is created through IT.

Study Questions

1. Explain how the balanced scorecard can be applied to the IT function.
2. How can you leverage the IT BSC as a management and alignment instrument?
3. Explain and illustrate the difference between outcome measures and performance drivers.
4. Explain the concept of the "cascade of scorecards."
5. Explain the aggregating and rolling-up mechanism of metrics and indicate which typical IT metrics you think should appear on the business-balanced scorecard.

Further Reading

Benbasat, I., Goldstein, D., and Mead, M., 1987, The Case Research Strategy in Studies of Information Systems, MIS Quarterly, vol. 11, no. 3, pp. 368–386.

Kaplan, R., and Norton, D., 1996, The Balanced Scorecard: Translating Vision into Action. Boston: Harvard Business School Press.

Van Der Zee, J.T.M., and De Jong, B., 1999, Alignment is Not Enough: Integrating Business and Information Technology Management with the Balanced Business Scorecard, Journal of Management Information Systems, Fall, vol. 16, no. 2, pp. 137–156.

Van Grembergen, W., 2000, The Balanced Scorecard and IT Governance, Information Systems Control Journal, vol. 2.

Van Grembergen, W. (Ed.), 2004, Strategies for Information Technology Governance. Hershey, PA: Idea Group Publishing.

Van Grembergen, W., and Van Bruggen, R., 1997, Measuring and Improving Corporate Information Technology Through the Balanced Scorecard Technique, in Proceedings of the European Conference on the Evaluation of Information Technology, Delft, The Netherlands.

Van Grembergen, W., and De Haes, S., 2005a, Measuring and Improving IT Governance through the Balanced Scorecard, Information Systems Control Journal, vol. 2.

Van Grembergen, W., and De Haes, S., 2005b, Measuring and Demonstrating the Value of IT, in IT Governance Domain Practices and Competencies (series of IT Governance Institute).

Van Grembergen, W., Saull, R., and De Haes, S., 2003, Linking the IT Balanced Scorecard to the Business Objectives at a Major Canadian Financial Group, Journal for Information Technology Cases and Applications (JITCA), vol. 5, no. 1.

Yin, 2002, Case Study Research: Design and Methods Third Edition (Applied Social Research Methods), Sage Publications Inc.

Websites

Balanced Scorecard Institute: www.balancedscorecard.org

Information Technology Alignment and Governance Research Institute: www.uams.be/ITAG

ISACA: www.isaca.org

IT Governance Institute: www.itgi.org

Power Financial: www.powerfinancial.com

Chapter 5
COBIT as a Framework for Enterprise Governance of IT

Abstract COBIT (Control Objectives for Information and Related Technologies) is a freely available industry framework that describes a set of best practices for management, control and assurance of information technology, and organizes them around a logical framework based on 34 IT processes. This chapter describes the COBIT framework and explains how it can be leveraged as an instrument for Enterprise Governance of IT.

5.1 Introduction

COBIT is developed by ISACA (Information Systems Audit and Control Association), an international professional membership association counting more than 60,000 members worldwide. COBIT initially originated mid-1990s out of the (financial) audit community, who were confronted more and more with automated environments. To guide their work in these IT environments, COBIT was initially developed as a framework for executing IT audit assignments (see Fig. 5.1). Building on this basis, the COBIT framework was developed further becoming a broader control and management framework, in 2000 with the addition of "Management Guidelines," including metrics and maturity models for IT processes. An important new release was issued in December 2005, COBIT 4.0, containing several new important governance concepts, such as the alignment of business and IT goals and their relationship with supporting IT processes, roles and responsibilities within IT processes and the inter-relationship between IT processes. With these new additions COBIT wants to continue to establish itself as a generally accepted framework for Enterprise Governance of IT. To date, the latest version COBIT 4.1 was released in 2007. The COBIT framework is freely available as a PDF download at www.isaca.org.

W. Van Grembergen, S. De Haes, *Enterprise Governance of Information Technology*, DOI 10.1007/978-0-387-84882-2_5,

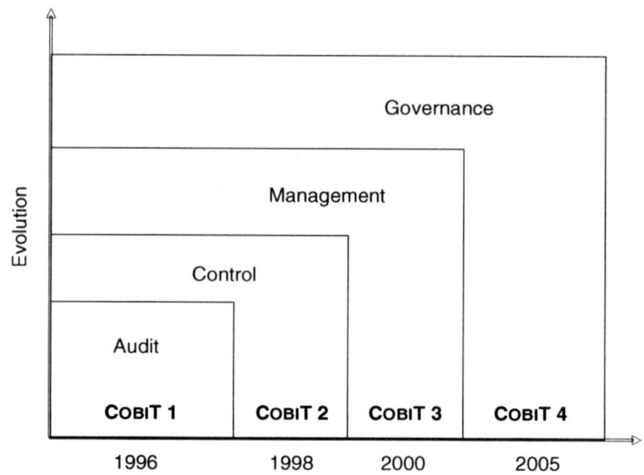

Fig. 5.1 History of COBIT

5.2 The COBIT Framework

The COBIT framework is developed around three concepts:

- Business goals/IT goals and Information Criteria
- IT processes
- IT resources

Each of these concepts is discussed in the following sections.

5.2.1 Business Goals/IT Goals and Information Criteria

A fundamental premise in the COBIT framework is that the investments in IT need to contribute to the achievement of the organization's objectives. Of course, this statement is made by many other frameworks as well, but COBIT tries to make this link between the business and IT more transparent in two ways.

The first method to clarify the link between business and IT is based on the *Information Criteria*. To satisfy the business objectives, the information that is delivered by IT to the business and its processes, needs to conform to certain quality criteria, which COBIT refers to as seven business requirements for information:

Effectiveness deals with information being relevant and pertinent to the business process as well as being delivered in a timely, correct, consistent and usable manner.

Efficiency concerns the provision of information through the optimal (most productive and economical) use of resources.

Confidentiality concerns the protection of sensitive information from unauthorized disclosure.

Integrity relates to the accuracy and completeness of information as well as to its validity in accordance with business values and expectations.

Availability relates to information being available when required by the business process now and in the future. It also concerns the safeguarding of necessary resources and associated capabilities.

Compliance deals with complying with those laws, regulations and contractual arrangements to which the business process is subject, i.e., externally imposed business criteria, as well as internal policies.

Reliability relates to the provision of appropriate information for management to operate the entity and exercise its fiduciary and governance responsibilities.

Because these information criteria are generic, they can be applied in each organization or business objective. For example, the business concern of "security" could be translated into the information criteria of "confidentiality," "integrity" and "availability." COBIT then provides, in its booklets, easy-to-use tables where the information criteria are linked to specific IT processes that are important to address the information criteria selected (see example in Fig. 5.2, P = primary link, S = secondary link).

However, the definitions of the information criteria are fairly abstract, making it more difficult to translate the information criteria to a specific situation (e.g., how to translate a business goal such as "business innovation" into information criteria?). In the context of further COBIT developments, a research was conducted together with UAMS – ITAG Research Institute in order to obtain a better view on business goals and IT goals and the way they support one another (see also Chapter 1). Based on this research, done in different industry sectors, a set of generic business and IT goals was identified and an analysis was done on how they are linked to each other. Figure 5.3 presents a matrix on how IT goals can support the achievement of business goals and this for companies in the financial sector: "P" represents a primary link and "S" a secondary link.

In this example we see that the IT goal "developing innovative IT services with a focus on information security" is an important goal in supporting the business goals "improving competitiveness through IT" and "improving customer orientation and service." This research resulted in the definition of 17 generic (IT related) business goals and 28 generic IT goals that now serve as a base for COBIT 4.1 (see Figs. 5.4 and 5.5). When combining both figures, they illustrate the relationship between business goals, IT goals and IT processes. Figure 5.4 lists the 17 generic IT-related business goals, organized according to the four perspectives of the business balanced scorecard, being *financial perspective, customer perspective, internal perspective* and *learning and growth perspective*. Each business goal is linked to one or more IT goals that support the business goal. These are indicated by numbers, representing the IT goals of Fig. 5.5. For example, the IT goal "ensure the satisfaction of end users with service offerings and service levels" supports the business goal "improve customer orientation and service."

		Effectiveness	Efficiency	Confidentiality	Integrity	Availability	Compliance	Reliability
PO1	Define a Strategic IT Plan	P	S					
PO2	Define the Information Architecture	S	P	S	P			
PO3	Determine Technological Direction	P	P					
PO4	Define the IT Organisation and Relationships	P	P					
PO5	Manage the IT Investment	P	P					S
PO6	Communicate Management Aims and Direction	P					S	
PO7	Manage Human Resources	P	P					
PO8	Manage quality	P	P		S			S
PO9	Assess Risks	S	S	P	P	P	S	S
PO10	Manage Projects	P	P					
AI1	Identify Automated Solutions	P	S					
AI2	Acquire and Maintain Application Software	P	P		S			S
AI3	Acquire and Maintain Technology Infrastructure	S	P		S	S		
AI4	Enable operation and use	P	P		S	S	S	S
AI5	Procure IT resources	S	P				S	
AI6	Manage Changes	P	P		P	P		S
AI7	Install and accredit solutions and changes	P	S		S	S		
DS1	Define and Manage Service Levels	P	P	S	S	S	S	S
DS2	Manage Third-Party Services	P	P	S	S	S	S	S
DS3	Manage Performance and Capacity	P	P			S		
DS4	Ensure Continuous Service	P	S			P		
DS5	Ensure Systems Security			P	P	S	S	S
DS6	Identify and Allocate Costs		P					P
DS7	Educate and Train Users	P	S					
DS8	Manage service desk and incidents	P	P					
DS9	Manage the Configuration	P	S			S		S
DS10	Manage Problems	P	P			S		
DS11	Manage Data				P			P
DS12	Manage the physical environment				P	P		
DS13	Manage Operations	P	P		S	S		
M1	Monitor and evaluate IT performance	P	P	S	S	S	S	S
M2	Monitor and evaluate internal control	P	P	S	S	S	S	S
M3	Ensure regulatory compliance						P	S
M4	Provide IT governance	P	P	S	S	S	S	S

Fig. 5.2 COBIT processes and information criteria
ITGI, 2007a, COBIT 4.1, on-line available at www.itgi.org.

Additionally, for each business goal, the most relevant information criteria are indicated. The relevant information criteria for IT goals can be found in Fig. 5.4, together with the IT processes that support the IT goal. These are indicated with the process indices, explained later on in this chapter. For example, the IT process

Business Goals \ IT Goals	Developing innovative IT services with a focus on information security	Fulfilling SLA's with business departments	Increasing IT department efficiency	Integration and consolidation of different IT departments	IT disaster recovery and business continuity	IT governance	IT strategic alignment	Lowering cost of transaction processing	Making IT measurable	Optimizing the IT infrastructure	Rapid development of new IT services	Reduce amount of IT insourcing	Standardizing IT systems	Taking IT measures to satisfy Basel II requirements
Achieving compliance with Basel II regulations					S									P
Improving competitiveness through IT	P									S	P			
Improving customer orientation and service	P		S	P	S				P	S				
Post-merger integration and consolidation				P						S		S	S	
Reducing operational cost			P	P	S			P	P	P		P	P	
Reducing transaction cost			P	S				P	P	S			S	
Risk management	S	P	S	S	P			S				P	S	
Shortening service development lifecycle									S		P			
Tailoring solutions for different target groups	P													

Fig. 5.3 Linking business and IT goals in the financial sector
Van Grembergen, W., De Haes, S., and Moons, J., 2005, IT Governance: Linking Business Goals to IT Goals and COBIT Processes, Information Systems Control Journal, vol. 4.

DS1, which stands for "define and manage service levels," may help achieving the aforementioned IT goal "ensure the satisfaction of end users with service offerings and service levels." In this way a cascade is formed from business goals to IT goals to IT processes.

5.2.2 *IT Processes*

COBIT 4.1 defines 34 IT processes, categorized into four domains: planning and organization, acquisition and implementation, delivery and support, monitoring en evaluation (Fig. 5.6). The domain "Planning and organization" concerns the identification of the way IT can best contribute to the achievement of the business objectives. Therefore it needs strategy and tactics for the information architecture, technology architecture, a good structured IT organization, budget control and management, the way management objectives are communicated (such as awareness around security), IT human resource management, quality management, risk assessment and management and project management.

The domain "Acquisition and Implementation" is concerned with the identification of IT solutions (insourcing or outsourcing), the acquisition and/or development and maintenance of software applications, the acquisition and maintenance of hardware and system software, the production of documentation and training of users, the acquisition of the necessary IT resources, the process for managing application changes and installing and accrediting solutions and changes.

The domain "Delivery and support" is concerned with the actual delivery of required services and contains those processes that deal with configuration management, problem management, data management, management of the physical environment (data centre and other facilities), computer operations

		BUSINESS GOALS	IT Goals										Effectiveness	Efficiency	Confidentiality	Integrity	Availability	Compliance	Reliability
Financial perspective	1	Provide a good return on investments of IT-enabled business investments	24											✔					
	2	Manage IT related business risks	2	14	17	18	19	20	21	22					✔	✔	✔		
	3	Improve corporate governance and transparency	2	18															✔
Customer perspective	4	Improve customer orientation and service	3	23									✔						
	5	Offer competiteve products and services	5	24									✔	✔					
	6	Establish service continuity and availability	10	16	22	23							✔				✔		
	7	Create agility in responding to changing business requirements	1	5	25								✔	✔					
	8	Achieve cost optimisation of service delivery	7	8	10	24								✔					
	9	Obtain reliable and useful information for strategic decision making	2	4	12	20	26						✔			✔			✔
Internal perspective	10	Improve and maintain business process functionality	6	7	11								✔	✔					
	11	Lower process costs	7	8	13	15	24							✔					
	12	Provide compliance with external laws and regulations	2	19	20	21	22	26	27						✔			✔	
	13	Provide compliance with internal policies	2	13											✔			✔	
	14	Manage business change	1	5	6	11	28						✔	✔					
	15	Improve and maintain operational and staff productivity	7	8	11	13							✔	✔					
Learning and growth perspective	16	Manage product and business innovation	5	25	28								✔	✔					
	17	Acquire and maintain skilled and motivated personnel	9										✔	✔					

(Information Criteria: Effectiveness, Efficiency, Confidentiality, Integrity, Availability, Compliance, Reliability)

Fig. 5.4 Business goals and IT goals
ITGI, 2007a, COBIT 4.1, on-line available at www.itgi.org.

#	IT GOALS	Processes											Information Criteria						
													Effectiveness	Efficiency	Confidentiality	Integrity	Availability	Compliance	Reliability
1	Respond to business requirements in alignment with the business strategy	PO1	PO2	PO4	PO10	AI1	AI6	AI7	DS1	DS3	ME1		✔			✔	✔		
2	Respond to governance requirements in line with board direction	PO1	PO4	PO10	ME1	ME3							✔	✔	✔			✔	✔
3	Ensure satisfaction of end-users with service offerings and service levels	PO8	AI4	DS1	DS2	DS7	DS8	DS10	DS13				✔						
4	Optimise use of information	PO2	DS11											✔		✔			
5	Create IT Agility	PO2	PO4	PO7	AI3									✔					
6	Define how business functional and control requirements are translated in effective and efficient automated solutions	AI1	AI2	AI6									✔	✔					
7	Acquire and maintain integrated and standardised application systems	PO3	AI2	AI5									✔	✔		✔			
8	Acquire and maintain an integrated and standardised IT infrastructure	AI2	AI5										✔	✔		✔			
9	Acquire and maintain IT skills that respond to the IT strategy	PO7	AI5										✔	✔		✔			
10	Ensure mutual satisfaction of third-party relationships	DS2											✔	✔					
11	Ensure seamless integration of applications into business processes	PO2	AI4	AI7									✔			✔	✔		
12	Ensure transparency and understanding of IT cost, benefits, strategy, policies and service levels	PO5	PO6	DS1	DS2	DS6	ME1	ME4					✔	✔				✔	✔
13	Ensure proper use and performance of the applications and technology solutions	P06	AI4	AI7	DS7	DS8							✔	✔		✔		✔	
14	Account for and protect all IT assets	PO9	DS5	DS9	DS12	ME2								✔				✔	
15	Optimise the IT infrastructure, resources and capabilities	PO3	AI3	DS3	DS7	DS9								✔					
16	Reduce solution and service delivery defects and rework	PO8	AI4	AI6	AI7	DS10							✔	✔		✔	✔		
17	Protect the achievement of IT objectives	PO9	DS10	ME2									✔	✔	✔	✔	✔	✔	✔
18	Establish clarity of business impact of risks to IT objectives and resources	PO9											✔		✔	✔	✔		
19	Ensure critical and confidential information is withheld from those who should not have access to it	PO6	DS5	DS11	DS12										✔			✔	
20	Ensure automated business transactions and information exchanges can be trusted	PO6	AI7	DS5												✔			
21	Ensure IT services and the IT infrastructure can properly resist and recover from failures due to error, deliberate attack or disaster	PO6	AI7	DS4	DS5	DS12	DS13	ME2					✔				✔		
22	Ensure minimum business impact in the event of an IT service disruption or change	PO6	AI6	DS4	DS12								✔				✔		
23	Make sure that IT services are available as required	DS3	DS4	DS8	DS13								✔				✔		
24	Improve IT's cost efficiency and its contribution to business profitability	PO5	DS6											✔					
25	Deliver projects on time and on budget meeting quality standards	PO8	PO10										✔	✔					
26	Maintain the integrity of information and processing infrastructure	AI6	DS5														✔		
27	Ensure IT compliance with laws and regulations	DS11	ME2	ME3	ME4													✔	
28	IT demonstrates cost-efficient service quality, continuous improvement and readiness for future change	PO5	DS6	ME1	ME4														✔

Fig. 5.5 IT goals and IT processes
ITGI, 2007a, COBIT 4.1, on-line available at www.itgi.org.

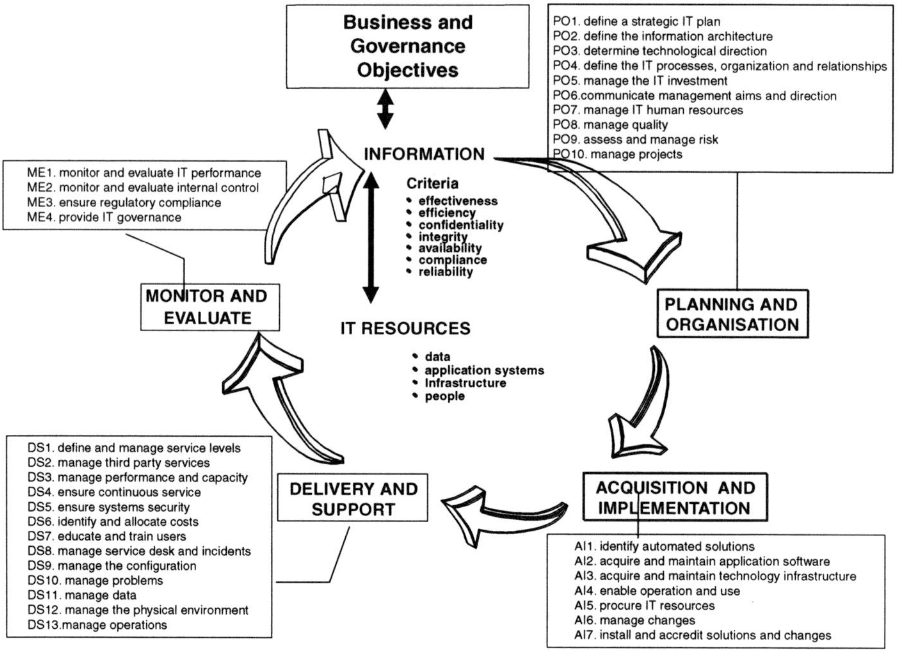

Fig. 5.6 Overall COBIT framework
ITGI, 2007a, COBIT 4.1, on-line available at www.itgi.org.

management and performance and capacity management of the hardware. Within this domain, we also find the definition of Service Level Agreements (SLAs), the management of third-party relationships, the assurance for continuous service (like a disaster recovery plan), security management, the identification and allocation of costs, education and training of users and the support and assistance for end users by means of a service desk.

The fourth domain "Monitor and evaluate" includes those processes that are responsible for the quality assessment in compliance with the control requirements for all previous mentioned processes. It addresses performance management, monitoring of internal control, regulatory compliance and providing IT governance.

Assignment Box 5.1: Most important IT processes

Work in teams and decide for which organization or sector you will do this assignment. Next, define the seven most important processes for that specific sector or organization, taking into account its business goals and IT goals. First, determine yourself the IT processes based on your knowledge of the organization/sector and then confront your solution with the generic business goals/IT goals/IT processes matrices as published in the COBIT 4.1 framework. You can download the COBIT framework at no cost at ISACA's website www.isaca.org.

5.2.3 IT Resources

COBIT refers to four IT-related resources that can be applied within the IT processes:

Information refers to the data in all their forms handled by the information systems, in whatever form is used by the business.
Applications are the automated user systems and manual procedures that process the information.
Infrastructure includes the technology and facilities (hardware, operating systems, database management systems, networking, multimedia, etc., and the environment that houses and supports them) that enable the processing of the applications.
People refers to the personnel required to plan, organize, acquire, implement, deliver, support, monitor and evaluate the information systems and services.

5.2.4 Overall COBIT Framework

According to the COBIT framework, information retrieved from IT systems is the result of a combined effort of IT-related resources, managed by IT processes. It is as such important that IT processes are managed and controlled in an effective way, so that the delivered information satisfies the defined quality standards.

Figure 5.5 summarizes the overall COBIT framework graphically. The organization defines the business and governance objectives, directly impacting the quality requirements of the IT information criteria. While managing the IT resources, the 34 generic IT processes, organized in four domains, can deliver the information to the business according the business and governance objectives.

For each of the 34 processes the COBIT framework defines control objectives, management guidelines and a maturity model. Within the COBIT 4.1 publication each process is typically described over four pages: two pages detailing the (high-level and detailed) control objectives, one page describing the management guidelines and one page for the maturity model. Following sections will further explore these different COBIT components.

5.3 COBIT Control Objectives

5.3.1 Control Objectives and Control Practices

For each of the 34 IT processes, COBIT describes control objectives. These control objectives can help the IT process owners to build a proper management and control system into the IT environment. An IT control objective is a statement of the desired result or purpose to be achieved by implementing control procedures in a particular IT activity. COBIT's control objectives can be seen as the requirements for effective management and control within each IT process. A good control comprises procedures, policies, practices and organizational structures designed to provide reasonable assurance that business objectives are achieved and undesired events are prevented or detected and corrected.

COBIT defines one high-level control objective and several detailed control objectives for each process. It is important to note that where possible, the control objectives were aligned with best practices for IT governance and other industry standards such as ITIL, CMMi and others. For instance processes DS8 — *manage service desk and incidents* and DS10 – *manage problems* are aligned with ITIL terminology. Furthermore, starting from the COBIT 4.x editions, the control objectives have been written in a more active format and as such they can be seen as more detailed process steps (sub-processes) or key management practices within the global IT process.

In total, COBIT 4.1 defines 34 *high-level* control objectives and 210 detailed control objectives. As an example, Fig. 5.7 presents the high-level control objective of process DS1 – *define and manage service levels*, giving a one-page summary of the process by describing the IT/business goals it supports (*that satisfies the business requirements for IT of*), its most important goals (*is achieved by*), its different important activities (*is managed by*) and some metrics that can be applied for its monitoring (*and is measured by*).

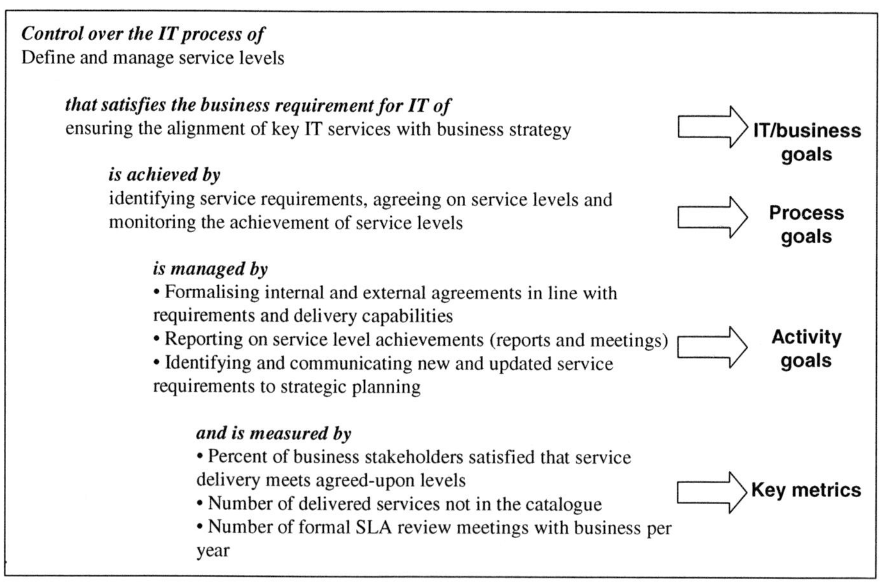

Fig. 5.7 High-level control objective for DS1 – define and manage service levels ITGI, 2007a, COBIT 4.1, on-line available at www.itgi.org.

An overview of the detailed control objectives for process DS1 can be found in Fig. 5.8. The control objectives or sub-processes for this process emphasize the importance of the existence of a Service Level Management framework, the definition of services and the Service Level Agreement (SLA). Additionally an SLA should be further detailed into operational level agreements containing the more technical aspects. Finally, performance, control and reporting procedures must be integrated and all agreements should be reviewed on regular basis.

DS1.1 Service level management framework

Define a framework that provides a formalized service level management process between the customer and service provider. The framework should maintain continuous alignment with business requirements and priorities and facilitate common understanding between the customer and provider(s). The framework should include processes for creating service requirements, service definitions, SLAs, OLAs and funding sources. These attributes should be organized in a service catalogue. The framework should define the organizational structure for service level management, covering the roles, tasks and responsibilities of internal and external service providers and customers.

DS1.2 Definition of services

Base definitions of IT services on service characteristics and business requirements. Ensure that they are organized and stored centrally via the implementation of a service catalogue portfolio approach.

DS1.3 Service level agreements

Define and agree to SLAs for all critical IT services based on customer requirements and IT capabilities. This should cover customer commitments; service support requirements; quantitative and qualitative metrics for measuring the service signed off on by the stakeholders; funding and commercial arrangements, if applicable; and roles and responsibilities, including oversight of the SLA. Consider items such as availability, reliability, performance, capacity for growth, levels of support, continuity planning, security and demand constraints.

DS1.4 Operating level agreements

Define OLAs that explain how the services will be technically delivered to support the SLA(s) in an optimal manner. The OLAs should specify the technical processes in terms meaningful to the provider and may support several SLAs.

DS1.5 Monitoring and reporting of service level achievements

Continuously monitor specified service level performance criteria. Reports on achievement of service levels should be provided in a format that is meaningful to the stakeholders. The monitoring statistics should be analyzed and acted upon to identify negative and positive trends for individual services as well as for services overall.

DS1.6 Review of service level agreements and contracts

Regularly review slas and underpinning contracts (UCS) with internal and external service providers to ensure that they are effective and up to date and that changes in requirements have been taken into account.

Fig. 5.8 Detailed control objectives for DS1 – define and manage service levels ITGI, 2007a, COBIT 4.1, on-line available at www.itgi.org.

Control objective DS8.1: Service desk

Establish a service desk function, which is the user interface with IT, to register, communicate, dispatch and analyze all calls, reported incidents, service requests and information demands. There should be monitoring and escalation procedures based on agreed-upon service levels relative to the appropriate SLA that allow classification and prioritization of any reported issue as an incident, service request or information request. Measure end users' satisfaction with the quality of the service desk and IT services.

Control practices DS8.1: Service desk

1. Establish a service desk as a single, initial point of contact for the reporting, monitoring, escalation and resolution of customer requests and incidents. Develop business requirements for the service desk, based on service definitions and SLAs, including hours of operation and expected response time to a call. Ensure that service desk requirements include identifying staffing, tools and integration with other processes, such as change management and problem management.
2. Ensure that there are clear instructions for service desk staff when a request cannot be immediately resolved by service desk personnel. Establish time thresholds to determine when escalation should occur based on the categorization/prioritization of the request or incident.
3. Implement the necessary support software and tools (e.g., incident management, knowledge management, incident escalation systems, automated call monitoring) required for operation of the service desk and configured in accordance with SLA requirements, to facilitate automated prioritization of incidents and rapid resolution.
4. Advise customers of the existence of the service desk and the standards of service they can expect. Obtain user feedback on a regular basis to ensure customer satisfaction and confirm the effectiveness of the service desk operation.
5. Using the service desk software, create service desk performance reports to enable performance monitoring and continuous improvement of the service desk.

Fig. 5.9 Control practices

For each Control Objective, COBIT also provides a set of Control Practices, which are defined as a necessary and sufficient set of practices to implement a control objective. These Control Practices are not included in the COBIT 4.1 Framework book but are contained in the COBIT Control Practices publication (this document is freely available in PDF format for ISACA members at www.isaca.org). Main reason is that these control practices are defined at a fairly detailed level and sometimes become more prescriptive, where the COBIT framework itself is more situated at a generic high-level. An example of control practices is provided in Fig. 5.9 for Control Objective DS8.1: Service Desk. First, the control objective is stated and, next, a set of control practices is defined to implement the control objective.

Assignment Box 5.2: Control practices

Work in teams. Select an IT process out of COBIT, and within the process, select two control objectives. For each control objectives, define a set of control practices, as a set of necessary and sufficient practices to implement the Control Objective. Then confront your solution with the control practices in the COBIT Control Practices book (this document is freely available for ISACA members or can be downloaded at minimal cost by assessing www.isaca.org).

5.3.2 Generic Process Controls and Application Controls

In the evolution from COBIT 3 to COBIT 4, the number of control objectives reduced from 318 to 210. The main reason for this reduction in control objectives was the extraction of generic process controls and application controls out of the IT processes.

From the COBIT 3 list of control objectives, all generic detailed control objectives, meaning those that apply to all processes, have been removed. These generic objectives have been defined in COBIT 4.1 as *process controls (PC)* (see Fig. 5.10) and together with the remaining detailed control objectives they provide a complete view of control requirements. These process controls deal

PC1 Process goals and objectives

Define and communicate specific, measurable, actionable, realistic, results- oriented and timely (SMARRT) process goals and objectives for the effective execution of each it process. Ensure that they are linked to the business goals and supported by suitable metrics.

PC2 Process ownership

Assign an owner for each IT process, and clearly define the roles and responsibilities of the process owner. Include, for example, responsibility for process design, interaction with other processes, accountability for the end results, measurement of process performance and the identification of improvement opportunities.

PC3 Process repeatability

Design and establish each key IT process such that it is repeatable and consistently produces the expected results. Provide for a logical but flexible and scaleable sequence of activities that will lead to the desired results and is agile enough to deal with exceptions and emergencies. Use consistent processes, where possible, and tailor only when unavoidable.

PC4 Roles and responsibilities

Define the key activities and end deliverables of the process. Assign and communicate unambiguous roles and responsibilities for effective and efficient execution of the key activities and their documentation as well as accountability for the process end deliverables.

PC5 Policy, plans and procedures

Define and communicate how all policies, plans and procedures that drive an IT process are documented, reviewed, maintained, approved, stored, communicated and used for training. Assign responsibilities for each of these activities and, at appropriate times, review whether they are executed correctly. Ensure that the policies, plans and procedures are accessible, correct, understood and up to date.

PC6 Process performance improvement

Identify a set of metrics that provides insight into the outcomes and performance of the process. Establish targets that reflect on the process goals and performance indicators that enable the achievement of process goals. Define how the data are to be obtained. Compare actual measurements to targets and take action upon deviations, where necessary. Align metrics, targets and methods with ITs overall performance monitoring approach.

Fig. 5.10 COBIT process controls
ITGI, 2007a, COBIT 4.1, on-line available at www.itgi.org.

with the importance of having a process owner identified, of making a process repeatable, of describing goals, objectives, roles and responsibilities, of measuring and managing performance and of defining policies, plans and procedures. They are defined in the introductory chapters of the COBIT framework book.

Regarding the application controls, all detailed control objectives from the COBIT 3 process DS11 – *manage data,* that are about the definition of application controls (AC), were removed. The assumption is that the definition of the application controls is not part of IT's responsibility. The business as any other business requirements has to define the application controls. IT is only responsible for implementing these controls in a correct way (as part of the AI processes). Of course, COBIT does acknowledge that, in practice, the definition of application control often is a joint effort between business and IT. Therefore, these application controls are still explained in the introductory chapters of the COBIT 4.1 publication. They typically address data origination and authorization controls, data input controls, data processing controls, data output controls and boundary controls (see Fig. 5.11).

AC1 Source data preparation and authorization

Ensure that source documents are prepared by authorized and qualified personnel following established procedures, taking into account adequate segregation of duties regarding the origination and approval of these documents. Errors and omissions can be minimized through good input form design. Detect errors and irregularities so they can be reported and corrected.

AC2 Source data collection and entry

Establish that data input is performed in a timely manner by authorized and qualified staff. Correction and resubmission of data that were erroneously input should be performed without compromizing original transaction authorization levels. Where appropriate for reconstruction, retain original source documents for the appropriate amount of time.

AC3 Accuracy, completeness and authenticity checks

Ensure that transactions are accurate, complete and valid. Validate data that were input, and edit or send back for correction as close to the point of origination as possible.

AC4 Processing integrity and validity

Maintain the integrity and validity of data throughout the processing cycle. Detection of erroneous transactions does not disrupt the processing of valid transactions.

AC5 Output review, reconciliation and error handling

Establish procedures and associated responsibilities to ensure that output is handled in an authorized manner, delivered to theappropriate recipient, and protected during transmission; that verification, detection and correction of the accuracy of output occurs; and that information provided in the output is used.

AC6 Transaction authentication and integrity

Before passing transaction data between internal applications and business/operational functions (in or outside the enterprise), check it for proper addressing, authenticity of origin and integrity of content. Maintain authenticity and integrity during transmission or transport.

Fig. 5.11 Application controls
ITGI, 2007a, COBIT 4.1, on-line available at www.itgi.org.

5.4 COBIT Management Guidelines

The management guidelines in COBIT 4.1 deliver more information for organizing, measuring and controlling a specific IT process. The management guidelines are summarized on one page (see Fig. 5.12), comprising for each COBIT process:

- The inter-relationship between the different IT processes, by means of *inputs* and *outputs*,
- An overview of important process tasks, including related roles and responsibilities (*RACI chart*),
- *Goals and metrics* on IT level, IT process level and IT process activity level.

From	Inputs
PO5	Cost-benefits reports
PO9	Risk assessment
PO10	Updated IT project portfolio
DS1	New/updated service requirements; updated IT service portfolio
*	Business strategy and priorities
*	Programme portfolio
ME1	Performance input to IT planning
ME4	Report on IT governance status; enterprise strategic direction for IT

Outputs	To				
Strategic IT plan	PO2…PO6	PO8	PO9	AI1	DS1
Tactical IT plans	PO2…PO7	PO9	AI1	DS1	
IT project portfolio	PO5	PO6	PO10	AI6	
IT service portfolio	PO5	PO6	PO9	DS1	
IT sourcing strategy	DS2				
IT acquisition strategy	AI5				

Inputs/outputs

Activities \ Functions	CEO	CFO	Business Executive	CIO	Business process owner	Head Operations	Chief Architect	Head Development	Head IT Admin	PMO	Compliance, audit, risk, security (CARS)
Link business goals to IT goals	C	I	A/R	R	C						
Identify critical dependencies and current performance	C	C	R	A/R	C	C	C	C	C		C
Build an IT strategic plan	A	C	C	R	I	C	C	C	C	I	C
Build IT tactical plans	C	I		A/R	C	C	C	C	C	R	I
Analyse programme portfolio	C	I	I	A/R	R	R	C	R	C	C	I

RACI

	IT	PROCESS	ACTIVITIES
GOALS	• Respond to business requirements in alignment with the business strategy. • Respond to governance requirements in line with board direction.	• Define how business requirements are translated in service offerings. • Define the strategy to deliver service offerings. • Contribute to the management of the portfolio of IT-enabled business investments. • Establish clarity regarding the business impact of risks on IT objectives and resources. • Provide transparency and understanding of IT costs, benefits, strategy, policies and service levels.	• Engaging with business and senior management in aligning IT strategic planning with current and future business needs • Understanding current IT capabilities • Providing for a prioritisation scheme for the business objectives that quantifies the business requirements • Translating IT strategic planning into tactical plans
METRICS	• Degree of approval of business owners of the IT strategic/tactical plans • Degree of compliance with business and governance requirements • Level of business satisfaction with the current state (number, scope, etc.) of the project and applications portfolio	• Percent of IT objectives in the IT strategic plan that support the strategic business plan • Percent of IT initiatives in the IT tactical plan that support the tactical business plans • Percent of IT projects in the IT project portfolio that can be directly traced back to the IT tactical plans	• Delay between updates of business strategic/tactical plans and updates of IT strategic/tactical plans • Percent of strategic/tactical IT plans meetings where business representatives have actively participated • Delay between updates of IT strategic plan and updates of IT tactical plans • Percent of tactical IT plans complying with the predefined structure/contents of those plans • Percent of IT initiatives/projects championed by business owners

Goal & metrics

Fig. 5.12 COBIT 4.1 Management guidelines
ITGI, 2007a, COBIT 4.1, on-line available at www.itgi.org.

5.4.1 Inputs/Outputs

For each process, COBIT defines a list of inputs the process should receive from other processes and a list of possible outputs to send to other processes. For example process PO1 – *define a strategic IT plan* (Fig. 5.13) should receive a cost/benefits report from process PO5 – *manage the IT investment*. The process PO1 itself should send strategic and tactical IT plans to several other processes. Note that it is indicated that PO1 should also receive inputs from the business (indicated with a*, business strategy and the program portfolio).

Assignment Box 5.3: Inputs and outputs

Determine inputs and outputs for AI6 (Manage Changes) and confront your result with the COBIT Framework AI6 inputs and outputs (you can download the COBIT Framework publication at no cost via ISACA's website www.isaca.org).

5.4.2 RACI Diagram

COBIT defines for each process a RACI diagram, where the role and responsibilities related to important process activities are identified. RACI stands for

- *Responsible*: who is responsible for the activity
- *Accountable*: who is accountable for the activity, meaning who provides direction and authorizes the activity (is typically hierarchically higher than *responsible*)
- *Consulted*: who should be consulted for the activity
- *Informed*: who must be informed about the activity

The activities are derived from the control objectives often resulting in more detailed activities. It should be noted that accountabilities and responsibilities are very organization specific and depending on the hierarchical structure and culture within organizations. It is therefore advisable to use the COBIT RACI charts as a kind of template for discussing and determining the IT accountabilities and responsibilities within a specific organization.

From	Inputs
PO5	Cost-benefits reports
PO9	Risk assessment
PO10	Updated IT project portfolio
DS1	New/updated service requirements; updated IT service portfolio
*	Business strategy and priorities
*	Programme portfolio
ME1	Performance input to IT planning
ME4	Report on IT governance status; enterprise strategic direction for IT

Outputs	To				
Strategic IT plan	PO2...PO6	PO8	PO9	AI1	DS1
Tactical IT plans	PO2...PO7	PO9	AI1	DS1	
IT project portfolio	PO5	PO6	PO10	AI6	
IT service portfolio	PO5	PO6	PO9	DS1	
IT sourcing strategy	DS2				
IT acquisition strategy	AI5				

Fig. 5.13 Input/outputs for PO1 – define a strategic IT plan
ITGI, 2007a, COBIT 4.1, on-line available at www.itgi.org.

Activities \ Functions	CEO	CFO	Business Executive	CIO	Business process owner	Head Operations	Chief Architect	Head Development	Head IT Admin	PMO	Compliance, audit, risk, security (CARS)
Link business goals to IT goals	C	I	A/R	R	C						
Identify critical dependencies and current performance	C	C	R	A/R	C	C	C	C	C		C
Build an IT strategic plan	A	C	C	R	I	C	C	C	C	I	C
Build IT tactical plans	C	I		A/R	C	C	C	C	C	R	I
Analyse programme portfolios	C	I	I	A/R	R	R	C	R	C	C	I

Fig. 5.14 Roles and responsibilities (RACI diagram) for PO1 – define a strategic IT plan ITGI, 2007a, COBIT 4.1, on-line available at www.itgi.org.

Our example process PO1 – *define a strategic IT plan* shows that especially the business executives together with the CIO are responsible for the linking business goals to IT goals activity (Fig. 5.14). The PO1 RACI chart indicates that the CIO is accountable for building the IT tactical plans. For this activity the accountability is laid down at the right position. One could argue that ultimately the CIO is accountable for all IT processes. However, in practice the accountabilities for some activities could be brought down which is illustrated, e.g., by the RACI chart for DS4 — Ensure Continuous Service where the "Develop and Maintain IT continuous plans" activity is the accountability (see Fig. 5.15) of the Head Operations.

Assignment Box 5.4: RACI chart (1)

Define the RACI chart for AI6 (Manage Changes) and confront your result with the COBIT Framework AI6 RACI (you can download the COBIT Framework publication at no cost via ISACA's website www.isaca.org).

Assignment Box 5.5: RACI chart (2)

Figure 5.15 depicts the RACI chart of the DS4 process (Ensure Continuous Service). Make teams and discuss the attribution of the R, A, C and I for the different activities.

Activities \ Functions	CEO	CFO	Business Executive	CIO	Business process owner	Head Operations	Chief Architect	Head Development	Head IT Admin	PMO	Compliance, audit, risk, security (CARS)
Develop an IT continuity framework.		C	C	A	C	R	R	R	C	C	R
Conduct a business impact analysis and risk assessment.		C	C	C	C	A/R	C	C	C	C	C
Develop and maintain IT continuity plans.	I	C	C	C	I	A/R		C	C	C	C
Identify and categorise IT resources based on recovery				C		A/R		C	I	C	I
Define and execute change control procedures to ensure that the IT continuity plan is current.				I		A/R		R	R	R	I
Regularly test the IT continuity plan.				I	I	A/R		C	C	I	I
Develop a follow-on action plan from test results.				C	I	A/R	C	R	R	R	I
Plan and conduct IT continuity training.				I	R	A/R		C	R	I	I
Plan IT services recovery and resumption.		I	I	C	C	A/R	C	R	R	R	C
Plan and implement backup storage and protection.				I		A/R		C	C	I	I
Establish procedures for conducting post-resumption reviews.				C	I	A/R		C	C		C

Fig. 5.15 Roles and responsibilities (RACI diagram) for DS 4 – ensure continuous service ITGI, 2007a, COBIT 4.1, on-line available at www.itgi.org.

5.4.3 Goals and Metrics

For each of the 34 IT processes, COBIT defines goals on three levels (see Fig. 5.14). IT goals are located at the level of the IT department, the highest level within COBIT for defining goals (the business goals are not retained because they are often very closely linked to the IT goals). On a second level, process goals are defined for the IT process itself and fall under the responsibilities of the process owner. And finally, activity goals are identified on the level of activities defined within the process. Clearly, achieving activity goals must support the achievement of process goals, which in turn must support the achievement of IT goals. Note that the activities in the goals and metrics charts are different from the activities in the RACI charts.

In order to monitor all these goals, metrics are defined for each of them (Fig. 5.16). It is important to note there are two distinct metrics: key goal indicators and key performance indicators.

Key goal indicators (outcome measures in balanced scorecard terminology) are known as *lag indicators* and they measure the achievement of the defined goals. Three levels of key goal indicators (KGIs) are known within COBIT: KGIs for measuring the IT goals, KGIs for measuring the IT process goals and KGIs for measuring process activity goals. As an example, for process DS5 – *ensure system security* (see Fig. 5.17) one of the IT process goals is defined as "permit access to critical and sensitive data only to authorized users" and a possible KGI to measure this process goal is "number and type of suspected and actual access violations."

Key performance indicators (key performance drivers in the balanced scorecard terminology) are known as *lead indicators* and measure the means to achieve the goals on a next level, e.g., the KGI on the activity level becomes the KPI on the IT process level. In previous example "number and type of suspected and actual access violations" was identified as a KGI on IT process level for the IT process goal "permit access to critical and sensitive data only to authorized users." In order to reach this goal, several activity goals must be executed, such as "managing user identities and authorization in a standardized manner" (Fig. 5.17). This goal can be measured by a KGI on activity level such as "number and type of obsolete

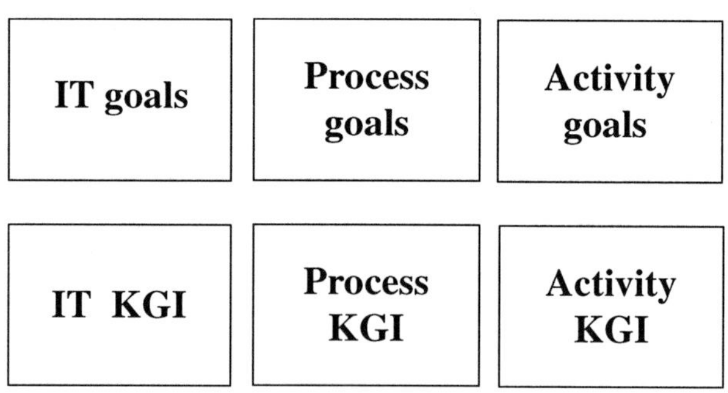

Fig. 5.16 Goals and metrics

	IT	PROCESS	ACTIVITIES
GOALS	• Ensure that critical and confidential information is withheld from those who should not have access to it. • Ensure that automated business transactions and information exchanges can be trusted. • Maintain the integrity of information and processing infrastructure. • Account for and protect all IT assets. • Ensure that IT services and infrastructure can resist and recover from failures due to error, deliberate attack or disaster.	• Permit access to critical and sensitive data only to authorised users. • Identify, monitor and report security vulnerabilities and incidents. • Detect and resolve unauthorised access to information, applications and infrastructure. • Minimise the impact of security vulnerabilities and incidents.	• Understanding security requirements, vulnerabilities and threats • Managing user identities and authorisations in a standardised manner • Defining security incidents • Testing security regularly
METRICS	• Number of incidents with business impact • Number of systems where security Requirements are not met • Time to grant, change and remove access privileges	• Number and type of suspected and actual access violations • Number of violations in segregation of duties • Percent of users who do not comply with password standards • Number and type of malicious code prevented	• Frequency and review of the type of security events to be monitored • Number and type of obsolete accounts • Number of unauthorised IP addresses, ports and traffic types denied • Percent of cryptographic keys compromised and revoked • Number of access rights authorised, revoked, reset or changed

Fig. 5.17 Goals and metrics for the Process DS5 – ensure system security ITGI, 2007a, COBIT 4.1, on-line available at www.itgi.org.

accounts," which is also a KPI for the IT process level. It is assumed that a lower score for this metric implicates a better indication for reaching the IT process goal.

Figure 5.18 shows the complete cascade of metrics for the IT/COBIT process "Ensure Systems Security" and illustrates clearly the relationship between KPIs

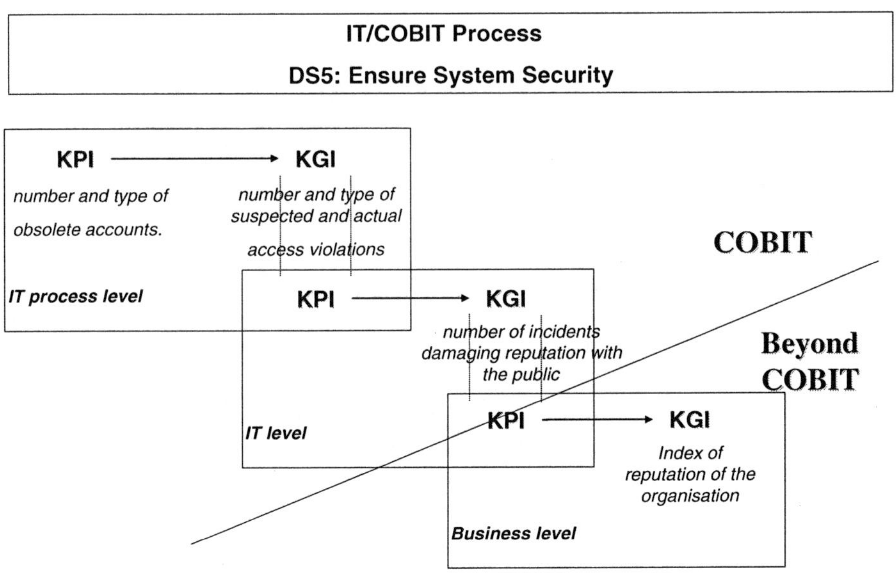

Fig. 5.18 Cascade of metrics

and KGIs. As already explained in previous chapter, *number and type of obsolete accounts* is a KGI at activity level but becomes a KPI at IT process level. Further, on IT process level *number and type of suspected and actual access violations* is defined as KGI for the IT process goal. We assume this is an important means, supporting the IT goal *ensure critical and confidential information is withheld from those who should not have access to it* (Fig. 5.17), which in turn is measured by the IT level KGI *number of incidents damaging reputation with the public*. This means, on IT level that the IT process KGI *number and type of suspected and actual access violations* now becomes a KPI, which is operating as lead indicator for the IT KGI *number of incidents damaging reputation with the public*. Next, this KGI can become a KPI for a business level goal like, for example, the organization's reputation, measured by *reputation index of the organization* (see Fig. 5.18). In the COBIT IT processes, metrics on business level are not included. The COBIT management guidelines only deliver IT-related goals and metrics, but as mentioned previously, guidance is provided on how IT processes and IT goals can support the business goals (Figs. 5.4 and 5.5).

Assignment Box 5.6: Goal and metrics

Define two metrics for each of the three levels (IT level, IT process level and activity level) for AI6 (Manage Changes) and confront your result with the COBIT Framework AI6 goals and metric chart (you can download the COBIT Framework publication at no cost via ISACA's website www.isaca.org).

Assignment Box 5.7: Metrics

Metrics should be SMART which means they should be Specific, Measurable, Actionable, Relevant and Timely. Discuss the SMARTness of the metrics for DS5 (Ensure System Security) as depicted in Fig. 5.17.

5.5 COBIT Maturity Models

A maturity model can be seen as a scoring technique for organizations to assess the maturity level of a specific process between 0 (not existent) and 5 (optimized). This instrument offers a comprehensible method for identifying and comparing the current (as-is) situation against the desirable (to-be) situation. Additionally, the organization can compare its situation against industry-specific best practices and standards. Gaps between the "as-is" and the "to-be" situation can be identified and specific actions to evolve toward the desirable situation can be set up. Whenever the maturity level of a process is being analyzed, it is important to apply the base principles of a maturity measurement: an organization can only evolve to a next maturity level, whenever all the criteria of that level are fulfilled.

0 Non-existent

Management has not recognized the need for a process for defining service levels. Accountabilities and responsibilities for monitoring them are not assigned.

1 Initial/Ad Hoc

There is awareness of the need to manage service levels, but the process is informal and reactive. The responsibility and accountability for defining and managing services are not defined. If performance measurements exist, they are qualitative only with imprecisely defined goals. Reporting is informal, infrequent and inconsistent.

2 Repeatable but intuitive

There are agreed-upon service levels, but they are informal and not reviewed. Service level reporting is incomplete and may be irrelevant or misleading for customers. Service level reporting is dependent on the skills and initiative of individual managers. A service level co-ordinator is appointed with defined responsibilities, but limited authority. If a process for compliance to service level agreements exists, it is voluntary and not enforced.

3 Defined process

Responsibilities are well defined, but with discretionary authority. The service level agreement development process is in place with checkpoints for reassessing service levels and customer satisfaction. Services and service levels are defined, documented and agreed-upon using a standard process. Service level shortfalls are identified, but procedures on how to resolve shortfalls are informal. There is a clear linkage between expected service level achievement and the funding provided. Service levels are agreed to but they may not address business needs.

4 Managed and measurable

Service levels are increasingly defined in the system requirements definition phase and incorporated into the design of the application and operational environments. Customer satisfaction is routinely measured and assessed. Performance measures reflect customer needs, rather than IT goals. The measures for assessing service levels are becoming standardized and reflect industry norms. The criteria for defining service levels are based on business criticality and include availability, reliability, performance, growth capacity, user support, continuity planning and security considerations. Root cause analysis is routinely performed when service levels are not met. The reporting process for monitoring service levels is becoming increasingly automated. Operational and financial risks associated with not meeting agreed-upon service levels are defined and clearly understood. A formal system of measurement of KPIs and KGIs is instituted and maintained.

5 Optimized

Service levels are continuously re-evaluated to ensure alignment of IT and business objectives, while taking advantage of technology including the cost-benefit ratio. All service level management processes are subject to continuous improvement. Customer satisfaction levels are continuously monitored and managed. Expected service levels reflect strategic goals of business units and are evaluated against industry norms. IT management has the resources and accountability needed to meet service level targets and compensation is structured to provide incentives for meeting these targets. Senior management monitors KPIs and KGIs as part of a continuous improvement process.

Fig. 5.19 Maturity model for the process DS1 – define and manage service levels
ITGI, 2007a, COBIT 4.1, on-line available at www.itgi.org.

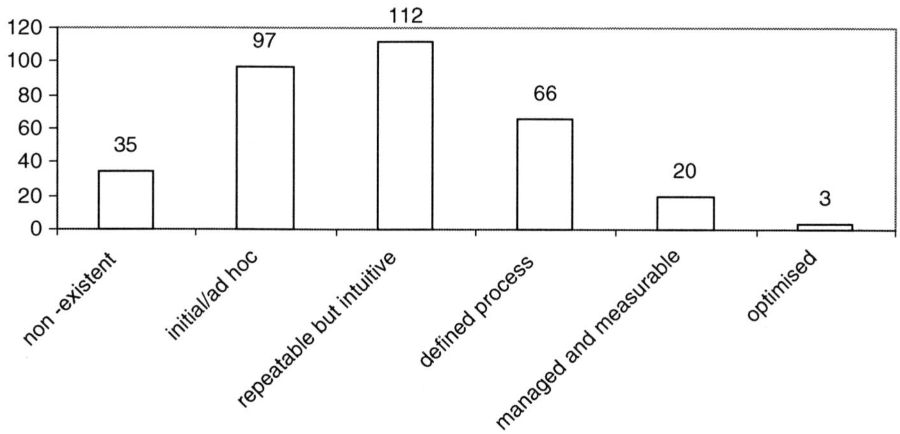

Fig. 5.20 Average maturity of DS1 – define and manage service levels
ITGI, 2007a, COBIT 4.1 – Benchmarking in COBIT Online, on-line available at www.itgi.org.

The maturity levels of the process DS1– *define and manage service levels* are listed in Fig. 5.19. If an organization reaches level 1 for this process, it is aware of the need to manage service levels, but the process is still informal. When the organization reaches maturity level 5, all defined service levels are continuously monitored and reviewed in order to guarantee an optimal alignment between business and IT objectives.

In its COBIT Online product (see infra), COBIT also provides benchmarking data regarding the maturity of processes (see Fig. 5.20, the numbers give the total population per maturity level). This benchmarking database shows that for a majority of the organizations the maturity level of the process DS1 – *define and manage service levels* hovers between 2 and 2.5. When further analyzing these results, organizations in the finance sector for example reached by average a higher score (between 2.5 and 3). These average numbers can help organizations analyzing their maturity level against industry best practices.

5.6 COBIT and Other Frameworks

Several standards and best practices, issued by both international standardization organizations and private organizations, exist in addition to COBIT for managing the different aspects of IT. When implementing IT control and IT governance, it may be important to know how these different standards and best practices relate.

COBIT can be seen as a kind of "umbrella" framework which addresses the full spectrum of IT processes. Several other standards and framework exist,

Guidance	Goals	Target audience
CMMi	Providing guidance to use when developing processes.	Systems & software developers/managers
COSO	Improve the ways of controlling enterprises by defining an integrated control system.	CxOs, users and internal auditors
ISO/IEC2700x (ISO17799)	Guidance for implementing information security	People responsible for information security
ISO/IEC TR 13335	Guidance on aspects of IT security management	Senior management, individuals responsible for security measures
ISO/IEC15408:2005	Definition of criteria for evaluation of IT security	Consumers, developers and evaluators
ITIL	Vendor-independent approach for service management	People responsible for IT service management
NIST 800-14	Baseline for establishing and reviewing IT security programs	Parties responsible for IT security in government organizations
PRINCE2	Definition of a project management method	Organizations of varying sizes (project managers)
PMBOK	A common lexicon for discussing, writing and applying project management.	Anyone interested in the profession of project management.
Tick IT	QMS for software development and certification criteria	Customers, suppliers and auditors

Fig. 5.21 Examples of more detailed IT governance standards/guidance

complementary to COBIT that focus at more specific aspects within IT or IT processes. Examples of such frameworks are provided in Fig. 5.21.

Figure 5.22 places the different standards and guidelines in a completeness classification diagram, using the vertical dimension for the detail of the standard/guidance in terms of technical and operational profundity and the horizontal dimension for the completeness of the standard/guidance with respect to COBIT.

The IT Governance Institute provides more guidance for practitioners on how COBIT maps onto other standards. More information can be found at www.itgi.org.

Assignment Box 5.8: COBIT and ITIL

Search at the Internet for information on ITIL (IT Infrastructure Library) and discuss and determine its relationship with COBIT. Discuss also the difference between ITIL2 and the recently published ITIL3 in relation to COBIT 4.1.

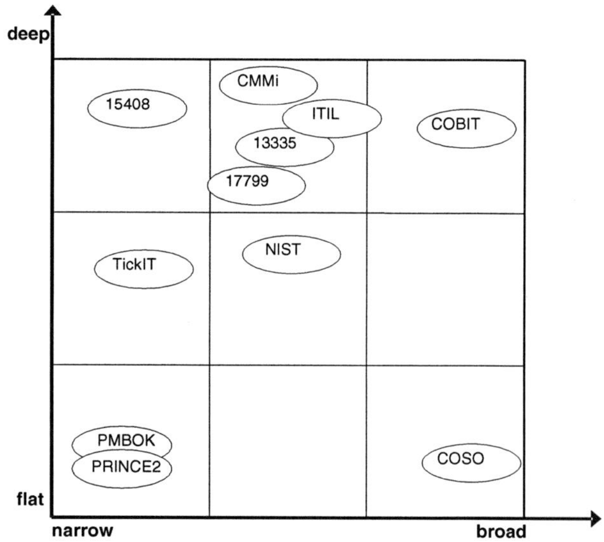

Fig. 5.22 Completeness classification of IT governance standards ITGI, 2006b, COBIT Mapping – Overview of International IT Guidance, 2nd Edition, from www.itgi.org.

5.7 COBIT and Compliancy for Sarbanes-Oxley

In response to well-known financial scandals, the United States introduced the Sarbanes-Oxley (SOX) law in 2002. This act intends to regain public trust into the capital markets by enhancing the accountability of executive management to their shareholders. With the higher attention for compliancy, IT governance and its frameworks has gained adoption into IT and business departments. The SOX law requires senior managers to take personal responsibility for the accuracy of the company's financial reports. It applies to all companies listed on the American stock exchange but also impacts those companies that deliver services to them.

Although the SOX-Act is defined with a strong financial perspective, the role of IT and the impact on the IT processes is fundamental. Financial reporting processes are heavily dependent upon reliable IT systems, which are in charge of the storage, processing, transfer and reporting of the financial data. Only a good working and controlled IT environment can sustain the integrity of the data and provide the basis for reliable reports.

With the SOX law the need arose for good and practical control frameworks. Where previously, internal control may have been organized ad hoc with no strict guidelines, the SOX-Act now specifically mentions the international control framework of the Committee of Sponsoring Organizations of the Treadway Commission (COSO). COSO defines internal controls as processes that are designed to offer a reasonable assurance regarding the achievement of those objectives related to the reliability of financial reporting, the effectiveness and efficiency of operations and compliancy with laws and regulations. The COSO framework is a broadly accepted framework for internal control of financial reporting, but it does not cover the control for the supporting IT processes. COBIT does fill in this gap and a good implementation of its framework offers management with the information to provide reasonable assurance that the necessary IT control mechanisms are in place for complete and correct reporting, as prescribed by SOX. As recognized by PCAOB and ITGI, there is no ready-made solution and each organization should carefully consider their company-relevant IT control objectives, in line with the business requirements for SOX compliancy.

Companies that want to make use of COBIT for their compliancy work may find guidance in the published ITGI document *Control Objectives for Sarbanes-Oxley* (ITGI, 2006a). This report is based on best practices and helps in making a company-specific SOX-compliancy plan for IT control objectives. It presents a selected list of 12 IT Control Objectives that play a crucial role in SOX compliancy (Fig. 5.23) and maps them to 14 COBIT processes and four IT general control domains, defined by PCAOB (U.S. Public Company Accounting Oversight Board): *Program development, Program changes, Computer Operations* and *Access to Programs and Data.*

These IT control objectives and their supporting IT processes do play an important role in the path toward compliancy. The first four processes in the list (Fig. 5.23) are important because wrongful or fraudulent procedures could already be introduced during the implementation or set up phase of financial systems. Afterward it is important that changes to an existing system are well controlled; especially during the emergency change process, non-controlled malfunctions may be introduced. Therefore, the fifth process in the list, *Manage changes* ensures that every modification to a financial system is correctly authorized and logged and that the necessary impact analyses and test

	COBIT	PCAOB IT General Controls			
IT Control Objectives for Sarbanes-Oxley	**Mapping to COBIT 4 Processes**	**Program development**	**Program changes**	**Computer operations**	**Access to programs and data**
1. Acquire and maintain application software	AI2	X	X	X	X
2. Acquire and maintain technology infrastructure	AI3	X	X	X	
3. Enable operations	AI4	X	X	X	X
4. Install and accredit solutions and changes	AI7	X	X	X	X
5. Manage changes	AI6		X		X
6. Define and manage service levels	DS1	X	X	X	X
7. Manage third-party services	DS2	X	X	X	X
8. Ensure systems security	DS5			X	X
9. Manage the configuration	DS9			X	X
10. Manage problems and incidents	DS8,DS10			X	
11. Manage data	DS11			X	X
12. Manage the physical environment and operations	DS12,DS13			X	X

Fig. 5.23 COBIT Control Objectives mapped to PCAOB IT general controls
ITGI, 2006a, IT Control Objectives for Sarbanes-Oxley, 2nd Edition, from www.itgi.org.

procedures take place. Other SOX-dependent IT processes apply to being "in control" over service levels and third-party services (*Is outsourced development under control?*), system security (*Are the financial reporting systems secured to prevent unauthorized use, modification, damage or loss of data?*), problem and incident management (*What is the process for reporting, logging and solving problems?*), data management (*Is data integrity assured?*) and operations management (*What are the controls over job scheduling, processing and error monitoring?*).

Other standards and frameworks such as ITIL and ISO 27000 may provide complementary elements for organizing internal control. For example, the ITIL processes, *Change Management*, *Service Level Management*, *Problem Management* and *Incident Management* will provide more detailed information in the area of Service Management, while the ISO 2700x series will complement the COBIT process *Ensure Systems Security.*

5.8 Adapting COBIT to Your Needs

COBIT did develop a generic framework, suitable for "any" organization. It does contain a lot of valuable information but by first reading the documentation it may be difficult to grasp the essence and/or the practical elements. For a practical approach it is important for an organization to rework and extract the necessary information and transform it to an organization-specific template. Some processes may be more important for one organization than another. The process DS 4 – *Ensure Continuous Service,* for example, will be of high importance in a financial organization. Indeed, if the IT systems of a commercial bank are not available for a certain time, this may have a negative impact on the financial results of the bank. On the contrary the same process will most probably have a lower priority for a bricks and stones factory, resulting in lower maturity level requirement. It is as such important that before starting with a COBIT implementation, there needs to exist a clear set of business goals and IT goals.

Summary

COBIT is seen more and more as a generally accepted framework for IT Governance. The essence of COBIT lies in the fact that IT processes and IT resources must support IT and business goals. This implicates that COBIT is not a cookbook with very precise recipes. The organization-specific environment is the starting point for implementing a good IT governance and it is important to take out those processes, components and elements from COBIT that could help in achieving the organization's own business and IT objectives.

COBIT defines 34 IT processes. For each of the 34 processes the COBIT framework defines control objectives, management guidelines and a maturity model. Several standards and best practices, issued by both international standardization organizations and private organizations, exist in addition to COBIT for managing the different aspects of IT. When implementing IT control and IT governance, it may be important to know how these different standards and best practices relate.

COBIT also provides a good framework to build up a control environment to comply with the Sarbanes-Oxley requirements.

Study Questions

1. Explain why COBIT should be regarded as a framework that enables the implementation of Enterprise Governance of IT.
2. Explain the four IT process domains in COBIT.
3. Explain the meaning of information criteria and how they can be used in practice.
4. Explain the relationship between the control objectives and the control practices and illustrate with an example.
5. Explain what is meant by application controls and why these are not specific IT management controls.
6. Explain how the IT balanced scorecard concepts are integrated in COBIT.
7. Explain the relationship between KGIs and KPIs and illustrate with an example.
8. Explain the difference between accountability and responsibility and illustrate with IT examples.
9. Explain how the maturity models can be used in practice.
10. Which IT COBIT processes are most important for SOX compliance and explain their relevance.

Further Reading

ITGI, 2006a, IT Control Objectives for Sarbanes-Oxley, 2nd Edition, from www.itgi.org

ITGI, 2006b, COBIT Mapping – Overview of International IT Guidance, 2nd Edition, from www.itgi.org

ITGI, 2007a, COBIT 4.1, from www.itgi.org

ITGI, 2007b, IT Assurance Guide, from www.itgi.org

Van Grembergen, W. (Ed.), 2004, Strategies for Information Technology Governance. Hershey, PA: Idea Group Publishing.

Van Grembergen, W., Van Brempt, H., and De Haes, S., 2007, Prioritizing and Linking Business and IT Goals in the Financial Sector, in Proceedings of the 40th Hawaii International Conference on System Sciences (HICSS).

Van Grembergen, W., De Haes, S., and Amelinckx, I., 2003, Using COBIT and the Balanced Scorecard as Instruments for Service Level Management, Information Systems Control Journal, vol. 4.

Van Grembergen W., De Haes S., Moons J., 2005, IT Governance: Linking Business Goals to IT Goals and COBIT Processes, Information Systems Control Journal, vol. 4.

Websites

Information Technology Alignment and Governance Research Institute: www.uams.be/ITAG

ISACA: www.isaca.org

IT Governance Institute: www.itgi.org

IT Governance using COBIT and Val IT, Student Book, 2nd Edition: www.isaca.org/cobitinacademia

IT Process Institute: www.itpi.org

Chapter 6
COBIT as a Framework for IT Assurance

Abstract In previous chapter, COBIT was introduced and discussed as a powerful framework to implement Enterprise Governance of IT. However, COBIT also provides in-depth support to execute IT assurance/audit assignments. This chapter explains how the COBIT concepts can be leveraged in the context of IT assurance. Readers who are not familiar with COBIT are recommended to first read Chapter 5 where the concepts of COBIT are explained.

6.1 Introduction

In 2007, the IT Governance Institute issued the "IT Assurance Guide – using COBIT" (the assurance guide is freely available for ISACA members or can be downloaded at minimal cost via ISACA's website www.isaca.org). This guide builds further on the earlier developed "IT Audit Guidelines – 3rd edition," released in 2000. The new IT Assurance Guide integrated all the new COBIT 4 concepts and also introduced new and innovative approaches for IT assurance.

An important evolution in the scope of the document, compared to the 2000 edition, is demonstrated in the new title, showing a shift from the word "audit" to "assurance." This shift stresses that this new guide is not only intended for the "pure audit assignment," independently reporting the audit committee of an organization, but also oriented toward management that wants to do self-assessments/assurance activities with the purpose of benchmarking and improving process performance.

It is also important to note that the IT Assurance Guide does not want to be a "manual" for IT assurance. It starts from the premise that the reader is knowledgeable about (IT) audit processes and explains how COBIT can be leveraged within the practices of the IT assurance professional.

W. Van Grembergen, S. De Haes, *Enterprise Governance of Information Technology*, DOI 10.1007/978-0-387-84882-2_6,

Basically, the IT Assurance Guide offers two elements:

- A detailed roadmap showing how typical IT assurance activities can be planned (IT assurance planning), scoped (IT assurance scoping) and executed (IT assurance execution) based on COBIT
- Detailed guidance in the IT assurance execution domain providing specific steps to test the control design, to test the outcome of the control objectives and to test the impact of control weaknesses, based on COBIT

Both aspects are discussed in more detail in the following sections.

6.2 The IT Assurance Roadmap

To support the IT assurance professional, the IT Assurance Guide offers a generic roadmap to execute IT assurance assignments. Acknowledging that each organization or professional will apply its own methodology, this generic approach distinguishes between three phases, as shown in Fig. 6.1.

The *planning stage* focuses on developing IT assurance plans (e.g., the IT assurance plan for next year) that enable the organization to balance the

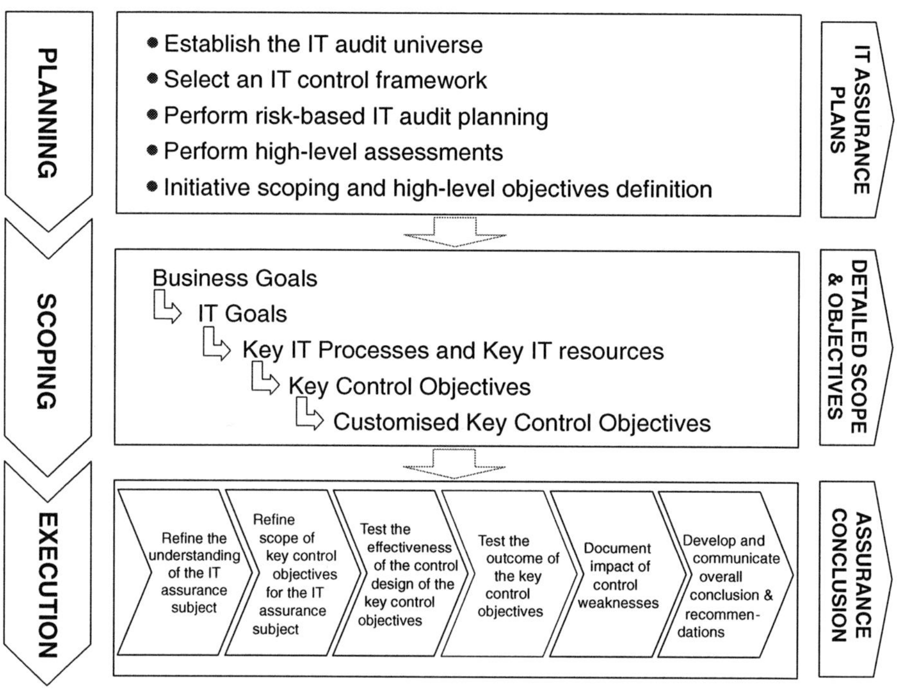

Fig. 6.1 Generic IT assurance roadmap
IT Assurance Guide, 2007b, online available at www.itgi.org.

limited assurance resources across the required assurance activities. To achieve this, the IT assurance professional first needs to define what the IT *assurance universe* is, i.e., what are all the elements that can be subjected to an assurance review? For COBIT, this assurance universe is encompassed by the combination of the business and IT goals, IT processes and IT resources. In relation to the IT resources, an understanding of the applications, data, infrastructure and people should be obtained. Typical questions such as which IT processes are relevant for which applications should be asked. Next, an appropriate *IT control framework* needs to be established against which the assurance activities will be executed. Of course, in this context of the IT Assurance Guide, COBIT is put forward as an appropriate control framework. To identify the areas that need prior attention in the complete assurance universe, the IT assurance professional can apply *risk-based analysis* (which areas have a high likelihood of impacting business outcomes?) or *high-level maturity assessments* (which areas appear to be very low in maturity?). The outcomes of these analysis and assessments can help in developing the scope (which areas have great risk exposure?), and appropriate resource allocation for the (e.g., yearly) IT assurance plans.

The *scoping stage* is focused at the level of one single IT assurance activity. At this stage, a detailed scope and control framework has to be developed. This scoping process should be based on relevant business goals and IT goals, and derived from that, IT processes and IT resources. Within those IT processes, appropriate control objectives and by extension control practices need to be selected to create a detailed control framework for the specific assurance assignment. This cascade of business goals, IT goals, IT processes, control objectives and control practices was also discussed in previous chapter (Chapter 5). In fact, the scoping process for the purpose of Enterprise Governance of IT or for the purpose of IT assurance is completely equivalent.

The *execution phase* encompasses the effective testing activities to be done by the assurance professional. Main activities focus on testing the control design, testing the outcomes of the control objectives and testing the impact of control weaknesses, ultimately leading to the communication of conclusions and recommendations. These testing steps are discussed in more detail in the next section.

6.3 IT Assurance Execution

Next to some extra detailed planning and scoping activities (see first two boxes in Fig. 6.2), the IT Assurance execution steps mainly address the core testing activities that the assurance professional executes (boxes 3, 4 and 5 in Fig. 6.2). The IT Assurance Guide provides detailed material to the assurance professional helping him/her to test the control design, test the outcome of control objectives and test the impact of control weaknesses. As shown in Fig. 6.2, the guidance

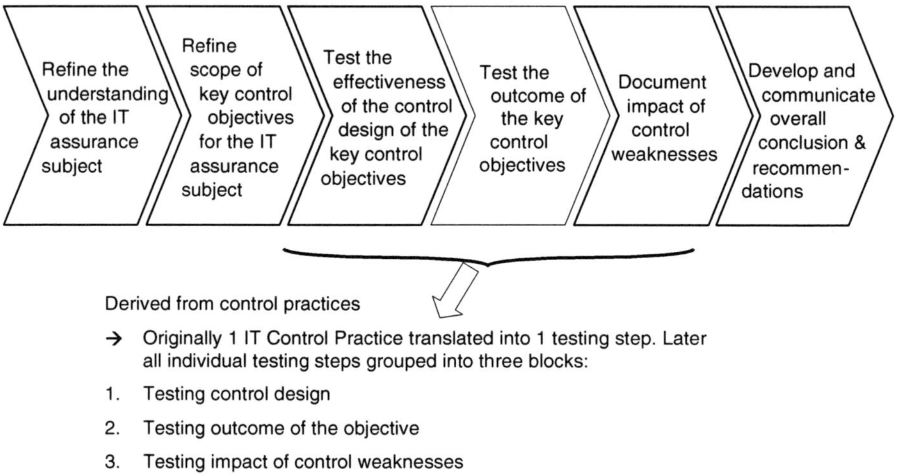

Fig. 6.2 Assurance steps derived from IT control practices
IT Assurance Guide, 2007b, online available at www.itgi.org.

developed in these three assurance execution stages is based on the COBIT IT Control Practices (cf. Chapter 5).

In the "IT Assurance Guide" development, initially all the IT Control Practices were translated into corresponding "testing/assurance steps" to be performed by the IT assurance professional to verify whether or not a specific control practice is in place. Later in the development, to avoid the danger of creating a "check-list approach," all testing steps were grouped into a logical sequence of three testing stages, as discussed in the following sections. From the above, it should be clear that, content wise, the testing steps provided in the IT Assurance Guide are similar to the Control Practices, but now written from the perspective of the IT assurance professional. For example, within the DS2 Manage Third-Party Services the first Control Practice for the DS2.1 Identification of all Supplier Relationships Control Objective is "Define and regularly review criteria to identify and categorise all supplier relationships according to the supplier type, significance and criticality of service. The list should include a category describing vendors as preferred, non-prefered or not recommended." The latter is translated into the Control Design test by "Enquire whether and confirm that a register of supplier relationships is maintained" (Fig. 6.3).

In the IT Assurance Guide publication, the detailed material of assurance steps is reported as shown in the template of Fig. 6.4. A template filled with some examples is provided in Fig. 6.5, for AI6.3 – *emergency changes*. As an extra piece of information for each control objective, risk and value statements are described, explaining the business value of having that specific control objective or business risk of not having this control objective. Next,

Control objective

Identify all supplier services, and categorize them according to supplier type, significance and criticality. Maintain formal documentation of technical and organizational relationships covering the roles and responsibilities, goals, expected deliverables, and credentials of representatives of these suppliers.

Control practice (first of two)

Define and regularly review criteria to identify and categorize all supplier relationships according to the supplier type, significance and criticality of service. The list should include a category describing vendors as preferred, non-preferred or not recommended.

Testing control design

Enquire whether and confirm that a register of supplier relationships is maintained.

Fig. 6.3 Control objective, practice and assurance step for DS2.1 – identification of all supplier relationships
IT Assurance Guide, 2007b, online available at www.itgi.org.

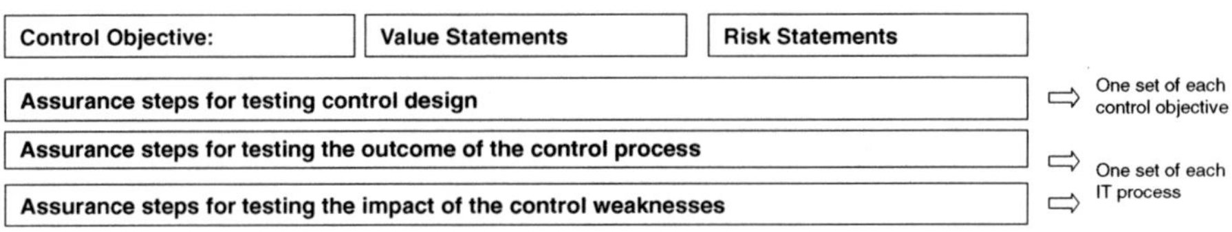

Fig. 6.4 IT Assurance steps in the IT assurance guide
IT Assurance Guide, 2007b, online available at www.itgi.org.

Control Objective: AI6.3 Emergency Changes

Establish a process for defining, raising, testing, documenting, assessing and authorising emergency changes that do not follow the established change process.

Value Statements

- Formally defined change impact expectations based on business risk and performance measurement
- Consistent change procedure

Risk Statements

- Unintended side effects
- Adverse effects on capacity and performance of the infrastructure
- Lack of priority management of changes

Assurance steps for testing control design

Enquire whether and confirm that the overall change management process includes emergency change procedures (e.g., defining, raising, testing, documenting, assessing and authorising emergency changes).

Assurance steps for testing the outcome of the control process

Inspect a sample of emergency changes and verify that they have been processed in accordance with the change management framework. Verify that procedures have been followed to authorise, document and revoke access after the change has been applied.

Assurance steps for testing the impact of the control weaknesses

Assess the time and cost of lack of formal emergency change standards and procedures (e.g., compromised security, failure to properly terminate additional access authorisations, unauthorised access to corporate information).

Fig. 6.5 IT Assurance steps in the IT assurance guide – example

at the level of a control objective, assurance steps for testing the control design are provided. The assurance steps for testing the control objective outcome and testing the impact of control weaknesses are provided at process level.

Important to recognize is that the IT assurance material provided are developed as a kind of library of potential assurance steps to be done, based on COBIT. This implies that these assurance steps give excellent material to create detailed assurance plans and programs, but it is still up to the assurance professional to apply professional judgment in selecting and adapting the relevant material out of the assurance guidance provided.

6.3.1 Testing Control Design

"Testing Control Design" (often also referred to as "testing the design effectiveness") covers the assurance steps to be performed to assess the adequacy of the design of controls. This assurance activity includes the evaluating of the appropriateness of control measures for the process under review by considering identified criteria, industry standard practices and applying professional judgment.

Figure 6.6 provides examples for a control objective in the COBIT IT process AI6 – *Manage changes*. The first assurance steps provided is "Enquire whether and confirm that the change management process allows business process owners and IT to request changes to infrastructure, systems or applications." These assurance steps typically are based on interviews with key stakeholders in the organization, leading to narratives describing the control measures applied in the organization.

The IT Assurance Guide uses typical generic testing methods such as enquire, confirm, observe and inspect. "Enquire and confirm" is about asking management questions to obtain an understanding of the processes and/or applications and includes the search and examination of exceptions and deviations. "Observe" is about the observation and description of the processes and procedures. "Inspect" includes the review of plans, policies and procedures, the tracing of transactions through the

- Enquire whether and confirm that the change management process allows business process owners and IT to request changes to infrastructure, systems or applications.
- Enquire whether and confirm that the overall change management process includes emergency change procedures (e.g. defining, raising, testing, documenting, assessing and authorizing emergency changes).

Fig. 6.6 Testing the control design
IT Assurance Guide, 2007b, online available at www.itgi.org.

processes/systems, physical inspection of the presence of documentation and assets, ...

To identify key interviewees in this assurance process, the assurance professional can leverage COBIT's RACI charts, looking for those people who are in the first place accountable (A) and responsible (R) (see Chapter 5) for these activities. Further, when asking for documentation the assurance professional can consult the inputs/outputs tables of COBIT, giving information on typical documentation to be expected in the process under review.

As indicated earlier, these assurance steps are provided for each individual control objective (cf. Fig. 6.4). This implies that, in total, 210 sets of assurance step for testing the control design are provided.

6.3.2 Testing the Outcome of Control Objectives

"Testing the outcome of control objectives" (often also referred to as "testing the operational effectiveness") addresses the assurance steps to be performed to ensure that the control measures established are working as prescribed, consistently and continuously. These assurance steps typically are about inspecting samples, re-calculations, etc. When looking for documentation to retrieve "evidence" in these activities, the assurance professional can consult the inputs/outputs tables of COBIT, giving information on typical documentation to be expected in this process.

The testing of the outcome in many cases is performed on the basis of samples. There are many factors that determine sample sizes. Figure 6.7 represents a common sample size used in practice by auditors to test the operating effectiveness of controls.

In the IT Assurance Guide, the assurance steps for testing the outcome of control objectives are not reported at the level of the control objective, but only at the level of a whole IT process (cf. 6.4). Figure 6.8 provides examples for the COBIT IT process AI6 – *Manage changes*, such as "inspect a selection of changes and determine if requests have been categorized."

Nature of control	Frequency of performance	Minimum sample size
Manual	Many times per day	25
Manual	Daily	25
Manual	Weekly	5
Manual	Monthly	2
Manual	Quarterly	2
Manual	Annually	1
Automated	Test one application of each programmed control activity (assures IT general controls are automated)	
IT general controls	Follow the guidance above for manual and programmed aspects of IT general controls	

Fig. 6.7 Guidance for sample size selection

- Inspect a selection of changes and determine if requests have been categorized.
- Inspect a selection of changes and determine if changes have been prioritized based on predefined criteria.
- Inspect a selection of changes and determine if changes have been assessed in a structured method (e.g. security, legal, contractual and compliance implications are considered and business owners are involved).
- Inspect a sample of emergency changes and verify that they have been processed in accordance with the change management framework. Verify that procedures have been followed to authorize, document, and revoke access after change has been applied.

Fig. 6.8 Testing the outcome of control objectives
IT Assurance Guide, 2007b, online available at www.itgi.org.

6.3.3 Testing the Impact of Control Weaknesses

If control weaknesses are identified based on previous steps, "Testing the impact of the control weaknesses" encompasses the assurance steps to document and report on potential business risks if specific control objectives are not met. The main issue here is that the assurance professional should not just report on control weaknesses (e.g., "we found evidence that there is no project management methodology"), but the assurance professional should demonstrate what the potential business impact of these weaknesses is (e.g., the likelihood of IT project failing increases, causing budgets over-runs or a longer time-to-market). Typical examples are provided in Fig. 6.9 for the example of the COBIT IT process AI6 – *Manage changes*. In most cases, the assurance professional tries to estimate potential cost, loss of time, business impact, etc., due to the control weaknesses. The IT assurance professional can leverage COBIT's goals and metrics tables, and risk and value drivers, to clarify the business issues at risk.

- Assess the time and cost of lack of formal change management standards and procedures (e.g. improper resource allocation, unclear roles and responsibilities, security breaches, lack of rollback procedures, lack of documentation and audit trails, inadequate training).
- Assess the time and cost of lack of formal impact assessment to prioritize and authorize changes.
- Assess the time and cost of lack of formal emergency change standards and procedures (e.g. compromised security, failure to properly terminate additional access authorizations, unauthorized access to corporate information).

Fig. 6.9 Testing the impact of control weaknesses
IT Assurance Guide, 2007b, online available at www.itgi.org.

6.4 IT Assurance in Practice

To execute IT assurance activities in practice, templates can be very helpful in supporting the assurance execution. These templates can be simple in nature, and as an illustration, some (non-prescriptive) examples are provided in this section, specifically in support of scoping and testing execution activities. Next section will also illustrate how some specific COBIT content components (without being exhaustive) can be helpful in the IT assurance work.

6.4.1 Templates for Scoping

Out of the planning phases of the assurance roadmap (see first phase in Fig. 6.1), detailed assurance assignments are defined (e.g., for the next year). When starting with such a specific assurance assignment, the detailed scope needs to be set first. As explained earlier, this scope analysis can be based on the identification and linking of relevant business goals and IT goals (see left section of Fig. 6.10, where business and IT goals can be defined and mapped), and derived from that, a set of IT processes in scope (see right section of Fig. 6.10, e.g. the five most important IT processes supporting the defined IT goals). Based on this analysis, IT

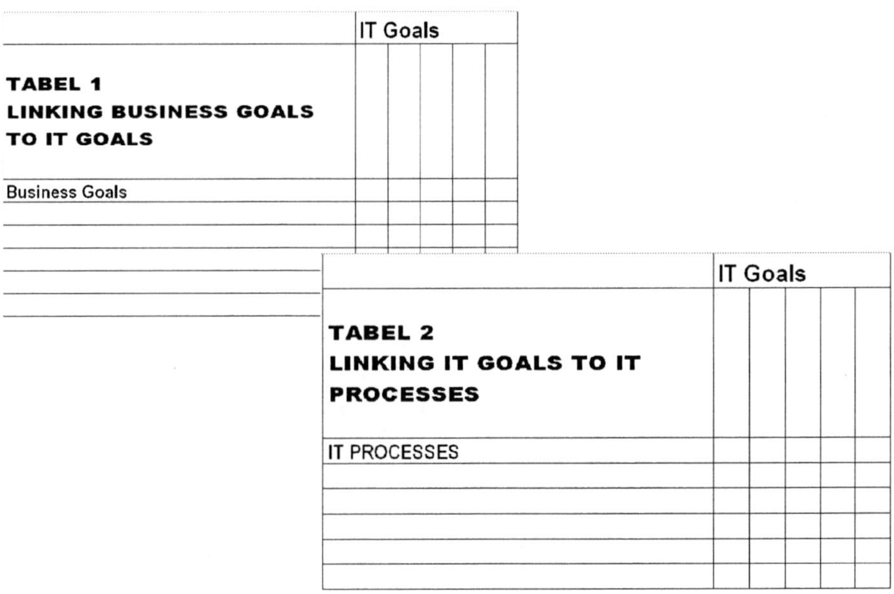

Fig. 6.10 Templates for value-based scoping

resources in scope also need to be defined (e.g., a set of core applications directly supporting core business processes).

Based on previous exercise, a set of IT processes is deducted from a value perspective (value-based scoping, i.e., IT processes in support of the achievement of business and IT goals). Depending on the context, it can be that this scope needs to be refined based on some risk insights and analysis. To support this, the IT Assurance Guide (and also the IT Control Practices) provides risk drivers for all control objectives within the IT processes, as shown in Fig. 6.11. Looking at the risk drivers of all control objectives within one process can help in refining the scope/selection of IT processes, based on risk insights. In the example below for the IT control objective DS1.3: Service level agreements, not having service level agreements can lead to failure in meeting customer requirements.

Control Objective DS1.3: Service Level Agreements	**Value Statements**	**Risk Statements**
Define and agree to SLAs for all critical IT services based on customer requirements and IT capabilities. This should cover customer commitments; service support requirements; quantitative and qualitative metrics for measuring the service signed off on by the stakeholders; funding and commercial arrangements, if applicable; and roles and responsibilities, including oversight of the SLA. Consider items such as availability, reliability, performance, capacity for growth, levels of support, continuity planning, security and demand constraints.	• Service responsibilities and IT objectives aligned with business objectives • Service quality enhanced due to proper understanding and alignment of service delivery • Service efficiency increased and costs reduced due to efficient deployment of IT services based on real needs and priorities	• Failure to meet customer service requirements • Inefficient and ineffective use of service delivery resources • Failure to identify and respond to critical service incidents

Fig. 6.11 COBIT components for risk-based scoping

Alternatively, easy-to-use templates can be leveraged that indicate a high-level risk profile for IT processes, based on an evaluation of importance, performance, responsibilities and accountabilities, formality, etc., as illustrated in Fig. 6.12. COBIT Online (available at www.isaca.org for ISACA members) provides similar templates that can be leveraged for these purposes.

RISK		**Importance** = how important for the organisation on a scale from 1 (not at all) to 5 (very) **Performance** = how well it is done from 1 (very well) to 5 (don't know or badly) **Formality** = is there a contract, an SLA or a clearly documented procedure (Yes, No or ?) **Audited?** = Yes, No or ? **Accountable** = Name or "dont' know"	Who does it?						
Importanc	Performan	CobiT's Domains and Processes	IT	Other	Outside	Don't Kno	Audited?	Formality	Who is accountable?
		Planning & Organisation							
		PO1 Define a Strategic IT Plan							
		PO2 Define the Information Architecture							
		PO3 Determine Technological Direction							
		PO4 Define the IT Processes, Organisation and Relationships							
		PO5 Manage the IT Investment							
		PO6 Communicate Management Aims and Direction							
		PO7 Manage IT Human Resources							
		PO8 Manage Quality							
		PO9 Assess and Manage Risks							
		PO10 Manage Projects							

Fig. 6.12 Templates for risk-based scoping

Once the set of IT processes is defined, a set of control objectives within each process needs to selected, as a basis for the control framework. In support of this, COBIT Online (available at www.isaca.org for ISACA members) provides attributes that help in evaluating and comparing the importance of control objectives within an IT process. These attributes are (see Fig. 6.13):

CobiT Control Objectives			Attributes: Effectiveness	Expedience	Sustainanility	cost
Planning & Organisation						
PO1		Define a Strategic IT Plan				
	1,1	IT as Part of the Organisation's Long- and Short-Range Plan	H	L	M	L
	1,2	IT Long-Range Plan	H	M	M	M
	1,3	IT Long-Range Planning-Approach and Structure	M	L	M	M
	1,4	IT Long-Range Plan Changes	M	H	L	M
	1,5	Short-Range Planning for the IT Function	H	M	H	H
	1,6	Communication of IT Plans	M	H	M	L
	1,7	Monitoring and Evaluating of IT Plans	H	M	M	M
	1,8	Assessment of Existing Systems	H	L	H	H

Fig. 6.13 Control objective attributes
COBIT Online, online available at www.isaca.org for ISACA Members.

- Expedience, i.e., the speed and ease it takes, on average, to implement the control objective; e.g., a high (H) score means the control objective can be implemented quickly.
- Sustainability, i.e., the degree to which the control can continue to operate without maintenance and management attention due to changes in the environment, reduced discipline, changed priorities, etc. Automated procedures (e.g., automatic backup) and mechanisms where the stakeholder has a high expectation (e.g., a weekly performance report) are generally more sustainable over time than procedures and mechanisms that require certain people's behavior and discipline.

- Effectiveness, i.e., the degree to which the control objective – compared to other control objectives for this process – contributes to achieving the process goals and mitigates the risks, irrespective of efficiency, cost, etc.
- Cost (effort), i.e., the investment in people and money to implement a control objective. There is usually a strong relationship between cost and expedience because high cost implies many activities, and investments are required to implement the control objective which generally means that implementation will not be expedient.

When the relevant control objectives are selected, appropriate control practices need to be defined. In the IT Control practices, COBIT provides a necessary and sufficient set of practices to implement a control objective (see example in Fig. 6.14 for DS8.1: service desk). Of course, you can also directly go to the IT Assurance guide where – as explained in previous paragraphs – the IT Control practices are translated into assurance tests; however, COBIT also states that this set is not the only workable set and organizations are free to develop their own specific set of practices required to implement a control

DS8.1 Service desk control objective

Establish a service desk function, which is the user interface with IT, to register, communicate, dispatch and analyze all calls, report incidents, service requests and information demands. There should be monitoring and escalation procedures based on agreed-upon service levels relative to the appropriate SLA that allow classification and prioritization of any reported issue as an incident, service request or information request. Measure end users' satisfaction with the quality of the service desk and IT services.

DS8.1 Service desk control practices

1. Establish a service desk as a single, initial point of contact for the reporting, monitoring, escalation and resolution of customer requests and incidents. Develop business requirements for the service desk, based on service definitions and SLAs, including hours of operation and expected response time to a call. Ensure that service desk requirements include identifying staffing, tools and integration with other processes, such as change management and problem management.
2. Ensure that there are clear instructions for service desk staff when a request cannot be immediately resolved by service desk personnel. Establish time thresholds to determine when escalation should occur based on the categorization/prioritization of the request or incident.
3. Implement the necessary support software and tools (e.g. incident management, knowledge management, incident escalation systems, automated call monitoring) required for operation of the service desk and configured in accordance with SLA requirements, to facilitate automated prioritization of incidents and rapid resolution.
4. Advise customers of the existence of the service desk and the standards of service they can expect. Obtain user feedback on a regular basis to ensure customer satisfaction, and confirm the effectiveness of the service desk operation.
5. Using the service desk software, create service desk performance reports to enable performance monitoring, and continuous improvement of the service desk.

Fig. 6.14 Control practices

objective. So based on the organizational context and the COBIT material provided, a set of control practices can be defined.

Once the control practices are defined for all the retained control objectives within the selected IT processes, the control framework is ready against which the assurance activities will be executed.

6.4.2 Templates for Testing

Figure 6.15 provides a template for testing the control design, at the level of a specific control objective (example DS8.1: service desk). Based on the control practices defined, assurance steps are developed based on professional judgment, and based on the assurance steps material is provided in the IT assurance guide. Required contact persons for interviewing (first column "contact person") are defined based on COBIT's RACI chart, and made organization specific (second column "contact person"). The assurance steps are then translated into a detailed and organization-specific assurance approach (column "design effectiveness approach"), describing exactly what needs to be done. After execution, findings and conclusions are recorded. An elaborated example of this approach is provided in Fig. 6.15.

Figure 6.16 provides a template, with examples, for testing control objectives outcomes for the COBIT IT process DS8.4: incident closure against (column 1),

Control Objective	Assurance steps	Contact person	Contact person	Design effectiveness approach	Design effectiveness findings	Design effectiveness conclusion
DS8.1 Service Desk	Is a service desk in place, which is the single point of contact with IT? In this service desk, all calls, reported incidents, service requests and information demands must be registered, communicated, dispatched and analysed.	Service desk manager Incident manager	Call center manager Contact center manager Open systems manager	1. Verify if a qualified service desk is in place, which acts as a single point of contact 2. Obtain the incident management procedure and validate if calls, reported incidents, service requests and information demands must be registered, communicated,	1. There is one number (505) know by all employees 2. Obtained the incident management procedures which include that all calls, reported incidents, service requests and information requests must be registered, communicated,	PASS
	Are monitoring and escalation procedures available, based on agreed service levels, that allow classification and prioritisation of any reported issue as an incident, service request or information request?	Service desk manager Incident manager	Call center manager Contact center manager Open systems manager	1. Obtain the incident management procedure and validate if the monitoring and escalation procedures are included that allow the classification of calls	1. All reported incidents are scaled from 1–6 (6 = low) based on two parameters: persons impacted & urgency. An SLA is in place and defines a resolution time for each reported incident. The priority of the incident increases if the incident remains in an "open" status.	PASS
	Are procedures in place to measure end users' satisfaction with the quality of the service desk and IT services	Service desk manager Incident manager	Call center manager Contact center manager Open systems manager	1. Obtain the procedures in which the users' satisfaction is measured.	1. No monitoring process in place that focusses on the service desk. A yearly questionnaire is sent to all employees oto measure employees' satisfaction.	FAIL

Fig. 6.15 Templates for testing control design
IT Assurance Guide, 2007b, online available at www.itgi.org.

	Control Objective	Assurance steps	Contact person	Contact person	Operating effectiveness approach	Operating effectiveness findings	Operating effectiveness conclusion
DS8.4 Incident closure	Are procedures for timely monitoring of clearance of customer queries in place (closing incident)?	Service desk manager Incident manager	Call center manager Contact center manager Open systems manager	1. Select a number of closed incidents (based on frequency) and verify if is has been closed within the timeframe listed in the procedure.	1. 25 tickets selected at random and verified that the tickets were closed after the resolution time indicated in the SLA. 2 tickets were not closed in the timeframe defined. However, the monitoring report for the month is within the defined exception rates (exception noted: 2/25)	EFFECTIVE
	Is for every resolved incident the root cause (if known) document?	Service desk manager Incident manager	Call center manager Contact center manager Open systems manager	1. Select a number of closed incidents (based on frequency) and verify that the root cause of the incident has been documented	1. 25 tickets selected at random and verified that the tickets indicated the resolution. 15 tickets stated "setting changed" and 10 tickets indicated the details of the resolution (Exceptions noted 15/25)	NOT EFFECTIVE
	Has every action taken been agreed with the customer?	Service desk manager Incident manager	Call center manager Contact center manager Open systems manager	1. Select a number of closed incidents (based on frequency) and verify that the action taken has been agreed upon with the customer	1. 25 tickets selected at random and verified that the tickets indicated the contact with the initiator for closing. Not the case for 17 tickets. (Exceptions noted 17/25)	NOT EFFECTIVE

Fig. 6.16 Templates for testing control objective outcomes
IT Assurance Guide, 2007b, online available at www.itgi.org.

assurance steps are developed and cross-checked against the IT Assurance Guide (column 2), supplemented with RACI chart information (columns 3 and 4) and then translated into a specific operating effectiveness approach (column 5), findings (column 6) and conclusions (column 7).

Figure 6.17 finally provides an example template on how control weaknesses can be reported, providing a short description of the control weakness and how it

FINDINGS	
Description	**Detection**
DS8.1: There is no monitoring process in place that focuses on the quality of the service desk and the end-users' satisfaction	Testing
RISK	
Description	**Classification**
IT management is not informed on how the business perceives the service desk in particular and the IT department in general. The lack of information can cause a disconnect between business and IT (i.e. no perception of added value by IT). Is also prevent the implementation of an effective continuous improvement process.	High
RECOMMENDATION	
Description	**Priority**
Organize regular user satisfaction surveys via the different available media (intranet, phone,...) and use this information to compare the responses of the satisfied users with the dissatisfied users. This information can also be used to enable continous improvement.	1

Fig. 6.17 Templates for testing impact of control weaknesses
IT Assurance Guide, 2007b, online available at www.itgi.org.

was detected (findings), clarifying the business risk and its classification, ultimately leading to prioritized recommendation.

Assignment Box 6.1: Developing an IT assurance program

Develop assurance steps for testing control design and testing control objective outcomes for COBIT IT Process "Manage third-party services," leveraging the templates provided in this chapter.

Confront your results with the material in the IT Assurance Guide and the IT Control Practices (both publications can be downloaded at minimal cost accessing ISACA's website www.isaca.org).

Assignment Box 6.2: Case study

Case background

Delta Lighting Design (DLD), founded in 1989, creates and assembles high-quality lighting products. The major goal of the company is to develop lighting products that are unique in concept and that appeal to a broad audience. Major processes within DLD are product design and development, procurement and ordering of components, assembling and sales. DLD recently developed a strategic road map to align its IT with its overall business strategy with the help of a local consulting firm. DLD needed to align its IT infrastructure, processes and applications with its strategic goals. The company knew that to compete more effectively, it would have to improve its customer focus and supply chain efficiency and support these areas with transparent IT solutions, compliant with the company's strategic IT vision. The company's main goals in undertaking a transformation of its IT infrastructure and processes were to support the creation of a comprehensive business, achieve profitable growth, reduce costs and improve customer focus and supply chain efficiency. With this clear vision of where it needed to go, DLD sought a consulting partner with expertise in the assembling industry to develop the business case for implementing new IT infrastructure and processes, including recommendations for new major IT application installations and integration across its functional areas.

The consultancy firm teamed with DLD to deliver the company's IT strategy plan, including the business case for required investments. The team used the consultant's proprietary methodology to evaluate DLD's strategic IT processes. The resulting road map aligns the company's IT strategy with its larger business goals and addresses the business requirements and issues. The actual implementations of recommended IT solutions will be completed during the next 2 years, delivering a solid return on investment (ROI) once the implementation is completed. The most important part of the solution was the implementation of an enterprise resource planning (ERP) system. The common ERP system is the key to DLD's cost reductions and profitable growth through the integration of production, supply and customer service. It is expected that through this ERP implementation, a better fusion between IT and business will be achieved, enabling a more efficient supply chain and improved logistics for purchasing and distribution. Further, DLD expects increased assembling efficiency by a more optimal labor utilization, purchase price reduction, significant cost reduction through consolidation into one IT platform, reduced application development time and more efficient finance and administration through integrated business processes.

Case questions

Answer questions 1 and 2 as the CIO of DLD. Answer questions 3 and 4 as the auditor for DLD:

1. Identify which COBIT processes and control objectives are relevant to handle the process of defining and implementing the IT strategy defined in the case. This can be done by assessing *COBIT 4.1* at ISACA's website, www.isaca.org/cobit and listing the processes and control objectives that you think might improve the IT/business strategic processes within DLD. Be prepared to justify your selection of the relevant processes and control objectives.
2. The case description contains concrete business goals that must be supported by IT. Use the charts titled Linking Business Goals to IT Goals and Linking IT Goals to IT Processes in Appendix I of *COBIT 4*.1 to translate DLD's business goals into relevant IT goals and IT processes. Be prepared to justify your selection of the relevant IT goals and IT processes.
3. You are confronted in this case with the IT strategy process. Identify which of the PO1 *Define a strategic IT plan* and AI1 *Identify automated solutions* COBIT control objectives are most appropriate to consider in designing an audit plan, and justify your selection of the relevant control objectives.
4. The solution was to bring in an ERP package. Identify which of the AI2 *Acquire and maintain application software* and AI5 *Procure IT resources* COBIT control objectives are most appropriate to consider in designing an audit plan, and justify your selection of the relevant control objectives.

IT Governance using COBIT and Val IT, caselets, 2nd Edition. Available on www.isaca.org (We refer to this publication for other caselets on IT Governance and IT Assurance).

Summary

COBIT is a powerful framework to implement Enterprise Governance of IT. However, COBIT also provides in-depth support to execute IT assurance assignments. To support this, COBIT's IT Assurance Guide offers two elements.

- A detailed roadmap showing how typical IT assurance activities can be planned (IT assurance planning), scoped (IT assurance scoping) and executed (IT assurance execution) based on COBIT
- Detailed guidance in the IT assurance execution domain providing specific steps to test the control design, test the outcome of the control objectives and test the impact of control weaknesses, based on COBIT

The IT Assurance execution steps mainly address the core testing activities that the assurance professional executes. The IT Assurance Guide provides detailed material to the assurance professional helping him to test control design, test the outcome of control objectives and test the impact of control weaknesses. Important to recognize is that the IT assurance materials provided are developed as a kind of library of potential assurance steps to be done, based on COBIT. This implies that these assurance steps give excellent material to create detailed assurance plans and programs, but it is still up to the assurance professional to apply professional judgment in selecting and adapting the relevant material out of the assurance guidance provided.

To execute IT assurance activities in practice, templates can be very helpful in supporting the assurance execution. These templates can be simple in nature, and as an illustration, some examples were provided in this chapter. Other COBIT components such as inputs/outputs, RACI charts, goals and metrics, control practices can also be helpful in supporting the IT assurance activities.

Study Questions

1. Discuss the difference between IT audit and IT assurance.
2. Explain the relationship between the COBIT Framework, the IT Control Practices and the IT Assurance Guide.
3. Explain and illustrate value-based scoping for IT assurance.
4. Explain and illustrate risk-based scoping for IT assurance.
5. Explain and illustrate how the process maturity models can be helpful in scoping for IT assurance.
6. Expedience, sustainability, effectiveness and cost are attributes in evaluating and comparing control objectives within an IT process. Explain and illustrate.
7. Explain the three main phases – planning, scoping and execution – of the IT Assurance Roadmap.
8. Explain and discuss the three core testing activities – testing control design, testing outcome of the control objective and testing impact of control weaknesses – to be executed by the IT Assurance Professional.
9. Explain how inputs/outputs, RACI charts and goals & metrics can be helpful in executing IT assurance activities.
10. In reporting on control weaknesses the assurance professional should focus on business risk issues. Explain and illustrate.

Further Reading

IT Governance using COBIT and VAL IT, caselets, 2nd Edition, from www.isaca.org
ITGI, 2007a, COBIT 4.1, from www.itgi.org
ITGI, 2007b, IT Assurance Guide, from www.itgi.org
Van Grembergen, W. (Ed.), 2004, Strategies for Information Technology Governance. Hershey, PA: Idea Group Publishing.
Van Grembergen, W., and De Haes, S., 2008, Implementing Information Technology Governance: Models, Practices and Cases, IGI Publishing

Websites

Information Technology Alignment and Governance Research Institute: www.uams.be/ITAG
ISACA: www.isaca.org
IT Governance Institute: www.itgi.org
The Institute of Internal Auditors: www.theiia.org

Chapter 7
Val IT as a Framework for Enterprise Governance of IT

Abstract Val IT is a relatively new framework issued by the IT Governance Institute, which mainly focuses on the business responsibilities in IT value creation. This framework starts from the premise that value creation out of IT investments is a business responsibility in the first place. To support business people in organizing and developing these responsibilities, Val IT presents a set of IT-related business processes and associated key management practices, management guidelines and maturity models. Val IT is complementary to COBIT and follows the same structure and templates as provided in the COBIT manuals.

7.1 Introduction

The first edition of Val IT was released in 2006 by the IT Governance Institute, as a complementary framework to COBIT (see previous Chapters 5 and 6). Main premise was that, in order to create business value from IT, not only IT but even more the business had to take up its responsibility. In the COBIT evolution, these business responsibilities were gradually incorporated in its COBIT IT processes. However, COBIT still focuses in the first place on IT processes, which are owned by the IT department. With the emergence of Val IT, the IT Governance Institute wanted to emphasize more on the business responsibilities in IT value creation, by defining a set of IT-related business processes. These business processes, and associated management practices, are required to ensure that the business takes ownership for business value creation from IT and are of course very closely related and intertwined with COBIT's IT processes.

In 2008, a new version of Val IT was released, Val IT 2.0. This new edition defines 22 IT-related business processes. Also, the strong link and integration with COBIT is stressed by embracing COBIT's structure and templates. Major benefits of the latter is that people who are familiar with COBIT's concepts and structure, fairly easily will understand Val IT's structure as well. This structural alignment is illustrated in the definition of Val IT 2.0: "Val IT supports the enterprise goal of creating optimal value from IT-enabled investments at an affordable cost, with an acceptable level of risk. As such, Val IT is guided by a

W. Van Grembergen, S. De Haes, *Enterprise Governance of Information Technology*, DOI 10.1007/978-0-387-84882-2_7,

set of principles applied in value management processes that are enabled by key management practices and are measured by performance against goals and metrics" (ITGI, 2008).

It should be acknowledged that, while Val IT addresses IT-related business responsibilities, the likelihood of the business automatically accepting and adopting this framework could be rather low. Because of IT's history in process-oriented thinking and designing, and automating business processes, we believe that IT is in a unique position to guide the business in adopting Val IT-based practices and in this way crafting a more value creating organization, levering IT.

7.2 Principles and Definitions of Val IT

The Val IT processes are built around a set of core principles and definitions. These principles and definitions are discussed in the following sections (the Val IT framework is freely available via ITGI's website www.itgi.org).

7.2.1 Principles of Value Creation

Val IT is built around a set of fundamental principles for IT value creation, as shown in Fig. 7.1.

In the first place, Val IT does not talk about IT projects but only about IT-enabled investments. This stresses the point that there are no pure "IT projects" (except for, e.g., IT infrastructure projects, etc.), but only business projects in many cases, with a large IT component. These IT-enabled investments should be managed as a portfolio of investments, implying that the organizations should compare and evaluate individual investments across the whole portfolio of investments in the organization (also non-IT-related investments). To be able to compare individual investments, the business cases should include the full

IT-enabled investments will:

- Be managed as a portfolio of investments
- Include the full scope of activities required to achieve business value
- Be managed through their full economic life cycle

Value-delivery practices will:

- Recognize there are different categories of investments that will be evaluated and managed differently
- Define and monitor key metrics and respond quickly to any changes or deviations
- Engage all stakeholders and assign appropriate accountability for the delivery of capabilities and the realization of business benefits
- Be continually monitored, evaluated and improved

Fig. 7.1 Val IT principles
ITGI, 2008, Val IT 2, on-line available at www.itgi.org.

scope of activities required to achieve business value. This statement refers back to the premise that IT in itself will not create business value. For example, the successful delivery of a new CRM application, in time, budget and functionality, will not create business value. Business value will only be created when the marketing and sales people are using the CRM application to increase sales and profit. Therefore, the IT projects, delivering a technical capability, should be supplemented with the business projects and processes such as training, the definition of new business processes, change management, etc. Finally, IT-related investment should be managed throughout the entire life cycle. Main issue here is that, when developing a business case, it should address not only the costs incurred by the initial investments, but also costs during the operational stages of the investment. Indeed, it is important to have a transparent view of all operational costs throughout the full life cycle, as it can far outweigh the cost of the initial investment in the business case.

To achieve all of the above, the organization needs to apply a set of value management practices. These practices should recognize that there are different categories of investments that will be evaluated and managed differently. This implies that the business has to clarify what type of investments the organization can make (e.g., strategic investments, management information investment, transactional investments and infrastructure investments) and what the criteria are to evaluate each type of investment. The value management practices should also address the definitions and monitoring of key metrics for each investment and the definition and acceptance of all accountabilities (both business and IT) in the delivery of business benefits out of investments. Finally, all value management practices should be continuously monitored and evaluated, and improved where necessary.

7.2.2 Definitions of Projects, Programmes and Portfolios

Organizations in the field have different interpretations regarding what is meant by a "project," a "programme" and a "portfolio." The developers of Val IT recognize this diversity in interpretations. However, to be able to develop the Val IT process framework on a consistent basis, a specific Val IT terminology is put forward and defined. Organization can of course continue to use their own terminology, but it is important to understand that Val IT used the below definitions in developing the Val IT framework (see Fig. 7.2).

A project is a structured set of activities concerned with the delivery of a defined technical capability based on an agreed schedule and budget. Projects are defined at the level of the delivery of IT applications and solutions, such as a CRM application or a new website, which are necessary but not sufficient to achieve a required business outcome. A programme is a structured grouping of projects that are both necessary and sufficient to achieve a business outcome and deliver value. A programme therefore is the combination of the "IT project" and

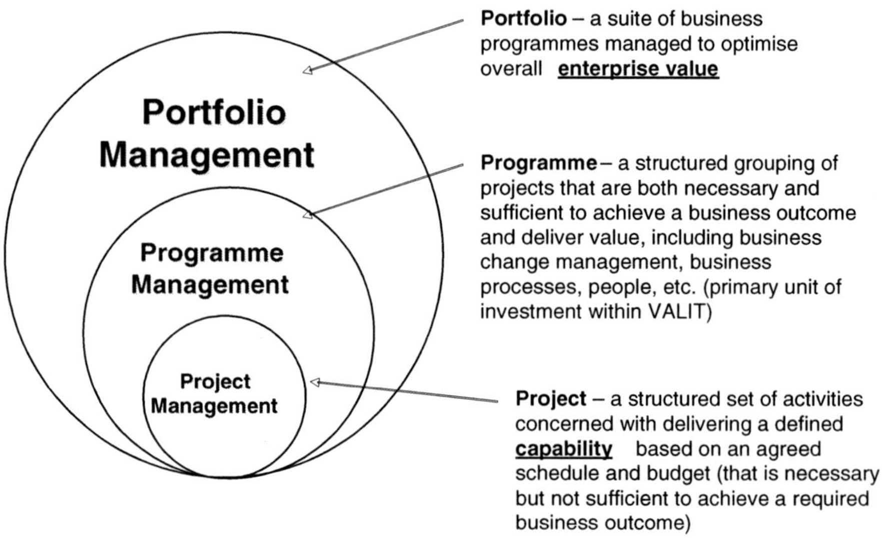

Fig. 7.2 Project, programmes and portfolios
ITGI, 2008, Val IT 2, on-line available at www.itgi.org.

all other business-related projects such as defining new business processes, providing training, managing change, etc. Finally, the suite of investment programmes, including also those with no IT involvement, is to be managed as a portfolio in order to optimize to total value creation for the organization.

7.3 Val IT Processes and their Key Management Practices

Starting from the above-mentioned principles and definitions, a set of 22 IT-related business processes is presented. These business processes are required to realize business value out of IT-enabled investments (Fig. 7.3).

The 22 processes are categorized into three domains: value governance (VG), portfolio management (PM) and investment management (IM). Each domain covers a set of IT-related business processes, each process having an index number starting with the VG for Value Governance, PM for Portfolio Management and IM for Investment Management.

Value governance addresses the structures and processes required to ensure that value management practices are embedded in the organization. Value governance deals amongst others with the engagement of the leadership (VG1), the definition and implementation of value management practices (VG2) and the integration of the latter into the organization's financial management processes (VG4). It also address the fact that portfolio types and criteria need to be defined by the business (VG3), that effective governance monitoring

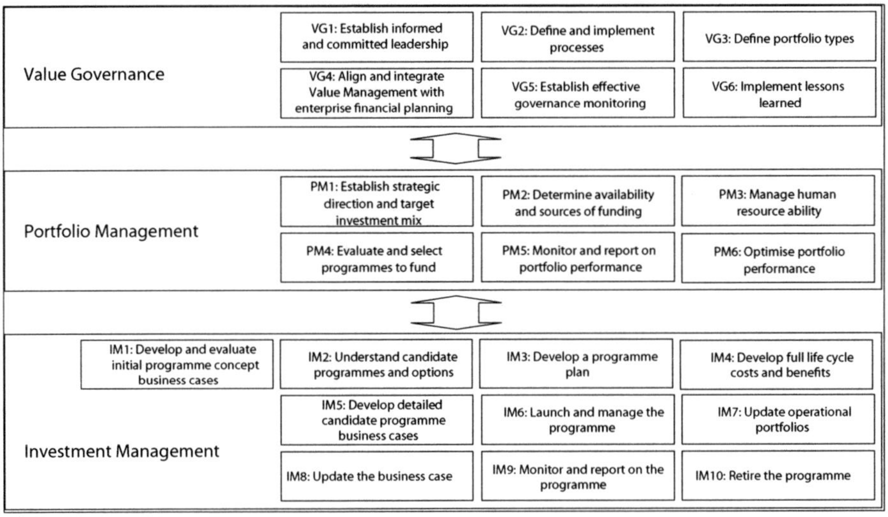

Fig. 7.3 Val IT domains and processes
ITGI, 2008, Val IT 2, on-line available at www.itgi.org.

should be established over the value management practices (VG5) and that there should be a continuous improvement cycle through implementing lessons learned (VG6). It is clear that these processes are defined at a higher level in Val IT and encompass "necessary conditions" to enable a value-based approach in portfolio and investment management.

Portfolio management addresses the processes required to manage the whole portfolio of IT-enabled investments. This domain starts with stating that the strategic direction of the organization should be clarified and that the target portfolio mix should be defined (PM1). Also, the available resources in terms of funding (PM2) and human resources (PM3) need to be inventoried. Based on detailed business cases arising from the investment management processes (see next paragraph, processes IM1–IM5), investment programmes are selected and moved into the active portfolio (PM4). The performance of this active portfolio needs to be continuously monitored and reported upon (PM5) and optimized (PM6), based on performance reports coming out of the investment management processes (see next paragraph).

The processes in the Investment Management domain is situated at the level of one single IT-enabled investment. The first five processes in investment management are about the emergence of new investment opportunities in the organization (IM1) and the development of detailed business cases (IM5) for the approved opportunities, including analyses of alternative courses (IM2) of actions, definition of a detailed programme plan (IM3) and full cost/benefits analysis (IM4). After approval of detailed business cases (PM4, see previous paragraph), investment programmes need to be launched (IM6), monitored

(IM8) and if required, business cases need to be updated (IM9). All investment programmes need to be retired (IM10), bringing programmes to an orderly closure when there is agreement that the desired business value has been achieved or when it is clear it will not be achieved. Also, changes to operational IT portfolios as a result of the investment programme need to be incorporated in the portfolios of IT services, assets or resources (IM7).

Each of these 22 processes is clearly defined and specified into more detailed key management practices (in COBIT terms: the control objectives). An example is provided in Fig. 7.4, for IM1 – *develop and evaluate an initial programme concept business case*. This process is about recognizing investment opportunities, making small initial business cases for them and, based on that, select those investments that are interesting for further detailed business case development.

IM1 Develop and evaluate an initial programme concept business case

Recognize investment opportunities, classify each with respect to the investment portfolio categories, and identify a business sponsor. Clarify expected business outcome(s), provide a high-level view of all initiatives required to achieve the expected outcomes, and how they would be measured. Provide an initial, high-level estimate of benefits and costs as well as the key assumptions and major risks, and obtain the appropriate sign-offs. Determine whether the opportunity merits further work to support development of a detailed business case, considering strategic alignment, benefits and expenditures, resource constraints, risks and fit with the overall investment portfolio.

IM1.1 Recognize investment opportunities

Recognize investment opportunities to create value in support of the business strategy and to address operational and compliance issues. Classify each opportunity with respect to the investment portfolio categories. Clarify expected business outcome(s) and identify, at a high level, business, process, people, technology, and organizational initiatives required to achieve the expected outcomes. These requirements must be owned by business managers acting as business sponsors for the overall opportunity, including the necessary IT projects.

IM1.2 Develop initial programme concept business case

Develop the initial programme concept business case to describe the business outcome(s) to which the potential programme will contribute, the nature of the programme's contribution, and how that contribution would be measured. High-level benefits, both financial and non-financial, and expenditures for the full economic life cycle of the programme should be estimated. Key assumptions should be stated and key risks should be identified, along with their potential impact and mitigation strategies.

IM1.3 Evaluate the initial programme concept business cases

Perform an initial triage of the programme concept business cases looking at strategic alignment; benefits, both financial and non-financial; expenditures required; resources needed and contention for them; risks; and fit with the overall investment portfolio. Determine whether the programme concept has sufficient potential to justify proceeding to full programme definition and evaluation. If the decision is to proceed, the CIO should sign off on the technical aspects of the programme, and the business sponsor should approve and sign off on the initial programme concept business case.

Fig. 7.4 Val IT IM1 process and its key management practices
ITGI, 2008, Val IT 2, on-line available at www.itgi.org.

7.4 Val IT Management Guidelines

The management guidelines in Val IT deliver more information for implementing, organizing and measuring specific Val IT processes. Similar to COBIT, the management guidelines are summarized on one page (see Fig. 7.5 for example IM1 – *develop and evaluate the initial programme concept business case*), comprising for each Val IT process:

- the relationship with other Val IT processes, by means of inputs and outputs,
- an overview of important process tasks, including related roles and responsibilities (RACI chart),
- goals and metrics on Val IT domain (value governance, portfolio management, investment management) level, Val IT process level and Val IT activity level.

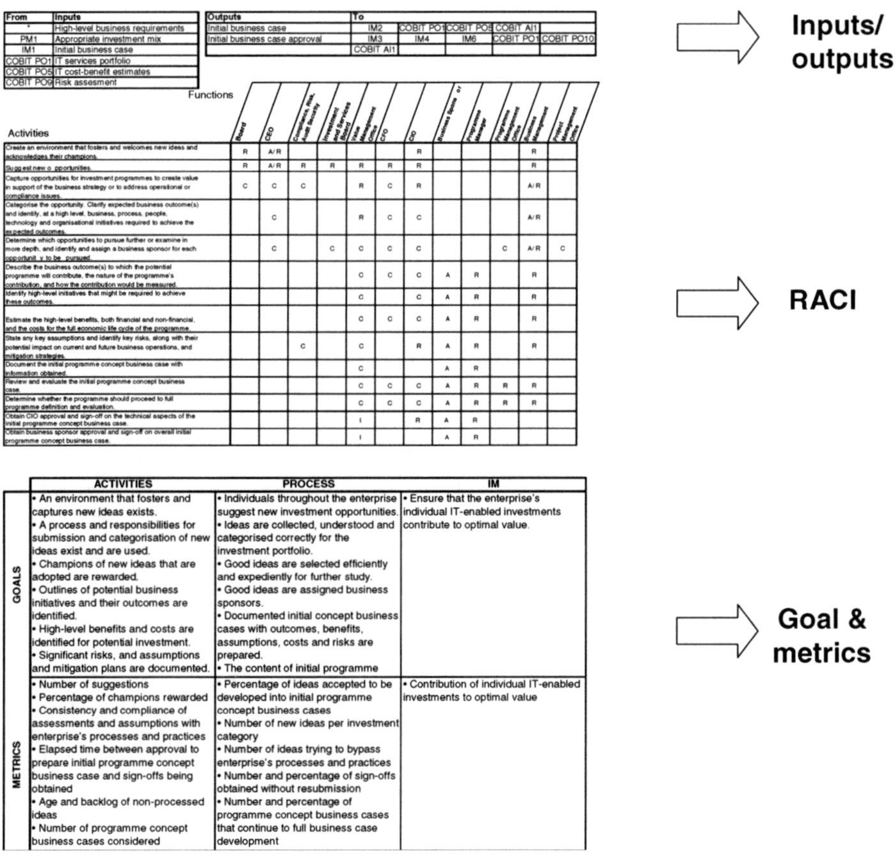

From	Inputs
*	High-level business requirements
PM1	Appropriate investment mix
IM1	Initial business case
COBIT PO1	IT services portfolio
COBIT PO5	IT cost-benefit estimates
COBIT PO9	Risk assesment

Outputs	To				
Initial business case	IM2	COBIT PO1	COBIT PO5	COBIT AI1	
Initial business case approval	IM3	IM4	IM6	COBIT PO1	COBIT PO10
	COBIT AI1				

Activities \ Functions	Board	CEO	Compliance, Risk, Audit Security	Investment and Services Board	Value Management Office	CFO	CIO	Business Sponsor	Programme Manager	Programme Management Office	Business Management	Project Management Office
Create an environment that fosters and welcomes new ideas and acknowledges their champions.	R	A/R					R				R	
Suggest new opportunities.	R	A/R	R	R	R	R	R				R	
Capture opportunities for investment programmes to create value in support of the business strategy or to address operational or compliance issues.	C	C	C		R	C	R				A/R	
Categorise the opportunity. Clarify expected business outcome(s) and identify, at a high level, business, process, people, technology and organisational initiatives required to achieve the expected outcomes.		C			R	C	C				A/R	
Determine which opportunities to pursue further or examine in more depth, and identify and assign a business sponsor for each opportunity to be pursued.		C		C	C	C	C			C	A/R	C
Describe the business outcome(s) to which the potential programme will contribute, the nature of the programme's contribution, and how the contribution would be measured.					C	C	C	A	R		R	
Identify high-level initiatives that might be required to achieve these outcomes.					C		C	A	R		R	
Estimate the high-level benefits, both financial and non-financial, and the costs for the full economic life cycle of the programme.					C	C	C	A	R		R	
State any key assumptions and identify key risks, along with their potential impact on current and future business operations, and mitigation strategies.			C		C		R	A	R		R	
Document the initial programme concept business case with information obtained.					C			A	R			
Review and evaluate the initial programme concept business case.					C	C	C	A	R	R	R	
Determine whether the programme should proceed to full programme definition and evaluation.					C	C	C	A	R	R	R	
Obtain CIO approval and sign-off on the technical aspects of the initial programme concept business case.					I		R	A	R			
Obtain business sponsor approval and sign-off on overall initial programme concept business case.					I			A	R			

	ACTIVITIES	PROCESS	IM
GOALS	• An environment that fosters and captures new ideas exists. • A process and responsibilities for submission and categorisation of new ideas exist and are used. • Champions of new ideas that are adopted are rewarded. • Outlines of potential business initiatives and their outcomes are identified. • High-level benefits and costs are identified for potential investment. • Significant risks, and assumptions and mitigation plans are documented.	• Individuals throughout the enterprise suggest new investment opportunities. • Ideas are collected, understood and categorised correctly for the investment portfolio. • Good ideas are selected efficiently and expediently for further study. • Good ideas are assigned business sponsors. • Documented initial concept business cases with outcomes, benefits, assumptions, costs and risks are prepared. • The content of initial programme	• Ensure that the enterprise's individual IT-enabled investments contribute to optimal value.
METRICS	• Number of suggestions • Percentage of champions rewarded • Consistency and compliance of assessments and assumptions with enterprise's processes and practices • Elapsed time between approval to prepare initial programme concept business case and sign-offs being obtained • Age and backlog of non-processed ideas • Number of programme concept business cases considered	• Percentage of ideas accepted to be developed into initial programme concept business cases • Number of new ideas per investment category • Number of ideas trying to bypass enterprise's processes and practices • Number and percentage of sign-offs obtained without resubmission • Number and percentage of programme concept business cases that continue to full business case development	• Contribution of individual IT-enabled investments to optimal value

Fig. 7.5 Val IT management guidelines
ITGI, 2008, Val IT 2, on-line available at www.itgi.org.

7.4.1 *Inputs/Outputs*

For each process, Val IT defines a list of inputs that the process should receive from other processes and a list of possible outputs to send to other processes. Also, inputs/outputs outside Val IT to/from business processes and to/from COBIT are addressed. For example process IM1 – *develop and evaluate an initial programme concept business case* (Fig. 7.6) should receive high-level business requirements for the business, the appropriate investment mix from PM1 – *establish strategic direction IT* and cost/benefits estimates from COBIT process PO5 – *manage the IT investment*. The process IM1 itself should send initial business cases and its approvals to several other processes in Val IT (IM2 – *understand candidate programmes and implementation options*, IM3 – *develop the programme plan*, IM4 – *develop full life cycle costs and benefits*, IM6 – *launch and manage the programme*) and COBIT processes (PO1 – *define a strategic IT plan*, PO5 – *manage the IT investment*, PO10 – *manage projects* and AI1 – *identify automated solutions*).

From	Inputs
*	High-level business requirements
PM1	Appropriate investment mix
IM1	Initial business case
COBIT PO1	IT services portfolio
COBIT PO5	IT cost-benefit estimates
COBIT PO9	Risk assesment

Outputs	To				
Initial business case	IM2	COBIT PO1	COBIT PO5	COBIT AI1	
Initial business case approval	IM3	IM4	IM6	COBIT PO1	COBIT PO10
	COBIT AI1				

Fig. 7.6 Input/outputs for the IM1 process – develop and evaluate an initial programme concept business case
ITGI, 2008, Val IT 2.0, on-line available at www.itgi.org.

Assignment Box 7.1: Define inputs and outputs

Access the Val IT publication on the ITGI website www.itgi.org and discuss the key management practices of PM4: evaluate and select programmes to fund. Afterward, determine the inputs from other Val IT processes and outputs to other Val IT processes for PM4 and compare your solution to the one in the management guidelines of this process. Evaluate also the inputs from and outputs to the COBIT IT processes.

7.4.2 *RACI Diagram*

Val IT defines for each process a RACI diagram, where the role and responsibilities related to important process activities are identified. RACI stands for

- *Responsible*: who is responsible for the activity
- *Accountable*: who is accountable for the activity, meaning who provides direction and authorizes the activity (is typically hierarchically higher than *responsible*)
- *Consulted*: who should be consulted for the activity
- *Informed*: who must be informed about the activity

Each Val IT process is subdivided into a set of activities, which are derived from the key management practices (see previous section). Next, for each activity, it is indicated who in the organization, i.e., which role, should be accountable, responsible, consulted and informed. Val IT uses a different set of roles compared to COBIT (see Chapter 5): COBIT addresses mainly IT roles, while Val IT mainly focuses on business roles. This again stresses Val IT's focus on the business involvement in value creation. There is only one IT role included in the RACI chart, more specifically the CIO. Everything delegated to the CIO will be handled in more detail in COBIT. The definition of the roles used in Val IT's RACI chart is provided in Fig. 7.7. An interesting new role being promoted

Role	Suggested definition
Board	The group of the most senior executives and/or non-executives of the enterprise, who are accountable for the governance of the enterprise and have overall control of its resources
Business sponsor (incl. service owner)	The individual accountable for delivering benefits and value to the enterprise from an IT-enabled business investment programme
Business unit executives/ managers	Business individuals with roles with respect to a programme
Compliance, audit, risk and security (CARS)	The function(s) in the enterprise responsible for compliance, audit, risk and security
Chief Executive Officer (CE0)	The highest ranking officer, who is in charge of the total management of the enterprise
Chief Financial Officer (CF0	The most senior official of the enterprise, who is accountable for financial planning, record keeping, investor relations and financial risks
Chief Information Officer (CIO)	The most senior official of the enterprise, who is accountable for IT advocacy; aligning IT and business strategies; and planning, resourcing and managing the delivery of IT services and information, and the deployment of associated human resources
Investment and services board (ISB)	A management structure primarily accountable for managing the enterprise's portfolio of investment programmes and existing/current services and, thus, managing the level of overall funding to provide the necessary balance between enterprise-wide and specific line-of-business needs
Head of Human Resources	The most senior official of an enterprise who is accountable for planning and policies with respect to all human resources in that enterprise
Programme Manager	The individual responsible for the achievement of the programme's objectives
Programme Management Office (PgMO)	The function responsible for supporting programme managers and gathering, assessing and reporting information about the conduct of their programmes and constituent projects
Project Management Office (PMO)	The function for supporting project managers; defining and propagating standardised methodologies; and gathering, assessing and reporting information about the conduct of their projects
Value Management Office (VMO)	The function that acts as the secretariat for the ISB in managing investment and service portfolios, including assessing and advising on investment opportunities and business cases, value governance/management methods and controls, and reporting on progress in sustaining and creating value from investments and services

Fig. 7.7 Roles in Val IT's RACI charts
ITGI, 2008, Val IT 2.0, on-line available at www.itgi.org.

here is the Value Management Office (VMO). The VMO is defined as the function that acts as the secretariat for the Investment and Services Board in managing investment and service portfolios, including assessing and advising on investment opportunities and business cases, value governance/management methods and controls, and reporting on progress sustaining and creating value from investments and services.

For the example Val IT process IM1, it seems that the main accountability for developing and evaluating initial business cases is assigned to the business sponsor, while new opportunities can be suggested across the enterprise (R's assigned to CEO, CFO, CIO and Business Management) (Fig. 7.8).

Assignment Box 7.2: Define roles and responsibilities

Access the Val IT publication on the ITGI website www.itgi.org and discuss the key management practices of VG5: establish effective governance monitoring. Afterward, define the main responsibilities and accountabilities for VG5 and compare your solution with the VG5's RACI chart.

7.4.3 Goals and Metrics

For each of the 22 IT-related business processes, Val IT defines goals on three levels (see Fig. 7.9):

- Val IT domain level: these are goals defined at the level of the domain of value governance, portfolio management and investment management
- Val IT process level: these are goals at the level on one individual Val IT process
- Val IT activity level: these are goals of activities within the Val IT process

Clearly, achieving activity goals must support the achievement of process goals, which in turn must support the achievement of Val IT goals. This is again an application of the cause-and-effect relationship cascade as is used in COBIT.

In order to monitor all these goals, metrics are defined for each of them (Fig. 7.9). It is important to note there are two distinct metrics: key goal indicators and key performance indicators.

Key goal indicators (outcome measures in balanced scorecard terminology) are known as lag indicators and they measure the achievement of the defined goals. Three levels of key goal indicators (KGIs) are known within Val IT: KGIs for measuring the Val IT domain goals, KGIs for measuring the Val IT process goals and KGIs for measuring Val IT process activity goals. As an example, for Val IT process IM1 – *develop and evaluate initial programme concept business case* (see Fig. 7.10) one of the Val IT process goals is defined as "Individuals throughout the enterprise suggest new investment opportunities" and a possible KGI to measure this Val IT process goal is "Number of new ideas per investment category."

Key performance indicators (key performance drivers in the balanced scorecard terminology – see Chapter 4) are known as lead indicators and measure the effectiveness of the process execution. The key performance indictors (KPIs)

Activities / Functions	Board	CEO	Compliance, Risi k, Audt Security	Investment and Services Board	Value Management Office	CFO	CIO	Business Sponsor	Programme Manager	Programme Management Office	Business Management	Project Management Office
Create an environment that fosters and welcomes new ideas and acknowledges their champions.	R	A/R					R				R	
Suggest new opportunities.	R	A/R	R	R	R	R	R				R	
Capture opportunities for investment programmes to create value in support of the business strategy or to address operational or compliance issues.	C	C	C		R	C	R				A/R	
Categorise the opportunity. Clarify expected business outcome(s) and identify, at a high level, business, process, people, technology and organisational initiatives required to achieve the expected outcomes.		C			R	C	C				A/R	
Determine which opportunities to pursue further or examine in more depth, and identify and assign a business sponsor for each opportunity to be pursued.		C		C	C	C	C			C	A/R	C
Describe the business outcome(s) to which the potential programme will contribute, the nature of the programme's contribution,and how the contribution would be measured.					C	C	C	A	R		R	
Identify high-level initiatives that might be required to achieve these outcomes.					C		C	A	R		R	
Estimate the high-level benefits, both financial and non-financial, and the costs for the full economic life cycle of the programme.					C	C	C	A	R		R	
State any key assumptions and identify key risks, along with their potential impact on current and future business operations, and mitigation strategies.			C		C		R	A	R		R	
Document the initial programme concept business case with information obtained.					C			A	R			
Review and evaluate the initial programme concept business case.					C	C	C	A	R	R	R	
Determine whether the programme should proceed to full programme definition and evaluation.					C	C	C	A	R	R	R	
Obtain CIO approval and sign-off on the technical aspects of the initial programme concept business case.					I		R	A	R			
Obtain business sponsor approval and sign-off on overall initial programme concept business case.					I			A	R			

Fig. 7.8 Roles and responsibilities (RACI diagram) IM1 process – develop and evaluate initial business case ITGI, 2008, Val IT 2.0, on-line available at www.itgi.org.

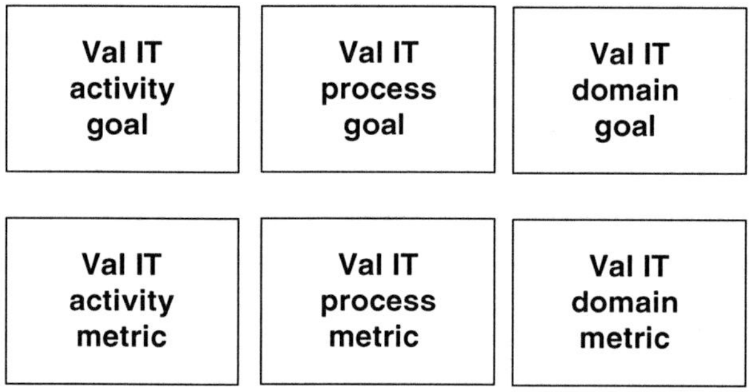

Fig. 7.9 Val IT goals and metrics

define measures that determine how well the process is performing in enabling the goal to be reached. This means there is an important causal relationship between KGIs and KPIs. In the previous example the KGI "Number of new ideas per investment category" was identified on Val IT process level for the Val IT process goal "Individuals throughout the enterprise suggest new investment opportunities." In order to reach this goal, several Val IT process activity goals must be executed, such as "Environment that fosters and captures new ideas exists" (Fig. 7.10). This Val IT process activity goal can be measured by a KGI on the Val IT process activity level, which also represents a KPI on the Val IT process level,

	ACTIVITIES	PROCESS	IM
GOALS	• An environment that fosters and captures new ideas exists. • A process and responsibilities for submission and categorisation of new ideas exist and are used. • Champions of new ideas that are adopted are rewarded. • Outlines of potential business initiatives and their outcomes are identified. • High-level benefits and costs are identified for potential investment. • Significant risks, and assumptions and mitigation plans are documented.	• Individuals throughout the enterprise suggest new investment opportunities. • Ideas are collected, understood and categorised correctly for the investment portfolio. • Good ideas are selected efficiently and expediently for further study. • Good ideas are assigned business sponsors. • Documented initial concept business cases with outcomes, benefits, assumptions, costs and risks are prepared. • The content of initial programme	• Ensure that the enterprise's individual IT-enabled investments contribute to optimal value.
METRICS	• Number of suggestions • Percentage of champions rewarded • Consistency and compliance of assessments and assumptions with enterprise's processes and practices • Elapsed time between approval to prepare initial programme concept business case and sign-offs being obtained • Age and backlog of non-processed ideas • Number of programme concept business cases considered	• Percentage of ideas accepted to be developed into initial programme concept business cases • Number of new ideas per investment category • Number of ideas trying to bypass enterprise's processes and practices • Number and percentage of sign-offs obtained without resubmission • Number and percentage of programme concept business cases that continue to full business case development	• Contribution of individual IT-enabled investments to optimal value

Fig. 7.10 Goals and metrics for the process IM1 – develop and evaluate initial programme concept business case
ITGI, 2008, Val IT 2.0, on-line available at www.itgi.org.

such as "Percentage of champions rewarded." It is assumed that a higher score for this metric implicates a better indication for reaching the process goal.

It is important to note that a KGI on one level becomes a KPI on a higher level. For example, on Val IT process level "Number of new ideas per investment category" was defined as KGI for the Val IT process goal of "Individuals throughout the enterprise suggest new investment opportunities." This KGI at Val IT process level is of course an important enabler for the goals at the level of the Val IT domain goals, and as such becomes a KPI for that level. For example, if there is a higher "number of new ideas per investment category," the likelihood increases for achieving the Val IT domain goal of "Ensuring the enterprise's IT-enabled investments contribute to optimal value."

Assignment Box 7.3: Define goals and metrics

Access the Val IT publication on the ITGI website www.itgi.org and discuss the key management practices of IM4: develop full life cycle costs and benefits. Afterward, define two metrics for each level of the IM4 process and compare your solution with the IM4 goals and metrics chart.

7.5 Val IT Maturity Models

A maturity model can be seen as a scoring technique for organizations to assess the maturity level of a specific process between 0 (not existent) and 5 (optimized). This instrument offers a comprehensible method for identifying and comparing the current (as-is) situation against the desirable (to-be) situation. Additionally, the organization can compare its situation against industry-specific best practices and standards. Gaps between the "as-is" and the "to-be" situation can be identified and specific actions to evolve toward the desirable situation can be set up. Whenever the maturity level of a process is being analyzed, it is important to apply the base principles of a maturity measurement: an organization can only evolve to a next maturity level, whenever all the criteria of that level are fulfilled.

Val IT provides two types of maturity models, each time developed at the level of the Val IT domains value governance, portfolio management and investment management (in contrast with COBIT, where maturity models are developed for each of the individual 34 processes (cf. Chapter 5)). In the first place, a maturity model is provided by defining in short paragraphs each of the maturity levels for a specific Val IT domain. The example for Value Governance is shown in Fig. 7.11. At level 0 the enterprise has not yet adopted even the most basic value management practices recommended by Val IT. At level 5 the enterprise is able to quantify the value it is creating through business change investments, whether or not they involve IT, and has the means to continue to improve the creation of value in the future. Clearly levels 1–4 represent intermediate stages on the journey to creating optimal value.

0 Non-existent when

The enterprise sees IT as an end in itself and the focus is on delivery of technology. There is no recognition of the strategic need for a benefits focus or to establish clear linkage between technology investments and expected business benefits.

1 Initial when

Investment processes are *ad hoc* and business cases are rarely required. Simple financial metrics may exist, primarily related to IT solution delivery costs. Tools and skills depend on individuals. IT holds the budgets and there is little business involvement in the investment management process. There is no consistent or effective management and tracking of total costs, benefits and risks.

2 Repeatable when

Intuitive processes emerge for the development of business cases, but are not clearly defined or formalized. The primary focus is on costs but there is increasing rigor around benefits. The programme view is emerging and different tools are being used. IT still holds the budgets but there is increasing business involvement in defining major investment programmes. Financial metrics exist for costs, business benefits and risks, but there is no consistent and effective monitoring or management of benefits and risks.

3 Defined when

Standards exist and tools emerge for the development of business cases including high-level benefits, both financial and non-financial, costs, and risks. For most major investments the focus is on clarity of business outcomes, identification of the full scope of initiatives required to achieve the outcomes, and risk. Expertise and skills exist both within IT and the business for assessing and estimating tangible and intangible benefits as well as for assessing business and technology risks. IT and business have clear responsibilities for the development of business cases which distinguish between intermediate and business benefits. Accountability for approval of business cases is established.

4 Managed when

Board and executive management are committed to investment management. Business cases are comprehensive, complete and regularly updated, and include programme and benefits realization plans. Standardized programme/project planning tools are used to automate and monitor the management of IT-enabled investments. Investment management skills are available and clear roles and responsibilities for business and IT stakeholders are assigned. A benefit monitoring process is in place to ensure planned benefits are achieved and sustained. Scorecards are used to summarize programme composition and health.

5 Optimized when

Financial and non-financial benefits, costs and risks of investment programmes are continuously monitored and adjusted to optimize their value over their full economic life cycle through retirement. Investment management processes and skills are improved based on lessons learned and tools are integrated with enterprise systems. Executive management assigns accountability for managing full economic life cycle costs, financial and non-financial benefits, and risks. When business cases are updated to reflect changes in requirements or programme performance, management re-evaluates the business case to determine whether it should still be pursued.

Fig. 7.11 Maturity model for investment management
ITGI, 2008, Val IT 2.0, on-line available at www.itgi.org.

The maturity models as presented above are in fact a summary of more detailed maturity models developed around a set of attributes:

- Awareness and communication
- Responsibility and accountability
- Goal setting and measurement
- Policies, standards and procedures
- Skills and expertise
- Tools and automation

For each of these attributes, specific maturity scales are provided for each Val IT domain. An illustration for IM is provided below (Fig. 7.12), where "awareness and communication" at level 0 implies that there is no recognition of the strategic need for a benefit focus, while level 2 entails an increasing awareness that IT is an important enabler for business value creation.

	Awareness and communication	Responsibility and accountability	Goal setting and measurement	Policies standards and procedures	Skills and expertise	Tools and automation
0	The enterprise sees IT as an end in itself and the focus is on delivery of technology. There is no recognition of the strategic need for a benefits focus or to establish clear linkage between technology investments and expected business benefits.					
1	...	...	...	...	...	...
2	There is increasing management awareness that IT is a business enabler and of the need to take a business value view of IT enabled investments.	IT function still holds the budget but there is increasing business involvement in defining major investment programmes although accountabilities are not always clear and causes of failure often are not appropiately attributed.	Financial metrics exist for costs, and business benefits and risks are considered. There is no consistent nor effective monitoring nor management of business risks	Intuitive processes emerge for development of business cases, but are not clearly defined nor formalised. Business cases are not required for all investments. The primary focus is on costs but there is an increasing rigour around benefits. A programme view is emerging but not universally accepted.	Skills exist, largely within the IT function, for estimating expenditures, business outcomes and benefits resulting from new IT enabled investments.	A number of one-off tolls exist and are increasingly customised, and different tools are used by different groups.
3	...	...	...	...	...	...
4	...	...	...	...	...	...
5	The board and executive management are proactive in regularly reviewing programme performance during the economic life cycle of all investments, whithin the context of the enterprise's overall portfolio of IT enabled investments, and initiating remedial actions as required	Executive management assigns accountability for managing full economic life cycle costs, and financial and non-financial benefits. There responsibilities effectively cascade through the enterprise. Continuous improvement processes are applied to all measurement processes and metrics.	Full economic life cycle costs and financial and non-financial benefits are monitored. When changes occur to the internal or external business environment, or when pgoramme business cases are updated to reflect changes in requirements or programme performance, management re-evaluates the business case for the programme to determine if it should still be pursued.	Feedback and continuous improvement exist. The programme is continuously monitored and adjusted to optimize its value over the full economic life cycle, up to and including retirement. Investment management processes are improved based on lessons learned.	Expertise is available to assess and report consistently on programme performance, both individually and as part of the overall investment portfolio, in line with the expected benefits during the full economic life cycle. Skills are continuously improved to meet enterprise goals.	Investment management tools are integraed with other enterprise tools to clearly communicate programme contribution to the business strategy.

Fig. 7.12 Maturity model attributes for investment management
ITGI, 2008, Val IT 2.0, on-line available at www.itgi.org.

It is clear that both maturity model presentations in fact mainly address the same issues and concerns. It is up to the organization to leverage the presentation most suited to its environment.

Summary

Val IT is a relatively new framework issued by the IT Governance Institute, which mainly focuses at the business responsibilities in IT value creation. This framework starts from the premise that value creation out of IT investments is a business responsibility in the first place. To support business people in organizing and developing these responsibilities, Val IT presents a set of 22 IT-related business processes and corresponding key management practices, management guidelines and maturity models.

Val IT is complementary to COBIT and follows the same structure and templates as provided in the COBIT manuals. Major benefit of this is that people who are familiar with COBIT's concepts and structure, fairly easily will understand Val IT's structure as well.

It should be acknowledged that, while Val IT addresses IT-related business responsibilities, the likelihood of the business automatically accepting and adopting this framework could be rather low. Because of IT's history in process-oriented thinking and designing, and automating business processes, we believe that IT is in a unique position to guide the business in adopting Val IT-based practices, in this way crafting a more value creating organization levering IT.

Study Questions

1. Describe the three domains of Val IT.
2. Describe the processes within Value Governance, Project Management and Investment Management.
3. Describe the differences and relationship between COBIT and Val IT.
4. Define the Val IT concepts of projects, programmes and portfolios.
5. Define the Val IT core principles.
6. Describe the roles defined in Val IT's RACI charts.
7. Describe the concepts of the Project Management Office (PMO) and the Value Management Office (VMO).
8. Describe and illustrate the concepts of KPI's and KGI's in the context of Val IT.
9. Define and describe the main responsibilities/accountabilities of the Board of Directors in the context of Val IT.
10. Define and describe the main responsibilities/accountabilities of the CIO in the context of Val IT.

Further Reading

ITGI, 2005, Optimising Value Creation from IT Investments, USA.
ITGI, 2008, Val IT 2.0, from www.itgi.org
Thorp, J., 2003, The Information Paradox, Mc. Graw-Hill.
Van Grembergen, W. (Ed.), 2004, Strategies for Information Technology Governance. Hershey, PA: Idea Group Publishing.
Van Grembergen, W., and De Haes, S., 2008, Implementing Information Technology Governance: Models, Practices and Cases, IGI Publishing.
Ward, J., Daniel, E., and Peppard, J., 2008, Building Better Business Cases for IT Investments, MIS Quarterly Executive, vol. 7, no. 1/Mar 1, 2008.

Websites

CIO.com: www.cio.com
Information Technology Alignment and Governance Research Institute: www.uams.be/ITAG
ISACA: www.isaca.org
IT Governance Institute: www.itgi.org

Chapter 8
Guidelines for the Implementation of Enterprise Governance of IT

Abstract There is no real "silver bullet" (the ideal way) for implementing and maintaining effective Enterprise Governance of IT within an organization. Having developed a high-level Enterprise Governance of IT model does not imply that governance is actually working in the organization. Conceiving the governance model is the first step, implementing it into the organization is the next challenging step. An important challenge is, how do you get started? This chapter provides some guidelines to get started and outlines a balanced scorecard for Enterprise Governance of IT, to manage and measure the outcome of the governance project. Readers who are not familiar with the balanced scorecard perspective should first read Chapter 4 on the IT Balanced Scorecard.

8.1 Getting Started

It became clear in previous chapters that Enterprise Governance of IT is a very broad concept and that each organization requires a specific approach applicable to its individual context. The question is, where and how to start?

To address the latter question, this textbook identified in Chapter 3 a key minimum baseline composed of seven practices that can be regarded as the necessary framework to implement Enterprise Governance of IT:

- IT steering committee
- IT project steering committee
- Portfolio management
- IT budget control and reporting
- CIO reporting to the CEO/COO
- IT leadership
- Project governance/management methodologies

It was demonstrated that high-performing organizations, in terms of business/IT alignment, are leveraging these seven practices as "necessary" components in their governance framework. Each (IT-intensive) organization should al least have these governance practices in place, regardless of other contingencies. Of course, these

W. Van Grembergen, S. De Haes, *Enterprise Governance of Information Technology*, DOI 10.1007/978-0-387-84882-2_8,

"necessary" (key minimum baseline) practices should be supplemented with other practices to build up a set of "necessary and sufficient" Enterprise Governance of IT framework. This "necessary and sufficient" governance framework will be different for every organization, depending on size, culture, etc., but it is best to focus on those practices that are perceived as highly effective and relatively easy to implement, as indicated in Chapter 2, such as an "IT governance officer/function," "service level management" and "business/IT account management."

In this domain of "sufficient" IT governance practices, a lot of relational mechanisms emerge as well such as "knowledge management" and "senior management giving the good example." Indeed, at the initial stages of an Enterprise Governance of IT project, a lot of attention should be given to relational mechanisms to ensure commitment of all the involved people in the process. Once the "governance culture" is embedded in the implemented structures and processes, these relational mechanisms require less attention. It is also important to point out that, in order for the Enterprise Governance of IT practices to be effective, they should be at least at a maturity level 2.

Out of the case research, it became clear that to get Enterprise Governance of IT effectively started in the organization, it should initially be regarded as a project, with a formal project organization supporting it. Once the governance practices are embedded into day-to-day operations, this project approach is not required anymore, moving the organization into a sustaining mode. It should, however, be taken into account that the introduction of a new concept or methodology (such as Enterprise Governance of IT) in an organization often raises resistance. To manage this, it is important to initially put a lot of focus on relational mechanisms and to have a senior sponsor in the organization act as the Enterprise Governance of IT guru. Based on the experiences from the case and qualitative research reported in this book, the following high-level 10-step implementation roadmap for Enterprise Governance of IT is suggested:

1. Obtain ownership/sponsorship at senior management/executive level.
2. Create awareness and involvement for the Enterprise Governance of IT initiative by business and IT senior and operational management.
3. Launch the Enterprise Governance of IT project, provide a formal project organization including project manager.
4. Assess the as-is situation (what is already in place?).
5. Define to-be situation, i.e., what will the ideal Enterprise Governance of IT state look like?.
6. Quickstart the Enterprise Governance of IT project with the seven necessary governance practices (highly effective, easy to implement).
7. Focus on relational mechanisms during initial phases to manage resistance.
8. Improve the Enterprise Governance of IT framework to create a necessary and sufficient IT governance framework.
9. Shift focus from relational mechanisms to improvement of the structures and processes once the Enterprise Governance of IT framework gets embedded into the organization.

10. In parallel, introduce a performance management system (balanced scorecard) to continuously monitor and improve the effectiveness of the Enterprise Governance of IT framework (see next section).

8.2 Measuring and Managing the Process of Enterprise Governance of IT

Today many organizations are in the process of implementing a combination of Enterprise Governance of IT structures, processes and relational mechanisms. An important aspect of the Enterprise Governance of IT implementation process is the measuring and evaluation part. It makes sense for CIOs, executive managers and board members to oversee the Enterprise Governance of IT status: how well it is doing and how it can be improved. For this purpose, a balanced scorecard (BSC) can be developed as a performance measurement system for the Enterprise Governance of IT process as a whole, enabling strategies for further improvement. With an Enterprise Governance of IT balanced scorecard, organizations can empower their board, CEO, CIO, executive management and the business and IT participants by providing them the necessary information to evaluate the Enterprise Governance of IT success and act upon to achieve a better alignment between business and IT and consequently reach better results. In this sense, the Enterprise Governance of IT scorecard can play an important role in an overall program that should be in place to enhance IT and corporate governance.

8.2.1 Building an Enterprise Governance of IT Balanced Scorecard

Figure 8.1 displays the mission statements, objectives and corresponding measures for the four dimensions of the proposed Enterprise Governance of IT balanced scorecard: corporate contribution perspective, stakeholder's perspective, operational excellence perspective and future perspective. The BSC not only is a performance management system but also provides a management system when causal relationships between metrics are properly implemented. The ultimate goal of the development and implementation of an Enterprise Governance of IT process is the attainment of a better alignment between business and IT and consequently achieving better financial results (business value). It is therefore logical that the Enterprise Governance of IT balanced scorecard starts with a corporate contribution perspective. As shown in Fig. 8.1, the other three perspectives have a cause relationship with corporate contribution and among each other cause-and-effect relationships. An illustration of these coupled metrics in a cause-and-effect relationship is: overall completed Enterprise Governance of IT education (future orientation) may enhance the level of IT/business planning (operational excellence), which in turn may

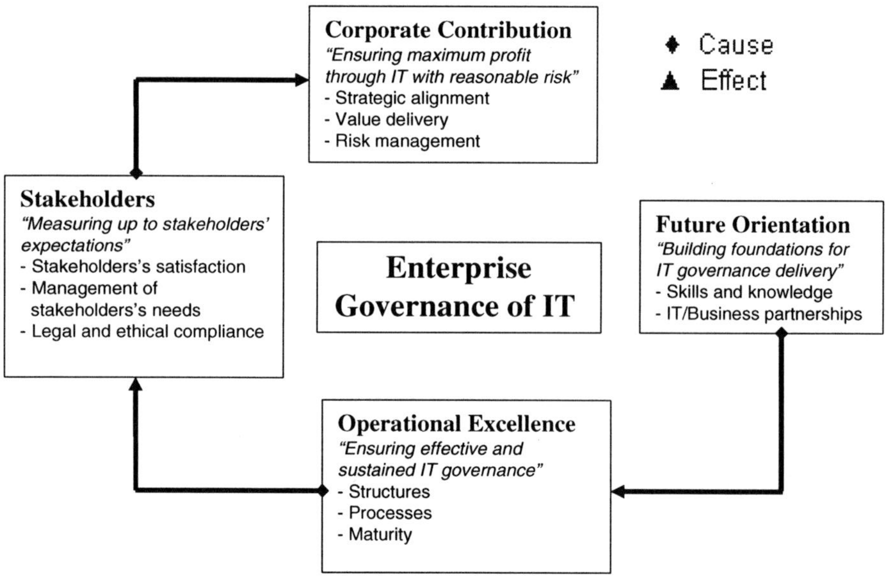

Fig. 8.1 Enterprise Governance of IT scorecard perspectives and its cause-and-effect relationships

improve stakeholders' satisfaction (stakeholders orientation), and have a positive effect on the strategic match of major IT projects (corporate contribution). The metrics of the main elements of Enterprise Governance of IT – structures, processes and relational mechanisms – can be found in the operational excellence and future perspective dimensions.

8.2.2 Metrics for an Enterprise Governance of IT Balanced Scorecard

The *corporate contribution* dimension evaluates the performance of the Enterprise Governance of IT process: a well-balanced Enterprise Governance of IT process must enhance business profit through IT while mitigating the risk related to IT (mission). The three key objectives, as depicted in Fig. 8.2, are strategic alignment, value delivery and risk management and are seen by the IT Governance Institute (2003) as main concerns of Enterprise Governance of IT.

The main measurement challenge is within the area of *strategic alignment*. As an overall metric, the *business/IT alignment maturity* model of Sledgianowski and Luftman is proposed. The measurement instrument is based on a survey to be completed by business and IT managers in the organization, addressing 22 attributes in six different domains: communication, competency and value measurement, governance, partnership, scope and architecture and skills. The

Perspective	Corporate contribution	
Mission	Ensuring maximum profit while mitigating IT related risks	
Objectives	***Strategic alignment***	
	Measures	Business/IT alignment maturity
		Strategic match of major IT projects
		Percentage of development capacity engaged in strategic projects
		Percentage of business goals supported by IT goals
	Value delivery	
	Measures	Business unit performance management
		Business value of major IT projects based on ROI, NPV, IRR, PB
		Ratio IT costs/total turnover
		IT costs charged back to the business
	Risk management	
	Measures	Number of new implemented IT security initiatives and security breaches
		Attainment of disaster recovery plans
		Number of IT audits performed and reported shortcomings

Fig. 8.2 Corporate contribution metrics

outcome is a business/IT alignment maturity score for the organization (see also Chapter 3). *Strategic match of major IT projects, percentage of development capacity engaged in strategic projects* and *percentage of business goals supported by IT goals* are specific strategic alignment concerns. Measuring the strategic match of IT projects can be done through a scoring technique as introduced by Information Economics (see also Chapter 3): typical scores are attributed from 0 to 5 whereby 0 means no match at all and 5 a perfect match of the IT project with the business strategy.

In the *value delivery* area, *business unit performance measurement* refers to the business results of the individual lines of business. Indeed, the ultimate responsibility for achieving and measuring the business value rests with the business units. Alternative metrics for value delivery assessment are the traditional financial evaluations such as the return on investment, net present value, internal rate of return and payback period (*business value of major IT projects based on ROI, NPV, IRR and PB*). A major concern of senior management is the level of the IT costs and their recovery respectively measured through *ratio IT costs/total turnover* and *percentage of IT costs charged back to the business.*

Regarding the *risk management* objective, a high level of security and disaster recovery should be attained and measured by the *number of implemented IT security initiatives and security breaches* and *attainment of disaster recovery plans*. The audit performance is measured through *number of IT audits performed and reported shortcomings*.

Figure 8.3 portrays the objectives of the *stakeholder's perspective:* stakeholders' satisfaction, management of stakeholders' needs and the legal/ethical compliance. This perspective evaluates the Enterprise Governance of IT process from the

Perspective	**Stakeholders orientation**	
Mission	Measuring up to stakeholders' expectations	
Objectives	***Stakeholders' satisfaction***	
	Measures	Stakeholders' satisfaction surveys on fixed times
		Number of complaints of stakeholders
		Index of availability of systems and applications
	Management of stakeholders' needs	
	Measures	Number of meetings with stakeholders
		Clear communication in place with CEO and board members
		Index of CEO/board involvement in new and major IT initiatives
		Number of major IT projects within SLA
	Legal and ethical compliance	
	Measures	IT adherence to Sarbanes-Oxley Act
		IT adherence to privacy regulations
		Adherence to IT code of ethics/IT code of conduct

Fig. 8.3 Stakeholders metrics

stakeholders' viewpoint including the board of directors, CEO and executive management, CIO and IT management, business and IT users, customers, shareholders and the community. It is important to point out that the scope of this stakeholder's perspective is much broader than the customer perspective of an IT Balanced Scorecard (see Chapter 4).

In relation to *stakeholders' satisfaction* the scores from satisfaction surveys (*stakeholders' satisfaction survey on fixed times*) for the aforementioned categories of stakeholders can be used. This can also be applied to the *number of complaints of stakeholders*. An overall specific metric for business users is the *index of availability of systems and applications*.

The *management of stakeholders' needs* are assessed through a set of performance metrics including measurements for the various stakeholder groups (*number of meetings with stakeholders*), more specific measurements for the board and CEO (*clear communication in place with CEO/board members* and *index of CEO/board involvement in new and major IT initiatives*) and specific measurements for the business users (*number of major IT projects within SLA*). Service Level Agreements (SLAs) as already pointed out in the previous section are an important governance instrument for enforcing levels of IT service that are acceptable by users and are attainable by their IT department and/or external providers.

Third objective within the stakeholder's perspective is the *legal and ethical compliance*. In their publication on the board balanced scorecard, Epstein and Roy (2004) state that "the company's reporting strategy is a powerful driver of stakeholder satisfaction, so accountable companies should provide transparent reporting to their internal and external stakeholders. . . ." Accountability and transparency can be enhanced through the adherence to government and IT community regulations. The Sarbanes-Oxley (SOX) Act for example focuses on the control and security of company's financial systems and consequently on its supporting IT processes. A crucial IT process in this context is "manage changes" as defined by COBIT (Control Objectives for Information and Related Technology), the internationally accepted IT control framework. The business objective of the manage changes process is "responding to business requirements in alignment with the business strategy, whilst reducing solution and service delivery defects and rework" (ITGI, 2007), and in this sense is a crucial supportive mechanism for Sarbanes-Oxley compliance. A specific metric for IT adherence to SOX could be the maturity level of the manage changes process evaluated on the basis of the maturity model as defined in the management guidelines of COBIT. Figure 8.4 illustrates maturity levels 0 and 5 for the manage changes process.

The *operational excellence* perspective identifies the key Enterprise Governance of IT practices (structures and processes) to be implemented and their corresponding metrics. As defined before, structures refer to the existence of responsible functions and committees, and processes to decision-making and monitoring. The operational excellence card of Fig. 8.5 gives a variety of metrics for governance structures and processes including an overall IT governance maturity measurement.

For the *structures* area three specific metrics regarding IT committees are retained: *number of meetings of IT strategy committee and IT steering committees, composition of IT committees* and *overall attendance of IT committees.* Taking the criticality of IT into account, boards should manage IT with high commitment and accuracy as it does with other critical areas such as audit, compensation and acquisitions. An instrument for achieving this is an IT strategy committee that supports the board in carrying out its IT governance duties. On the other hand, the detailed implementation of the IT/business strategies will be the responsibility of executive management assisted by a variety of steering committees overseeing major projects and managing priorities. Considering the importance of the IT strategy committee and the IT steering committees these committees need careful and close

Level 0: Non-existent
There is no defined change management process and changes can be made with virtually no control. There is no awareness that change can be disruptive for IT and business operations, and no awareness of the benefits of good change management.
Level 5: Optimized
The change management process is regularly reviewed and updated to stay in line with good practices. The review process reflects the outcome of monitoring. Configuration information is computer-based and provides version control. Tracking of changes is sophisticated and includes tools to detect unauthorized and unlicensed software. IT change management is integrated with business change management to ensure that IT is an enabler in increasing productivity and creating new business opportunities for the organization.

Fig. 8.4 Maturity levels for "manage change" process
ITGI, 2007, COBIT 4.1, from www.itgi.org.

Perspective	Operational excellence	
Mission	Ensuring effective and sustained IT governance	
Objectives	*Structures*	
	Measures	Number of meetings of IT strategy committee and IT steering committees
		Composition of IT committees
		Overall attendance of IT committees
		CIO member of executive management
	Processes	
	Measures	Level of IT strategy planning and business planning
		Number of hours spent on IT/business strategic issues
		Existence of an IT balanced scorecard and a business balanced scorecard
		Number of IT processes measured through a scorecard
		Number of IT processes covered by COBIT
		Number of business processes covered by Val IT
		Maturity levels of IT and IT related business processes
		Percentage of IT goals supported by IT processes
	Maturity	
	Measure	Overall level of the IT governance process maturity

Fig. 8.5 Operational excellence metrics

monitoring through the aforementioned measures. Besides the meeting frequency and the attendance, it should be monitored whether the right people are members, taking into account factors such as their profile and IT literacy. An ideal composition of an IT strategy committee would be: a board member as chairman, other board members, non-board independent members and ex-officio representation of key executives. *CIO member of executive management* is an indication of how important IT is considered within the organization.

The metric examples of the *processes* objective are focused on the level of and involvement in IT/business planning, the use of scorecards, the coverage by COBIT and Val IT and the maturity levels of the IT (COBIT) and IT-related business (Val IT) processes. *Level of IT strategy planning and business planning* can be monitored by the effective use of strategic models such as the competitive forces model and the value chain of Porter and the Strategic Alignment Model of Henderson and Venkatraman. As already illustrated in previous section, the balanced scorecard can be an effective management instrument. The *existence of an IT balanced scorecard and a business balanced scorecard* is very supportive for achieving a linkage between IT and business objectives. Establishing such a cascade of scorecards with rolling-up and aggregating metrics of the IT scorecard in the business balanced scorecard may help to realize the ultimate link between IT and business. This cascade mechanism can also be used between the IT scorecard and the scorecards at a lower level for the different IT processes (metric: *number of IT processes through a scorecard*). Outcome measures (key goal indicators) and performance drivers (key performance indicators) can be found in the management guidelines of COBIT for the 34 identified IT processes as well as the corresponding maturity models (metrics: *maturity levels of IT processes*). Regarding COBIT and Val IT two metrics are included: *number of IT processes covered by COBIT and number of IT-related business processes covered by Val IT*. *Percentage of IT goals supported by IT processes* is related to the corporate contribution measure "percentage of business goals supported by IT processes." A clear causal relationship between both metrics exists: if IT goals are not properly supported by IT processes, this may result in an insufficient IT support for the business.

The operational excellence card concludes with an *Enterprise Governance of IT maturity evaluation*. *Overall level of the Enterprise Governance of IT process maturity* can be assessed through the IT governance maturity model of ITGI. Such a maturity model provides a method for scoring that enables an organization to grade itself from non-existent (level 0) to optimized (level 5). According to this model (see Fig. 8.6), organizations that are situated in level 0 are characterized by a complete lack of any recognizable IT governance process. To move up to level 1, the organization needs to at least recognize the

0 Non-existent

Complete lack of any recognizable processes. Organization has not even recognized that there is an issue to be addressed.

1 Initial

There is evidence that the organization has recognized that the issues exist and need to be addressed. There are however no standardized processes but instead there are ad hoc approaches that tend to be applied on an individual or case by case basis. The overall approach to management is chaotic.

2 Repeatable

Processes have developed to the stage where similar procedures are followed different people undertaking the same task. There is no formal training or communication of standard procedures and responsibility is left to the individual. There is a high degree of reliance on the knowledge of individuals and therefore errors are likely.

3 Defined

Procedures have been standardized and documented, and communicated through training. It is however left to the individual to follow these processes, and any deviations would be unlikely to be detected. The procedures themselves are not sophisticated but are the formalization of existing practices.

4 Managed

It is possible to monitor and measure compliance with procedures and to take action where processes appear not to be working effectively. Processes are under constant improvement and provide good practice. Automation and tools are used in a limited or fragmented way.

5 Optimized

Processes have been refined to a level of best practice, based on the results of continuous improvement and maturity modeling with other organizations. IT is used in an integrated way to automate the workflow and provide tools to improve quality and effectiveness.

Fig. 8.6 IT governance maturity model
ITGI, 2003, Board Briefing on IT Governance, Second Edition, from www.itgi.org.

importance of addressing IT governance issues. Maturity level 5 at least implies an advanced and forward-looking understanding of IT governance issues and solutions, supported by an established framework and best practices of structures, processes and relational mechanisms. Maturity models such as the ITGI model have to comply with the basic principles of maturity measurement: one can only go to a higher maturity when all conditions described in a certain level are fulfilled. The level that an organization should target is of course dependent on the nature of the business: a business within the banking sector should probably strive to a higher IT governance level than a concrete factory.

The *future orientation* scorecard reports on the building foundations for governance delivery focusing on relational mechanisms. Relational mechanisms such as business/IT co-location, partnership rewards and incentives, shared understanding of business/IT objectives, cross-functional business/IT training and cross-functional business/IT job-rotation are of primordial importance. Enterprise Governance of IT structures and processes may be in place but when IT and business professionals do not understand each other and do not share the business/IT related problems, a successful alignment between both areas will not be achieved. Implementing the right relational mechanisms will be the crucial enabler for better governance structures and processes (operational excellence perspective), higher stakeholders' satisfaction (stakeholder perspective) and ultimately a higher governance performance (corporate contribution perspective). Figure 8.7 displays the two distinct objectives of the future orientation perspective: skills and knowledge and IT/business partnership.

Within the *skills and knowledge* area the cross-functional education and training metrics are predominant: *number and level of cross-functional business/IT training sessions, number of overall Enterprise Governance of IT training sessions, percentage Enterprise Governance of IT education per skill type*. A specific and important measure is the *number of Enterprise Governance of IT presentations for*

Perspective	**Future orientation**	
Mission	Building foundations for IT governance delivery	
Objectives	***Skills and knowledge***	
	Measures	Number and level of cross -functional business/IT training sessions
		Number of overall Enterprise Governance of IT training sessions
		Percentage completed Enterprise Governance of IT education per skill type
		Number of Enterprise Governance of IT presentations for CEO and board members
		Level and use of Enterprise Governance of IT knowledge management system
	IT/business partnership	
	Measures	Percentage of senior managers IT literate
		Percentage of IT managers business literate
		Level of business perception of IT value

Fig. 8.7 Future orientation metrics

CEO and board members capturing the communication efforts between the IT management team and its business hierarchy. *Level and use of Enterprise Governance of IT knowledge management system* refers to an intranet that all employees can access for seeking and sharing knowledge on the *Enterprise Governance of IT* practices within the organization.

IT/business partnership objectives report on the IT and business literacy of respectively senior business managers (*percentage of senior manager IT literate*) and the IT team (*percentage of IT managers business literate*). The importance of these two metrics is confirmed by Teo and Ang's study where the knowledge ability of IT management and top executives concerning business and IT were found to be the two crucial critical success factors in business/IT planning alignment. *Level of business perception of IT value* can be measured through scores indicating the level going from 1 (perceived as a cost) to 5 (IT seen as a driver/enabler).

The performance of the Enterprise Governance of IT process can be visualized using this generic Enterprise Governance of IT balanced scorecard. The corporate contribution perspective of this scorecard matches with the IT function's balance scorecard (see Chapter 4). Indeed, the ultimate goal for both scorecards is to obtain better corporate financial results. The main difference between both scorecards is that the other perspectives focus completely on the Enterprise Governance of IT process. Some of the metrics of the Enterprise Governance of IT BSC will, however, be rolled-up and/or aggregated in the IT BSC. Additionally, the board BSC will certainly import some relevant Enterprise Governance of IT measures.

Improving the Enterprise Governance of IT performance is the main reason for building and implementing an Enterprise Governance of IT scorecard. It must be clear that just measuring is not enough; the scorecard must be implemented as a management system. When the measurements indicate that there are major problems with risk management (corporate contribution), a possible strategy may involve the improvement of the disaster recovery planning (DRP) through a COBIT implementation (operational excellence), which in turn may need a cross-sectional business/IT training in COBIT and DRP (future orientation).

Assignment Box 8.1: Improve the Enterprise Governance of IT balanced scorecard

Review the proposed enterprise governance of IT balanced scorecard and improve it based on the Val IT processes and key management practices.

Summary

With an Enterprise Governance of IT balanced scorecard, organizations can empower their board, CEO, CIO, executive management and the business and IT participants by providing them the necessary information to evaluate the Enterprise Governance of IT success and act upon it to achieve a better alignment between business and IT and consequently reach better results. In this sense, the Enterprise Governance of IT scorecard can play an important role in an overall program that should be in place to enhance corporate governance. Currently, many organizations are introducing and implementing Enterprise Governance of IT processes. Using this proposed generic Enterprise Governance of IT BSC may help them to realize a successful implementation.

Study Questions

1. Explain the four perspectives of the Enterprise Governance of IT BSC: corporate contribution, stakeholders, operational excellence and future orientation.
2. Define and discuss typical metrics for each of the perspectives of the Enterprise Governance of IT Balanced Scorecard.
3. Explain the difference between an IT BSC and an Enterprise Governance of IT BSC.

Further Reading

Epstein, M.J., and Roy, M.-J., 2002, Measuring and Improving the Performance of Corporate Boards, The Society of Management Accountants of Canada, www.cma-canada.org

Epstein, M.J., and Roy, M.-J., 2004, How Does Your Board Rate? Strategic Finance, February, pp. 25–31.

Porter, M., 1998, Competitive Advantage: Creating and Sustaining Superior Performance. New York: Free Press.

Porter, M., 2001, Strategy and the internet, Harvard Business Review, March.

Teo, T., and Ang, J., 1999, Critical Success Factors in the Alignment of IS Plans with Business Plans, International Journal of Management Information, vol. 19.

Van Grembergen, W., 2002, Introduction to the Minitrack IT Governance and its Mechanisms, in Proceedings of the 35th Hawaii International Conference on Systems Sciences (HICSS).

Van Grembergen, W., and De Haes, S., 2006, Leveraging the Balanced Scorecard to Measure and Manage Information Technology Governance, in Proceedings of the 10th Information Resources Management (IRMA) International Conference, Hershey (PA).

Van Grembergen, W., De Haes, S., and Amelinckx, I., 2003, Using COBIT and the balanced scorecard as instruments for service level management, Information Systems Control Journal, vol. 4.

Van Grembergen, W., Saull, R., and De Haes, S. 2003, Linking the IT Balanced Scorecard to the Business Objectives at a Major Canadian Financial Group, Journal of Information Technology cases and applications.

Websites

Balanced Scorecard Institute: www.balancedscorecard.org

Information Technology Alignment and Governance Research Institute: www.uams.be/ITAG

ISACA: www.isaca.org

IT Governance Institute: www.itgi.org

Index

CPSIA information can be obtained at www.ICGtesting.com
Printed in the USA
LVOW082124281111

256888LV00006B/55/P

9 780387 848815